Palgrave Studies in the History of Economic Thought

Palgrave Studies in the History of Economic Thought publishes contributions by leading scholars, illuminating key events, theories and individuals that have had a lasting impact on the development of modern-day economics. The topics covered include the development of economies, institutions and theories.

The series aims to highlight the academic importance of the history of economic thought, linking it with wider discussions within economics and society more generally. It contains a broad range of titles that illustrate the breath of discussions – from influential economists and schools of thought, through to historical and modern social trends and challenges – within the discipline.

All books in the series undergo a single-blind peer review at both the proposal and manuscript submission stages.

For further information on the series and to submit a proposal for consideration, please contact the Wyndham Hacket Pain (Economics Editor) wyndham.hacketpain@palgrave.com.

More information about this series at
http://www.palgrave.com/gp/series/14585

Daniel Diatkine

Adam Smith and the Wealth of Nations

The Discovery of Capitalism and Its Limits

palgrave
macmillan

Daniel Diatkine
University of Paris-Saclay
Univ Evry, Evry, France

université evry val-d'essonne | université PARIS-SACLAY

LABORATOIRE

-PHARE-

PHILOSOPHIE, HISTOIRE ET ANALYSE
DES REPRESENTATIONS ECONOMIQUES

université PARIS-SACLAY

ISSN 2662-6578 ISSN 2662-6586 (electronic)
Palgrave Studies in the History of Economic Thought
ISBN 978-3-030-81599-8 ISBN 978-3-030-81600-1 (eBook)
https://doi.org/10.1007/978-3-030-81600-1

Cover illustration: amnach kinchokawat/Alamy Stock Photo

This Palgrave Macmillan imprint is published by the registered company Springer Nature Switzerland AG
The registered company address is: Gewerbestrasse 11, 6330 Cham, Switzerland

Contents

Introduction

The first aim of this book is to encourage the reader to read Adam Smith's *Inquiry into the Nature and Causes of the Wealth of Nations*,[1] which was not written for economists but for "legislators", that is to say for citizens. This is also how in France, for example, Nicolas de Condorcet (1743–1794) understood Adam Smith (1723–1790), when publishing a copious summary of his work (translated by his friend Rouché) in the "Library of the public man" (*Bibliothèque de l'homme Public*) in 1790.[2] The *Wealth of Nations*, along with Montesquieu's *The Spirit of Laws* and Aristotle's *Politics* among many others, was then perceived as one of the texts necessary for public education. Condorcet believed that it was essential for citizens to have a more than basic knowledge of Smith's work, during the early days of the French Revolution. Indeed, the *Wealth of Nations* was written as a criticism of privilege and the privileged. According to Smith, these were the consequences of the Dark Ages when solid alliances had been forged between princes and the urban bourgeoisies, united by their common struggle against the local lordships. In economic terms, such

[1] Quotations from the *Wealth of Nations* (henceforth *WON*) are taken from the reference version of *The Glasgow Edition of the Works and Correspondence of Adam Smith*, published by Oxford University Press for the bicentenary of Smith's book, and in which the *WON* is the second volume, edited by R. H. Campbell and A. S. Skinner, 1976.

[2] Condorcet's wife, Sophie de Grouchy, was the first person to translate Smith's other major work into French, *The Theory of Moral Sentiments (TMS)*, which is the first volume of the Glasgow reference edition.

privileges were expressed by monopolies (protections) granted by princes in favour of particular interest groups, such corporations, or particular companies, often in exchange for financial rewards. Furthermore, Smith showed that, beyond expedients or even pure corruption, there was a deeper bond of intellectual association between legislators (and so citizens) and merchants (or capitalists). The result of such collusion was what he called the *mercantile system*. This term designated both a political expression of *commercial society*, which characterised commerce in Western Europe, and the discourses by both scholars and merchants justifying this system. "Commercial society" was the term used by Smith at the same time as that of the "advanced state of societies". The use of these two concepts was not accidental. The commercial society was a *stage* (no doubt the ultimate one) in the historical development of societies. The advanced state of societies was—and is—characterised by an *economy* in which natural prices were defined by the fact that the sale of goods led to the same natural rate of profit to those "who bring them to the market".

In this way, Smith discovered capitalism in three dimensions: economic, historical and political. The political dimension of capitalism was the "mercantile system", and its economic dimension was designated in the *Wealth of Nations* by the term "advanced state of societies". Finally, Smith called the historical dimension of capitalism the "Age of Commerce", which succeeded the "Age of Hunters, the Age of Shepherds and the Age of Agriculture" hunter-gatherer, livestock and farming societies.[3] Taking into account all of these dimensions of capitalism creates both the richness and the difficulties of the *Wealth of Nations*.

It therefore becomes necessary to answer the following question: how and why is Smith considered by most of our contemporaries today as the spokesperson of the "rising bourgeoisie" given that he saw his most famous work as being a critique of eighteenth-century capitalism? Indeed, the criticism of the mercantile system, and therefore of the political dimension of capitalism, was the initial subject of Smith's book. For him, the mercantile system was *partial* because it stated there was an identity of the interests between the merchant and manufacturing classes (to use Smith's terms)—or the capitalists (to use the terminology of Anne Robert Turgot (1766–1997, p. 194 et sq.)—and the common interest. However, this

[3] *Lectures on Jurisprudence*, Glasgow Edition of the Works and Correspondence of Adam Smith, 14. Thereafter: LJ(A) or LJ(B).

was (and is) not the case, as Smith intended to demonstrate. While the interest of the two other classes which made up society (the landowners and the labourers) always went in the direction of the general interest, the same was not so for the interest of the class of merchants (or capitalists). Demonstrating these propositions is the subject of Book I of the *Wealth of Nations*. It must be emphasised particularity from the outset that, according to Smith, capitalism implies a society made up of social classes whose interests are different. Social conflicts *cannot therefore be reduced* only to individual conflicts. Smith states this proposition as being self-evident, and we shall see that he was in no ways original in this observation. A second characteristic completes this observation, namely that the general interest is distinct from the interest of each of these classes. This is all the more so as the general interest is not the sum of individual interests. Again, this proposition was not original as it was common to the whole tradition of classical political philosophy.[4] This view of economic and social phenomena is radically opposed to methodological individualism, a notion which dominates a significant part of the social sciences today, and according to which only individual behaviour should be taken into account.

Herein lies the main difficulty, which the reader has to overcome today, given the strong prevalence of the view that Smith was the founder of economic liberalism in which the interests of companies (entrepreneurs, capitalists) are identified with the general interest. If however we accept this first definition of economic liberalism, then the reader will be confronted with a first paradox: Smith attacked economic liberalism head-on by attacking what he called the "partiality" and therefore the injustice of the mercantile system. The mercantile system was unfair, but in a sense that had to be clarified immediately. It was not unjust in that the distribution of wealth was such that a share of wealth would be diverted to the benefit of capitalists, for example. The first socialists denounced this injustice. Instead, the mercantile system was unfair, according to Smith, because it was partial, because as a system of legislation, it confused the interest of a social class (that of merchants and manufacturers) with the general interest. The result of this partiality was threefold. Firstly, it reduced the rate of growth. Secondly, the defence of merchants' interests, and in particular of their exclusive control of colonial development, led to

[4] For a clear presentation, see Quentin Skinner (1998).

wars, which for the first time took place across much of the whole world.[5] We shall see how the political and economic situation of Great Britain in the aftermath of the Seven Years' War sheds light on some of the *political* proposals of the *Wealth of Nations*; this "first world war" having being won by Britain on the eve of the American War of Independence (1775–1783). Thirdly one may (perhaps) think that the "constitution" of Great Britain saved by the Glorious Revolution of 1688, then threatened to turn itself into a new form of tyranny (just as the Roman Republic fell to imperial tyranny), due to the immense extension of the British Empire after the Seven Years' War.

A second paradox must be underlined. Smith denounces the "partiality" of the British government which had adopted the mercantile system, and had thus adopted the interests of the merchants. Their interests were identified with those of the emerging British (colonial) Empire. But in doing so, Smith at the same time attacks what may have explained the astonishing rise of capitalism in Europe, for it was perhaps the first time, with the exception of "small commercial republics" (the Italian cities of the Renaissance and the United Provinces), that the ruling classes (the *landlords*, for the most part) fully legitimated the views of the merchants and the manufacturers by adopting them, as Smith showed.

Finally, I must immediately address a third paradox. By attacking the mercantile system, Smith attacked certain analytical propositions which were at its heart. These asserted that the interest rate of money was inversely proportional to the "abundance" of money available, then that low rate of interest enhance the price of lands and above all that this greater or lesser "abundance" of money was an essential factor and a measure of the enrichment of an economy. These propositions were theoretical targets of criticism by the *Wealth of Nations*, which devoted much of Book II to show not only that the interest rate depends above all on the real rate of profit, but also that all monetary phenomena only "hide" *real* wealth and *real* enrichment (i.e. capital accumulation). Money, in whatever form, therefore was pushed to the margins of economic analysis. Some economists still welcome this view today: others deplore it. But in any case, one ambition of this book is also to understand this marginalisation of money; and to do this, we must go far back in history.

[5] It is significant that historians qualify the Seven Years' War (1756–1763) as the first world war, because it took place not only in Europe but also in the Americas and in Asia.

I will first try to explain the origins of this critique by Smith, and we shall see that it was rooted in a reflection on the foundations of justice, once it was rid of its religious justifications. If the law and the institutions are not "natural", if they are "artifices"—i.e. human constructions—then they can and must be explained. David Hume (who was very close to Smith) had already shown that law and institutions are products of human understanding intended to channel greed; that is to say, above all, the desire for money which is the only passion "directly destructive of society". Smith extended this approach in two essential ways. On the one hand, for Smith, the law and institutions are products of the history of societies. They cannot therefore be explained solely by the principles of understanding—i.e. by psychology—but need also to be explained by history itself. On the other hand, Smith substituted the accumulation of capital for greed. The accumulation of capital was therefore the activity of merchants and manufacturers whose mercantile system and its institutions support and defend capital accumulation. Smith then quit the field of ethics to enter that of economics and politics.

This criticism of the mercantile system is not the only objective of the *Wealth of Nations*. This book will show that it was for Smith an important element of a much larger project, namely the science of the legislator (Haakonssen, 1981). For Smith, this was a science which was not so much what the legislator had to master, but a science which sought to examine the legislator and which made it possible to examine under what conditions the legislator (the citizens) could *actually govern with impartiality*. In other words, Smith was asking the question: what institutions would make it possible to transform the (partial and hence unjust) mercantile system into a "system of natural liberty" (an impartial and hence just system): i.e. a system which would allow capitalism to be channelled and controlled? For if, according to Smith, the accumulation of capital allowed the enrichment of the poorest, but at the same time the much faster enrichment of the richest, then capitalism is fraught with political threats.

It was therefore during his attack on the mercantile system that Smith "discovered" capitalism, just as Amerigo Vespucci discovered a New World. Like Vespucci, he did not name it. However, as Vespucci, Smith contrasted decisively the New World to the Old World, by opposing the "advanced state" of societies to their "early and rude state". This book thus highlights a remarkable peculiarity of the *Wealth of Nations*, namely that the mercantile system—the European form of capitalism as it was developing before Smith's very eyes—was a viable but dangerous economic model. But it was not the *only* viable economic model. The primitive state was also viable, even if both enrichment (and inequalities) were much lower there. Perhaps there is such a thing as a "system of natural liberty", as the North American English colonies seemed to suggest at the time. However, Smith was very dubious about its stability. This plurality of economic models was very characteristic of Smith. Yet apart from with Marx, it is not mentioned in any important text in economic literature.

However, the description of this discovery is not the only aim of this book. Another aim is to show how Smith's economic analysis, which is rooted both in the philosophical reflections of its author and in his political positions against the mercantile system, acquired its identity and hence its *autonomy*. If the mercantile system was characterised by the accumulation of capital, it was necessary for Smith to explain how the enrichment of some did not occur at the expense of others, but also allowed the enrichment of all—albeit unequally.

How this enrichment occurred was thus an initial question of economic theory. In his earliest texts, Smith already provided an answer, which he later used to inaugurate the *Wealth of Nations*. It was progress in the division of labour, following the "extent of the market", which explained the progress of labour productivity, of wealth per capita, and which in turn explained why the poorest Englishman was richer (in terms specified by Smith) than the richest Native Americans. And this held true despite the increase in inequalities to the advantage of those classes which did not work at all, whereas everyone was assumed to work among Native Americans.

Smith then went on to enrich this latter model decisively. The accumulation of capital—the fruit of savings—was itself a second cause of enrichment. It was this second cause that lay at the heart of the *Wealth of Nations*. It plays a decisive role in Smith's work, and capital, defined as the stock of wealth used for profit, became a central concept in Smith's analysis.

It is therefore necessary to understand how these two causes of enrichment are linked—the division of labour and the accumulation of capital—and also to understand how and in which sectors capital accumulation began and then spread. These questions are complicated, and economic theories have been forced to resort to simplifications in order to progress. This explains why some of these questions were subsequently marginalised or forgotten. This marginalisation or oversight also results from the multiple readings of the *Wealth of Nations* which have piled up for more than two hundred years, because what has happened to this book is what happens to major works: it has helped to generate readers, and some of these readers ultimately became economists.

Indeed, most readers of the *Wealth of Nations* who read the book as economists, read it with *their* specific questions in mind, and have often been pleased to find that Smith had *almost* said what they were saying. According to David Ricardo (1817–1951, p. 13), this is how Smith had "accurately defined the original source of exchangeable value". For Karl Marx (1863), Smith had "recognised the true origin of surplus-value". Or as Milton Friedman (1976) noted, "Smith's great importance for 1976, and his great achievement—as Hayek and others have so eloquently pointed out—is the doctrine of an 'invisible hand', his vision of the way in which the voluntary actions of millions of individuals can be coordinated through a price system without central direction". For Kenneth Arrow and Frank Hahn (1971, p. 1), the analysis of the functioning of the market put forward in the *Wealth of Nations* is "surely the most important intellectual contribution that economic thought has made to general understanding of social processes".

This astonishing diversity has been—as it should be—accompanied by a torrent of criticism commensurate with the homage paid to Smith. For Ricardo, Smith had "himself erected another standard of value" in an "inconsistent" manner (Ricardo, ibid.). For Marx, "Adam Smith is very copiously infected with the conceptions of the Physiocrats, and often whole strata run through his work which belong to the Physiocrats and are in complete contradiction with the views specifically advanced by himself" (Marx, ibid.). Or again, Murray Rothbard (2006, p. 435), who situated himself in the liberal Austrian tradition of Hayek and other, asserted "[t]he problem is that [Smith] originated nothing that was true, and that whatever he originated was wrong".

Such difficulties of interpretation reflect the fact that the *Wealth of Nations* produced its readers. They, in turn, have produced the *Wealth of Nations*. Thus, Ricardo was certain that Chapters 5 and 6 of Book I were introductions to Chapter 1 of his own book. Marx, for his part, found his theory of exploitation in the *Wealth of Nations* that Smith was supposed to have written in opposition to Sir James Steuart's analysis of profit. Today, the dominant reading of Smith, perfectly set out by Friedman or by Arrow and Hahn, associates the metaphor of the "invisible hand" with the behaviour of the market, ignoring that four hundred pages in the *Wealth of Nations* separate Smith's analysis of the market from his widely quoted metaphor (Grampp, 2000). Finally Rothbard goes full circle, as if Marx were right, by raising Smith to be the father of the theory of labour value, and so the mother of all socialisms.

Ricardo, Marx, Friedman, Arrow, Hahn and Rothbard are, or were, economists, and, like all economists, they are or were—more or less consciously—historians of economic thought as well. In a certain way, they practised economic theory retrospectively. This was (and is) inevitable, since they knew that they depended closely on former economists. This is because economic concepts like markets, price, money, etc. are the products of theoretical texts and not just words used in everyday life. This is inevitable and it is useful, because it helped them improve their understanding of their own theories. However, the words of the *Wealth of Nations* used in this way make it an unintelligible palimpsest. Indeed, all these superimposed readings, none of which is absurd, make this book into a seemly inextricable tangle of brilliant intuitions and gross errors.

Books specialising in the history of economic thought encounter similar difficulties. The two most important works seem to me to be those of Samuel Hollander (1973) and Tony Aspromourgos (2009) and they are authoritative. Both authors have read the *Wealth of Nations* as economists, and they consider, with good reason, that price determination is the economic question that determines all others. However, they provide fairly different answers to this. They naturally seek answers in Smith, but they seem to fail to imagine that Smith may not have asked this question. Their readings of the *Wealth of Nations* then reveal analytical inconsistencies, as if it were mutilated somehow to fit Procrustes' bed, while never actually meeting the analytical demands that were legitimately made of it.

One might therefore rightly be surprised by so many contradictory interpretations. Was Adam Smith an inconsistent genius? We need to try to elucidate this oxymoron. Yet, first, how can it be explained? In addition, how then can the coherence of the *Wealth of Nations* be restored?

To do this, we must try to adopt a different approach to that taken so far by economists. Instead of going back to later economic theories that seem to me, rightly or wrongly, relevant, I look *upstream* of the *Wealth of Nations*, using an approach already followed by *Historians of Ideas*, such as Donald Winch (1973), Knut Haakonssen (1981) or Emma Rothschild

(2002). These historians of political, but also economic and social ideas, sought above all to reconstruct the original philosophical *questions* which the *Theory of Moral Sentiments* (Smith's other major work) and the *Wealth of Nations* tried to answer. These questions have been *forgotten* as they have been covered by subsequent readings and interpretations by Smith. The originality of the work proposed here is to extend this approach by showing how the questions of economic theory, this time raised by the *Wealth of Nations*, followed from the philosophical and political positions of Smith.

Smith's answers to these questions are of course debatable. Some of them do still constitute a very solid knowledge base. However, in this book, I am not seeking alternative theories to contemporary approaches by using the *Wealth of Nations*. Nevertheless, Smith's examination of the historical nature of capitalism, its contributions and the dangers capitalism poses to humanity are still current and are very often forgotten.

A French version of this book was published in 2019 by the Éditions du Seuil, and received the Colbert Foundation Prize, awarded by the Institut de France.

It is the joint product of a seminar devoted to Hume and Smith organised for an M.Phil. degree (*DEA* then *M2 Recherche*) on the history of economic thought at the Université Paris 1 Panthéon-Sorbonne, the Université d' Évry and other universities. It owes much to the participants of this seminar over the years.

The book has also benefited from the material and intellectual help of the two research teams to which I have belonged successively: PHARE (Université Paris 1) and EPEE (Université Paris-Saclay, Univ Evry), as well as joint discussions within researchers at BETA (CNRS and Université de Strasbourg) and Triangle (CNRS and Université Lyon II). I also owe a lot to the seminars of CAESAR (Université Paris X Nanterre), and to the discussions with A. Berthoud, J. Cartelier and R. Frydman. I am particularly grateful also to Carlo Benetti, Jean Delemotte, Jean-Marc Gayman, André Hervier, André Lapidus, André Straus and Donald Winch, who gave me the benefit of their knowledgeable and challenging remarks.

Finally, this book has benefited from the very great skills in the history of monetary and financial theories of Sylvie Diatkine.

I would also like to thank Nicholas Sowels, Assistant Professor (Université Paris 1 Pantheon- Sorbonne), who translated a large part of this text, with my supervision.

It goes without saying that any errors are entirely mine.

References

Arrow, K., & Hahn, F. (1971). *General competitive analysis*. North Holland.

Aspromourgos, T. (2009). *The science of wealth: Adam Smith and the framing of political economy*. Routledge.

Friedman, M. (1976). *Adam Smith's relevance for 1976*. University of Chicago, Selected Papers Series, n°50b.

Grampp, W. (2000). What did Smith mean by the invisible hand? *Journal of Political Economy, 108*(3).

Haakonssen, K. (1981). *The science of a legislator, the natural jurisprudence of David Hume and Adam Smith*. Cambridge University Press.

Hollander, S. (1973). *The economics of Adam Smith*. The University of Toronto Press.

Marx, K. (1863). *Theories of surplus value*. https://www.marxists.org/archive/marx/works/1863/theories-surplus-value/ch03.htm#s1.

Ricardo, D. (1817–1951). *On the principles of political economy and taxation*. Cambridge University Press.

Rothbard, M. (2006). *An Austrian perspective on the history of economic thought, 1*. Mises Institute.

Rothschild, E. (2002). *Economic sentiments. Adam Smith, condorcet and the enlightment*. Harvard University Press.

Skinner, Q. (1998). *Liberty before Liberalism*. Cambridge University Press.

Turgot, A. R. J. (1766–1997). *Réflexions sur la formation et la distribution des richesses*. Flammarion.

Winch, D. (1978). *Adam Smith's politics*. Cambridge University Press.

Chronology

26 April 1711	Day of birth of David Hume.
16 June 1723	Day of Birth of Adam Smith (Kirkcaldy, Scotland).
1739–1740	Hume publishes *A Treatise of Human Nature*.
1737–1746	Smith's studies at the University of Glasgow, then at Baillol College, Oxford.
1740–1748	War of the Austrian Succession.
1741	First Hume's *Essays Moral and Political*.
1745	Hume's failure at the University of Edinburgh under the influence of an accusation of atheism (repeated failure in 1751 in Glasgow University).

1745–1746	Attempted insurrection of the Stuarts and Highlanders.
1748–1751	Smith gives private lessons in Edinburgh.
1749 (?)	Hume and Smith meet in Edinburgh.
1751	Smith is appointed Professor of Logic at the University of Glasgow.
1752	Smith succeeds Hutcheson as Chair of Moral Philosophy at the University of Glasgow.
1756–1763	Seven Year's war.
1759	Publication of the *Theory of Moral Sentiments*. Other editions: 1761, 1767, 1774, 1781, 1790.
1764	Smith resigns his chair and become tutor to the young Duke of Buccleuch, on the recommendation of his father-in-law, Sir Charles Townshend (1725–1767), an important politician who became Chancellor of the Exchequer in 1766.
1764–1766	Smith and his pupil joins Hume who is private secretary to the British Ambassador to Paris. After staying in Toulouse, he met Voltaire in Ferney. Back in Paris, Smith attended Mme d'Enville's salon, meeting Holbach and Helvetius, Quesnay and probably Turgot.
Late 1766	Smith returned to Great Britain and then Scotland. He began writing the *Wealth of Nations*.
9 March 1776	Publication of the *Wealth of Nations* by Strahan in London. Other editions of Smith's lifetime: 1778, 1784, 1786 and 1789.
15 August 1776	Death of David Hume. Smith is his executor.
1778	Commissioner of customs in Scotland.
17 July 1790	Smith's death in Edinburgh.

PART I

Preliminaries

CHAPTER 1

Smith and Economic Liberalism

On the 12th–15th April 1990, an international conference was held at the University of Nagoya to commemorate the bicentenary of Adam Smith's death.[1] It brought together historians, philosophers and economists specialised in the work of Smith, including most of the editors of the reference edition of his works: the Glasgow Edition, published in 1976–1978 by Oxford University Press. The conference participants studied *An Inquiry into The Nature and Causes of the Wealth of Nations* as a part—and certainly very important—of a work covering very broad disciplinary fields. Everyone was fully aware that Smith was undoubtedly a resolute opponent of monopolies, specifically in the sense of privileges granted by the State to certain companies. Yet Smith was surely not opposed to all political economy and all regulation. This can be easily seen when reading him. Accordingly, identifying the *Wealth of Nations* as the founding text of economic liberalism was not even discussed by the participants at the conference.

This book follows the perspective of the conference. It may therefore provoke readers' surprise, because the divergence between specialist views of Adam Smith's thinking and public opinion is very clear. For the

[1] The proceedings of this conference were published by Hiroshi Mizuta and Chuhei Sugiyama (1993).

D. Diatkine, *Adam Smith and the Wealth of Nations*, Palgrave Studies in the History of Economic Thought, https://doi.org/10.1007/978-3-030-81600-1_1

latter, the mere mention of Adam Smith's name has become a catchphrase closely associated with neoliberal views which celebrate the virtues of the "invisible hand" of the competitive marketplace.

However, the main aim of this book is not to show that this commonplace slogan has no solid foundations in the work of Smith. Yet argument is possible, and so I would like to clarify certain points as a forward.

It is important to recall that *economic* liberalism is a *doctrine* in the positive meaning of this term. Lawyers accept that, in certain cases, a doctrine may justify the decisions of a court, provided the doctrine emanates from an authoritative institution (for example, the university). More generally, a doctrine is a properly argued opinion.

A doctrine expresses a position in a legal or political *debate*. Consequently, a doctrine may only be understood in relationship to another, which it opposes. It is therefore difficult to define a doctrine positively, out of its context. It is easier to define economic liberalism *negatively*. Given that it is a doctrine, it argues *against* a discourse or rectifies a proposition. To understand this better, it may be useful to attempt a short history of the term liberalism.[2] In Sect. 1 below, I will start by showing that economic liberalism is different from the notion of *laissez-faire*. The next section then quickly describes the emergence of the term "political liberalism" in the language of the nineteenth century. I will then show (just as quickly) that economic liberalism, as a doctrine begins in France and only began to be used against the emerging workers' movements (Sect. 3). Finally, Sect. 4 recalls why the term *liberal* has a rather different meaning in the English-speaking/Anglo-Saxon world.

Section 1) The assertion of *laissez-faire* as a principle is often considered to be the first manifestation of economic liberalism.[3] This principle is widely attributed to Vincent de Gournay, as Count d'Albon (1775, pp. 136–137) wrote in 1775 in his *Eloge de François Quesnay*: "It was here that Quesnay met with the wise M. de Gournay, Intendant of Commerce, and a contemporary, whom he esteemed, whom he liked, and in whom, along with his disciples, he took pleasure in founding some of the hope of his country. Mr. Gournay reached this practical result by a different route: nobody, he said, does anything so useful to commerce as those who actually do it. They should not be subject to regulations. Nobody

[2] See D. Diatkine (2007) and especially Catherine Audard (2009).

[3] See: J. M. Keynes (1926).

is as interested in knowing whether a trading business, a factory, or a profession will be profitable, as the person actually willing to try it. There should therefore be no corporations, no juries, no exclusive privileges". … "It is thus necessary to free their work from these taxes which intercept their success … *Laissez les faire & laissez-les passer*".[4]

However, it is easy to show that the Count d'Albon was mistaken: *laissez-faire* was in fact much older. This is what Turgot (*Eloge de M. Vincent de Gournay*, [Turgot, 1970]), himself had said, a few years earlier, when he had precisely praised de Gournay: "It must also be said that M. de Gournay's alleged system has the particularity that it's general principles have been pretty much adopted by everyone; that, at all times, the wish to trade among all nations has been contained in these two words: freedom and protection, and above all freedom. We know what Mr. Le Gendre said to Mr. Colbert: '*laissez-nous faire*'".[5]

Laissez-faire therefore predated Gournay. However, the text by Count d'Albon allows us easily to enter one of the most common arguments in the eighteenth century, namely that nobody knows better than they themselves what is in their interest. This proposition was seen as a powerful attack on the absolutist dogma that obedience to the sovereign by divine right was required of subjects, just like obedience to the father was required of children, and obedience to divine laws was required of believers, because the monarch knew better what was good for his subjects than they did themselves. In opposition to absolutism, *laissez-faire* objected precisely that citizens were not subjects because they were not children. In the *Wealth of nations,* we find the idea that an individual

[4] My translation. "C'est ici que Quesnay s'est rencontré avec le sage M. de Gournay, Intendant du Commerce, son Contemporain, qu'il estima, qu'il aima & sur la personne & sur les disciples duquel il se plaisoit à fonder une partie de l'espoir de sa patrie. M. de Gournay étoit arrivé à ce résultat pratique, par une route différente: personne, disoit-il, ne fait si bien ce qui est utile au commerce que ceux qui le font; il ne faut donc point leur imposer des règlements. Personne n'est si intéressé à savoir si une entreprise de commerce, si un établissement de fabrique, si l'exercice d'une profession lui sera profitable ou non, que celui qui veut le tenter; il ne faut donc ni corporations, ni jurandes, ni privilèges exclusifs". … "il faut donc affranchir leurs travaux de ces impôts qui en interceptent le succès… *Laissez les faire & laissez-les passer*".

[5] My translation: "Il faut dire encore que ce prétendu système de M. de Gournay a cela de particulier, que les principes généraux en sont à peu près adoptés par tout le monde; que, de tout temps, le vœu du commerce chez toutes les nations a été renfermé dans ces deux mots: liberté et protection, et surtout liberté. On sait le mot de M. Le Gendre à M. Colbert: "laissez-nous faire"".

(provided *he* is adult, mentally sane, male, and not a servant, a slave, in military service, nor imprisoned) knows better than anyone *his* own interest. But this was a common place view in eighteenth-century Western Europe.

More generally, the principle of "letting nature do" had and has a very broad application, as we know, and can be found in the field of pedagogy (see *Emile* by Jean-Jacques Rousseau) or horticulture, etc. It means letting nature do its business, and not constraining nature by opposing it; instead using nature to better control it. Such *laissez-faire* requires attentive pedagogues and skilful gardeners, who watch over the reproduction of organisms to avoid ever-possible accidents.

In economics, a classic medical metaphor associates the free circulation of wealth with the free circulation of blood. The struggle by the Physiocrats for free trade in general, and for that of corn in particular, did not manifest their belief in a spontaneous competitive mechanism. Instead, it reflected more the view of the organic character of the body politic, which reproduces itself from one period to another, does so all the better when the circulation of wealth is not impeded. Yet this organism, like all organisms, may suffer accidents in reproduction (wars, epidemics, epizootics and disastrous crop failures), accidents that may require the attentive care of the sovereign for the organism to be preserved. The sovereign must therefore avoid obstacles to the circulation of wealth, as regulations on wheat trade tended to do. However, laissez-faire was not enough to always—and in all cases—ensure the reproduction of the social body. Thus, according to Quesnay, the distribution of net income operated by the owners between the sterile and productive classes could not be arbitrary, although it was not regulated by any market mechanism. It could not therefore be left unattended if reproduction was to be ensured. Here reproduction is the important notion. It characterise an organic conception of society. We all know what distinguishes an organism from a mechanism. We can disassemble a mechanism and reassemble it. This is never the case for an organism, where the whole is greater than the sum of the parts.

The principle of *laissez-faire* used to be mentioned above all in two crucial areas. The first was that of the wheat trade. We know that most of the spending on consumption by most people at the time was spent on the purchase of cereals. However, the price of cereals was very unstable, being sensitive to climatic and phytosanitary hazards. The spontaneous policy therefore consisted in trying to store cereals in times of good harvests. Yet, such preservation costs were very high. The protagonists of the *laissez-faire*, using some solid arguments, claimed this very expensive policy to be counterproductive. Allowing the sale of surplus wheat outside the region would maintain a "good price" of wheat and thus avoid the impoverishment of the countryside, and consequently that of the cities whose countryside are the markets.

The second area is still relevant today, and is well known as "Dutch disease" which hits economies benefiting from mining rents. This had been the case of the Spanish economy through which the precious metals from the Americas flowed. The Spanish government had tried to protect its economy by prohibiting—unsuccessfully—imports of goods and exports of precious metals.

This prohibitionist policy was quickly criticised, in particular when its implementation was planned in England, at the beginning of the seventeenth century. Its most famous opponent was Thomas Mun (1664–1895),[6] who is discussed later in this book, and who showed with some talent that this possibility would impoverish the economy rather than preserve its wealth. Such "sanguinary laws" (WON 436) would only act to worsen the economic situation, while merchants' import–export activities that such legislation sought to combat were in fact the cornerstones of general prosperity. This explains why we must understand the dialogue between Colbert and the merchant Legendre as follows. Colbert assumed (and this was the essence of Colbertism) that the interests of the kingdom were identical to the interests of the merchants, because only the latter were able to import precious metals lacking in the kingdom (or at least avoid their exportation). Therefore, the duty of the State was to help the merchants, and so he surely asked Legendre the question: "What must be done to help you?", to which Legendre replied, "laissez-nous faire" (let us do). Legendre's answer thus very simply stated that the interests of the merchants (who were obviously alone capable of knowing) were identical

[6] Mun was a director of the East India Compay (EIC), from 1615 until his death. In the 1620s, the pound sterling was attacked by the foreign-exchange markets, and the price of sterling silver rose. There was debate over why this happened. The newly created EIC, whose trade with India was in deficit as indeed had always been the case of trade between Europe and the Orient, was attacked. Mun defended the Company by demonstrating that the re-export of Asian products to the rest of Europe more than compensated for these deficits. See Lars Magnusson (1994).

to those of the State. However, as we shall see later, for Smith, this assertion characterised the partiality of the mercantile system which he set out to challenge root and branch in the *Wealth of Nations*. We are therefore faced with a curious paradox: the partisans of the mercantile system, which Smith criticises with vigour, in fact, defend some propositions considered as the ancestors of economic liberalism.

It was in this way that everybody in the eighteenth century judged Spain's policy to be ineffective, especially proponents of the mercantile system who were criticised by the *Wealth of Nations*. On the other hand, the free movement of wheat and corn led to intense and well-known debates, especially in France.

Laissez-faire, laissez-passer is untranslatable into English, and was a French doctrine emanating from royal intendant of the *Ancien Régime*. Yet, Hayek (1946), for example, who was an expert of economic liberalism was certainly not mistaken by denouncing the "false individualism" and holism of Continental thinkers.[7]

Section 2. "What is this word liberal,/That people of a certain kind/ use here and there?/ It is the diminutive of *liberty*".[8]

One example is enough to demonstrate that it is very difficult to define economic liberalism positively. In a book by M. Biziou (2003) entitled *Adam Smith et l'origine du libéralisme*, the author proposes this carefully worded definition of economic liberalism: "The minimum reasonable degree of state intervention". Such care in formulation is important, and here Biziou's is followed by all economists. Tracing the demarcation between the agenda and non-agenda is common, as far as I know, to all economists. Biziou is less concerned with the origins of economic liberalism than with the origins of British political economy, which he assumes to be the same as economic liberalism—an elision which is not his alone. Smith "had twins", so to speak—he brought forth into the world simultaneously liberalism and political economy, and the one has been taken for the other ever since.

We still lack a general treatment of the history of the term "economic liberalism". At the end of the Second Empire, Littré (1863–1872) made no mention in his dictionary entry "Libéral" of the economic dimension of the term. He proposed three meanings for the word. The first

[7] See F. Hayek (1946).

[8] "Qu'est-ce que ce mot libéral/Que des gens d'un certain calibre/Placent toujours tant bien que mal ?/ C'est le diminutif de libre". Écouchard Lebrun (1729–1807), cited by Littré (1863–1872).

and oldest is linked to the liberal arts that are the worthy activities of a free man. They are *ends* in themselves, as opposed to the mechanical arts, which are only *means* permitting the appropriation of goods. This opposition is a classical one and survives today in the expression "liberal professions". The second sense is clearly related to the first since it involves the idea of generosity, that practised by a free man "who likes to give", who therefore possesses the *freedom* to give because it is not subordinated to the *necessities* of work. Littré then gives a third sense whose connection with the previous two appears to him rather odd: this is political liberalism, which according to Balzac goes back, he thinks, to the opponents of the First Empire, Benjamin Constant and Madame de Staël. Here Littré cites from Germaine de Staël's book *Corinne* (VI, 3): "Florentines, possessed either by liberty or princes of a liberal character, are enlightened and peaceful". Littré thought that this third sense was imperfectly linked to the first two and assumed that it dated "at least from the Consulate". Today, on the other hand, Germaine de Staël's statement is hardly a surprise. She only attributes generosity to "Florentine princes" and hence to the state, that is, an openness of spirit and tolerance that is part of the second sense of "liberal" and which had until then been reserved for private individuals.

Here I would like to risk two conjectures.

Balzac's attribution to Benjamin Constant and Madame de Staël of this political sense of the term "liberalism" could be explained by the fact that the Consulate appears to be an optimal political regime to Germaine de Staël, Benjamin Constant and those close to them; Constant was nominated to the *Tribunat* (Lavisse, 1921, t.III, p. 78). At this precise moment, the first half of 1800, the regime had abandoned the official cult of the Republic (the "culte de l'être suprême) *Freedom of conscience* now seemed to typify Consulate policy, adopting a policy of religious indifference. Then from the summer of 1800, Bonaparte made overtures to the Catholic Church and prepared for the signing of the *concordat*. The break between the "Salm Hotel Group" and Bonaparte is probably linked to this change in religious policy.

This affirmation of freedom of conscience made by political liberalism will find its clearest expression in the course of the Restoration (1815–1830) among the opponents of the ultras under Louis XVIII and above all under Charles X; it is during the reign of the latter that the need for an alliance between the French Catholic Church and the monarchy will be stated most forcefully.

Section 3. However, it was in the course of the Restoration and the July Monarchy that the first critiques of industrialisation were aired. Not only do the first workers' demands for the regulation of the labour contract appear, but also a legitimist reaction describing workers' conditions, demanding measures such as the creation of relief funds and even the development of factory inspection. Under the July Monarchy, therefore, the need for regulation of the labour contract came, simultaneously, from the early stages of the workers' movement and also from some defenders of legitimist tradition.

My second conjecture is that economic liberalism arose to prevent any linkage between legitimism and the workers' movement, representing a threat to the July Monarchy from both right and left. Here I take up a point already raised by Gide and Rist (1944).[9] If my hypothesis is correct, in France, the connection between political liberalism (representing above all freedom of conscience and opposition to any official religion) and economic liberalism—probably called so by F. Bastiat (1849) advocating contractual freedom and opposing the right to work—came about as an attempt to counter this linkage of left and right. Support for this comes from Coquelin and Guillaumin's economic dictionary in which there is no entry for liberalism, but entries for "freedom of commerce" and "freedom to work", the first written by Molinari and the second by Garnier. The latter stated that "the freedom to work includes competition, the freedom of transactions and of commerce" since in the final analysis, the freedom to work is nothing but the freedom to exercise one's own right of property. Word for word here we find the classical identification of property and labour which allowed Tocqueville, for instance, to successfully oppose the inclusion of the right to work in the Declaration of Constitutional Rights issued by the Second Republic. Since the right to property was already included, the addition of the right to work (which is not "obviously" the right to wages) was said to be entirely redundant.

[9] Gide and Rist (1944) suggested that there was during the July Monarchy "…a conjunction of political and economic liberty, and these were melded into the same sect and bore the same name—liberalism. Economic liberty, that of work and transactions, was elevated to the same status as the freedom of conscience or the freedom of the press" (p. 382).

Section 4. I can complete these two conjectures with a brief examination of the occurrence of the terms "liberal" and "liberalism" in English. The existing etymological dictionaries[10] are here very close to Littré. This should be no surprise, since the origins of the words lie in Medieval Latin (*liber*) together with its academic connotations (the seven liberal arts). The political connotation appears to have been imported from France, but also from Spain since the first use of the term in its political sense occurred in French and Spanish (*liberales*), and this usage was adopted by English conservatives seeking to characterise their political opponents, stigmatising them as partisans of ideas contrary to English tradition. This represents therefore the moral and political significance of the term "liberal" in English usage throughout the remainder of the nineteenth century.

One has to wait until 1954 for the *Britannica World Language Dictionary* to include an entry on "Liberalism" which includes a mention for "economic liberalism", since the term expresses (a) a favourable attitude to reform and hostility to both conservatism and revolution; (b) an economic doctrine favourable to *laissez-faire*; (c) a doctrine opposed to conservatism; (d) in nineteenth-century Britain, a Catholic religious doctrine opposed to ultramontanes or Protestants and which favours a historical reading of the Bible.

The *Oxford English Dictionary* is more detailed and extends this semantic profusion. It notes that the word "liberal" has a different meaning outside Europe. It cites the *New York Times* for 23rd January 1940, arguing that the word "liberal" has become a source of some confusion, for whoever is not a conservative automatically becomes a "liberal", a "radical" or a "red", these three terms being employed as synonyms. In a similar way, "communist" and "liberal" were interchangeable in South Africa.

To link Smith to economic liberalism means that one considers Smith's doctrinaire while at the same time committing an obvious anachronism. Of course, economic liberals have seized upon the *Wealth of Nations* and Smith's authority is regularly invoked when the metaphor of the "invisible hand" is cited; this has itself become an icon of economic liberalism together with the profile of the Scottish philosopher that adorns the ties worn by members of the Mont Pélerin Society.

[10] Skeat, Etymological Dictionary 1879, 1882; Barnhardt, Dictionary of Etymology 1988.

Numerous texts have been penned, from Jacob Viner (1928) to Spencer Pack (1991, 2005) or Steven Medema and Warren Samuels (2005), all of which demonstrate how distant Smith was from economic liberalism. They have still failed to convince the most extreme liberals, some of whom like Murray Rothbard (1995) insist that Smith was the harbinger of Marx.

This controversy will have no end, and like the wider assimilation of liberalism to economic theory, it blocks our path to the most important point: pursuit of the linkages woven by Smith between economic theory and practical policy. And to do so, I intend to consider the criticisms that Smith made of what he called the "mercantile system".

Smith's criticisms of the mercantile system are very sharp indeed; and in making such criticisms, he is aiming at the greater part of contemporary economic policy as well as its underlying principles.

It can of course be said that he is criticising a "particular" type of state intervention; but here again, it is not for me a matter of where he draws the line between the agenda and the non-agenda of the state, but instead to understand how Smith perceived political practice. I start from the perspective long since opened by the work of Donald Winch (1978) and Knud Haakonssen (1981). This involves "…what Smith can legitimately be said to have intended, rather than with what he might be said to have anticipated or foreshadowed" (Winch, 1978, p.1). Let us therefore examine how Smith criticised what he called, after Mirabeau (1763), the mercantile system.

The mercantile system is quite different from the usual adversaries of economic liberalism: socialism, planned economies, welfare states are not discoveries of Bastiat, Barone or Hayek. By contrast, we find in Smith (and in Mirabeau) the *invention* of a mercantile system. Nobody is ever cited as a proponent or defender of this system. Smith's adversaries (first among them Sir James Steuart, who is cited not once) study *political œconomy*. And I will come back on this point. Smith's critique could just as well be entitled "critique of political œconomy". By that, I want to suggest that the mercantile system is, for Smith, no less than the economy of his time and the discourses that seek to come to terms with it.

So Smith wrote *Wealth of Nations against his own invention*. The genesis and description of the mercantile system take up the most part of Books III and IV, the political difficulties to which this leads being dealt with in the fifth and last book of the work.

A characteristic feature of the mercantile system appears if one makes a comparison with the way that Smith presents the other system that he criticises, the "agricultural system", or Physiocracy. The latter is purely theoretical and will therefore never do any kind of harm.[11]

By contrast, the mercantile system is not only a body of theoretical propositions ("speculations" which will be examined in due course) but also a set of political practices associated with these propositions.

This set of practices is minutely described in Book IV, culminating in the analysis of the colonial system, a system which is raised to the status of a caricature with the conquest of Bengal by the East India Company during the Seven Years' War.

This critique is all the more effective because Smith, and this is unusual enough to demand emphasis, begins by outlining a seductive *theory* for his adversary. The mercantile system is *not therefore* the result of ignorance of the fundamental laws of economics. Instead, the mercantile system is held to be the outcome of connivance between merchants and the legislator. These are the *interests*, more or less conscious, that are defended by the ruler. The mercantile system is also the outcome of a history; it expresses a kind of historical *necessity*. But if it were necessary, could it be transformed? And if so, how? This question of political practice and its relation to theory is one that will haunt the entire history of Marxism and the workers' movement. I believe that this issue finds its first expression in the pages of the *Wealth of Nations*. And this is the more important difference with economic liberalism of today.

[11] "That system which represents the produce of land as the sole source of the revenue and wealth of every country has, so far as I know, never been adopted by any nation, and it at present exists only in the speculations of a few men of great learning and ingenuity in France. It would not, surely, be worth while to examine at great length the errors of a system which never has done, and probably never will do any harm in any part of the world" (WON, 663).

References

Albon, Comte d'. (1775). *Eloge historique de François Quesnay*. de Knapen.
Audard, C. (2009). *Qu'est-ce que le libéralisme?* Gallimard.
Bastiat, F. (1849). *Protectionnisme et communisme*. Paris, Guillaumin.
Biziou M. (2003). *Adam Smith et l'origine du libéralisme*. P.U.F.
Diatkine, D. (2007). Le suffrage et le marché: la critique par Smith du système mercantile est-elle libérale ? *Cahiers d'Economie Politique* (52).
Gide, C., & Rist, C. (1944). *Histoire des doctrines économiques, depuis les Physiocrates jusqu'à nos jours*. Larose et Tenin.
Haakonssen, K. (1981). *The science of a lagislator*. Cambridge University Press.
Hayek, F. (1946). *Individualism: True and false*. Blackwell.
Keynes, J. M. (1926). *The End of Laissez-Faire*. Hogarth Press.
Lavisse, E. (Ed.). (1921). *Histoire de la France contemporaine*. Hachette.
Littré. (1863–1872). *Dictionnaire de la langue française*. Hachette.
Magnusson, L. (1994). *The shaping of an economic language*. Routledge.
Medema, S. G., & Samuels, W. J. (2005). Freeing Smith from the "free market": On the misperception of Adam Smith on the economic role of government. *History of Political Economy*, *37*(2), 219–226.
Mirabeau. (1763). *Philosophie rurale, ou Economie Générale et politique de l'agriculture*. Amsterdam, Libraires associés.
Mizuta, H., & Sugiyama, C. (1993). *Adam Smith*. London, Mac Millan Press.
Mun, T. (1664–1895). *England's treasure by foreign trade* or *the Balance of foreign trade is the rule of our treasure*. https://en.wikisource.org
Pack, S. (1991). *Adam smith's critique of the free market economy*. Billing & Sons.
Pack, S. (2005). Freeing Smith from the "free market": On the misperception of Adam Smith on the economic role of government. *History of Political Economy, 37*(2), 219–226.
Rothbard, M. (2006). *An Austrian perspective on the history of economic thought* (Vol. 1). Mises Institute.
Turgot, . (1970). *Ecrits Economiques*. Calmann-Lévy.
Viner, J. (1928). Adam Smith and laissez faire. In John Maurice Clark et al., *Adam Smith 1776–1926*. Chicago, University of Chicago Press.
Winch, D. (1978). *Adam Smith's politics*. Cambridge University Press.

CHAPTER 2

Hume's Challenge: Hume's Theory of Promise

The mercantile system is a partial system and that is why it can be dangerous. This book wishes to shed light on this proposal, which seems to be as important as it is obscure. It is therefore necessary to understand what Smith means by "system" and "partiality" in Smith's work. This elucidation will be the subject of the next chapter. It requires a detour through the work of Smith's friend, David Hume (1711–1776).

Historians of ideas like Duncan Forbes (1976), Donald Winch (1978) or Knut Haakonssen (1981) have underlined the close links between Hume and Smith, especially in the field of political philosophy. Here I want only to remember the importance of the "Sceptical Whiggism" in their political philosophy. The political issue concerns the fragility of the regime inherited from the Glorious Revolution. This fragility is revealed by the inconsistency in Whiggism's theory of the social contract, which attempts to explain this Revolution as a return to the old theory of contract denied by the absolutist practice of James II. As we know,

A first version of this chapter, translated by Keith Tribe, is published under the title Hume's *Treatise of Human Nature* and "Liberalism of Freedom" in R. Ege and H. Iggersheim (2011).

D. Diatkine, *Adam Smith and the Wealth of Nations*, Palgrave Studies in the History of Economic Thought, https://doi.org/10.1007/978-3-030-81600-1_2

Hume was a firm adversary of social contract theories, and, more generally attempted to demonstrate that rules of justice are artificial and require controlling the insatiable passion for possessions. Yet, if rules of justice are artifices, then there is no more room for the idea of a natural (divine) right. On the contrary, such artifices are the products of human understanding. I emphasise this point because I will show in the next chapters how Smith developed this position in two important ways. The first was Smith's attempt to prove that those artifices were not (only) the products of understanding: they were in fact the *products of history*. The second one qualified the insatiable passion for possessions as the *accumulation of capital*. Smith then dropped psychology in favour of economics and history.

The Hume's central thesis based his theory of justice on a set of necessary artifices. This was a sensitive issue for two reasons:

1. Regarding justice as an artificial virtue (as Hume affirms), meant making a clean break with theories of natural law and the social contract. It therefore meant running two risks. First of doing away with what has always seemed to be one of the most precious ramparts protecting the individual against the omnipotence of government; secondly the risk, very real, to be accused of irreligion.
2. Hume challenged traditional opinion concerning justice. For him, what was astonishing was not that we obey the law (in its most general sense) because we are afraid of punishment, but that *we actually want* to obey the law. Of course, we often infringe the law, when our interest is stronger than our sentiment of obligation. However, if we are not perverse, then we will judge ourselves to be guilty. How is this possible?

Before responding to this question, I want to show that Hume's theory relies on the partiality of sympathy to show that the feeling of justice or injustice cannot emanate from this (I). This is why the rules of justice are necessary artifices (II), and at the heart of these artifices lies the necessity of keeping one's promises. However, *seen in isolation*, this archetypal act of fairness—which quite simply lays the foundations for trust (in society, in others and in oneself)—cannot be justified by either private or social utility.

Sympathy is Partial

Hume's theory of justice is set out in the third and last Book of the *Treatise of Human Nature.*[1] Hume explains very simply why rules of Justice are indispensable. In the Second Book, he had explained how passions—and only passions—are the motors of action. So, only passions may limit passions. There is only one passion which is never limited by any other passion, namely cupidity or interest: "No one can doubt, that the convention for the distinction of property, and for the stability of possession, is of all circumstances the most necessary to the establishment of human society, and that after the agreement for the fixing and observing of this rule, there remains little or nothing to be done towards settling a perfect harmony and concord. All the other passions, beside this of interest, are either easily restrain'd, or are not of such pernicious consequence, when indulg'd. *Vanity* is rather to be esteem'd a social passion, and a bond of union among men. *Pity* and *love* are to be consider'd in the same light. And as to *envy* and *revenge,* tho' pernicious, they operate only by intervals, and are directed against particular persons, whom we consider as our superiors or enemies. *This avidity alone, of acquiring goods and possessions for ourselves and our nearest friends, is insatiable, perpetual, universal, and directly destructive of society*. There scarce is any one, who is not actuated by it; and there is no one, who has not reason to fear from it, when it acts without any restraint, and gives way to its first and most natural movements. So that upon the whole, we are to esteem the difficulties in the establishment of society, to be greater or less, according to those we encounter in regulating and restraining this passion" (Hume, [1739–1740] 1983, pp. 491–492).

The denunciation of chrematistic as a destructive passion of society has been well-known since Aristotle's *Politics*. However, Hume's novelty lay in his attempt to found a theory of justice as an artificial virtue; as a means "to regulate" this passion. I insist on this point because we will see that one of the most important novelties of the *Wealth of Nations* is founded exactly on this. The "avidity of acquiring goods"—insatiable and perpetual, but not universal—is transformed into capital accumulation. As we shall see later, if accumulation of capital allows enrichment, it is not without dangers and the dangers here according to Smith were not moral, but political.

[1] Hume ([1739–1740] 1983), thereafter quoted as THN.

Traditionally, moral judgement concerns judgements relating to human actions and covers three principal domains: ugly and beautiful, good and bad, just and unjust. British moral philosophy called on *sympathy*, as we will see. However, Hume's new proposition in this domain resides in the affirmation whereby sympathy allows us to bring moral judgements to bear concerning the first two domains, but certainly not the third. According to Hume, sympathy is inevitably partial, whereas justice is impartial by definition. Therefore sympathy cannot make judgements concerning what is just or unjust. It is thus the role of artifices to allow such judgements to be made. This must be examined.

Hume thus uses the generally accepted theories of moral judgement of his time, developed by Shaftesbury then Hutcheson, to produce a devastating critique of these same theories. The stakes are high and are above all political, since it is not only the theories of natural law that are in question, but also the political principles that legitimate the political regime that resulted from the 1688 revolution. It is also theoretical, since Hume would develop his own theory based on this critique.

The initial question posed by Hume is that of moral judgement moral, that is, the question of knowing what is implied by the statement: "X is a virtuous man".

Hume's response (Hume, [1739–1740] 1983, p. 471) is deployed in two phases. Hume admits the existence of a "moral sense", which procures of its own accord this particular pleasure or displeasure that makes us judge a given action as virtuous or not. Indeed, this sentiment, which makes us praise or blame, this pleasure or pain which inevitably accompanies it, are characterised by the fact that they stem from a general character, without any relationship whatsoever with our specific interest (Hume, [1739–1740] 1983, p. 472).

From this moral sense, then, comes the judgement concerning what Hume calls natural virtues (and natural vices). Of course, it is the knowledge of the reasons for the action that allow us to judge it, and this knowledge is procured for us through sympathy, that is, the property that is deemed profoundly human of being able to put oneself, as a spectator, in the place of the actor and to experience in some way the feelings experienced by that person. This social experience provided by sympathy is partial and procures the "habits" that engender moral judgement concerning *good or bad*. However, this moral sense is not at all pertinent for making judgements regarding what is *just or unjust*.

It is important to note that if sympathy is partial, this is because it can only deal with close and specific objects. It is clear that it is because of this characteristic that it is inevitably partial. In order to gain access to general and far-removed principles—those of justice—artifice is required. This point merits further comment, since it engages Hume's conception of partiality. Being partial, of course, means mistaking one part for the whole. However, it is characteristic of Hume to associate the part to that which is particular and contingent. The whole, however, is understood as though it was general and necessary. Therefore, it is because sympathy can only take the particular and contingent into consideration that it is partial. It is clear that the construction of artifices must also allow judgements of a general nature to be formulated.

The problem posed by Hume is thus to describe which process allows us to pass from specific judgement, which is partial since it is limited, to a judgement that is impartial since it is general. In other words, Hume must describe how we manage to formulate judgments regarding what is just and unjust, independently of any reference to a "moral sense". If Hume can take up this challenge, he can demonstrate why justice is an artificial virtue.

Rules of Justice Are Not the Results of Sympathy

What does the notion of artifice mean here? If justice is an artificial virtue, this is because nothing in the operation of sympathy allows us to isolate the rules of justice.

To return to one of Hume's examples, it is certainly not selfishness that obliges me to repay a loan when it is due. It is not benevolence either (since people other than the lender may need the loan amount), or even an action in the public interest, since the lender may be a "vicious man who deserves the hatred of all mankind".[2] Similarly, the exemplariness of the act cannot be claimed, since the "loan may be secret", and no moralist would conclude that duty and obligation disappear with publicity (Hume, [1739] 1983, p. 597). It therefore follows that the immediate reason for the just act can only be the desire for one's action to conform with general rules. What might this proposition mean exactly? How can we desire something other than that which conforms to our particular,

[2] A little further on (Hume, [1739] 1983), p. 497), Hume is more precise: this creditor who "deserves the hatred of all mankind" is "a seditious bigot", a characteristic loaded with meaning in the eighteenth and twenty-first centuries.

private interest? This question not only pertains to investigating how we can *construct* the common good—which was posed by Hobbes and to which he responded by the theory of *covenant* forming the basis of the Leviathan—but above all, it asks *why it is that we desire it*? In other words, the surprising element is not the fact that laws exist, but that we *want to* obey them (or, what amounts to the same thing *in this context*, the fact that we feel guilty when we infringe them).

If Hume is right, it is clear that he is shutting the door on any attempts (such as those of Shaftesbury and Hutcheson) that aim to found the law on a moral sense that is inherent to each individual.

Justice is an artificial virtue. This thesis is difficult, provocative and dangerous,[3] since it raises an obvious difficulty in its turn. If justice is artificial, how does it distinguish itself from what is arbitrary? The obvious power of the theory of natural law resides in the fact that it closely associates the natural and the universal. Hume, in his critique in this particular domain, risks assigning a comfortable and sinister scepticism to us once again, one that is very fashionable in our post-modern times, whereby human rights are not universal, but local, circumstantial and thus contingent. Hume must therefore demonstrate that this artifice is not contingent but necessary.

No spontaneous individual process resulting from sympathy can therefore explain the production of the rules of justice. This is why they are artifices. Yet, they are necessary to society. I must firstly explain that this necessary character of justice involves two different meanings: on the one hand, as an artifice, justice is necessary because the rules of justice are *inevitably constructed* according to the rules of understanding, which are necessary rules, and on the other hand, it is because justice is a *general* system that it is socially necessary.

Now I will show an example—that of the right of ownership—of the way in which Hume attempts to explain how *custom*, that is, practice, allows rules of justice to be developed.

All of the rules that fix the right of ownership make up a set of conventions. Hume carefully distinguishes between conventions and contracts,

[3] Hume was very sharply attacked on this point when he was a candidate in 1744 for a chair at the University of Edinburgh. William Wishart, who directed this university, accused him of undermine the foundations of morality by denying the natural and therefore essential difference between good and bad, just and unjust. Cf. Eugenio Lecaldano (2008).

which are exchanges of promises. It is clear that Hume will seek to demonstrate how the right of ownership is independent, since it logically precedes the contract. In fact, he states that this convention is not of the same nature as a promise. This is a difficult point that warrants explanation. For Hume:

> I observe, that it will be for my interest to leave another in the possession of his goods, *provided* he will act in the same manner with regard to me. He is sensible of a like interest in the regulation of his conduct. When this common sense of interest is mutually express'd, and is known to both, it produces a suitable resolution and behaviour. And this may properly enough be call'd a convention or agreement betwixt us, tho' without the interposition of a promise; since the actions of each of us have a reference to those of the other, and are perform'd upon the supposition, that something is to be perform'd on the other part. Two men, who pull the oars of a boat, do it by an agreement or convention, tho' they have never given promises to each other. (Hume, [1739] 1983, p. 490)

This famous quote raises several issues. Firstly, it is difficult to imagine that this convention is not the product of a rational calculation; secondly, it is not clear that no promise was involved in the convention. Jonathan Harrison (1981, p. 58) claimed, not without a certain degree of plausibility, that Hume's statement here is contradictory, since it is difficult to imagine that no promise—at least implicit—exists in the agreement between two men deciding to abstain from violating their respective properties. If one man says to another: "I will not take your goods if you do not take mine" and the other responds "I agree", it is hard not to see in this exchange of words an exchange of promises that are tacit at the least. Likewise, the example of the boaters seems likely to attract similar criticism.

According to Harrison, then, each of the parties involved would consider the other to be guilty of acting in bad faith if the other did not fulfil his engagement. In these conditions, it is of course the whole edifice developed by Hume regarding promises and contracts that threatens to fall, since moral judgement now seems to logically precede the convention. This is why Harrison proposes to interpret Hume's position as involving the simultaneity of the conventions concerning both ownership and promises.

In my opinion, such an analysis merely postpones the difficulty, but does not resolve it, since it calls into question the principle of causality. As we shall see, in Hume's analysis, the promise is inevitably a consequence of ownership.

However, Hume's text is particularly clear. Let us examine the example of the boaters once again. Since, in this case, the "common sense of interest" is "mutually express'd", it seems obvious that what he means is that each boater knows that the free-rider strategy is a losing one, because *each party* knows that the effort *of both* is required for the journey. It is therefore unthinkable that one of the rowers can abstain from rowing without losing all hope of attaining his goal. Clearly, we can interpret this example in terms of a cooperative game, in which each rower is obliged to adopt a cooperative strategy for fear of losing too much, since the free-rider strategy is, in this case, very penalising. But what is important is that the two boaters together act like *one single* rower, since no alternative strategy is possible. In this case, the act of cooperation does not involve even an implicit exchange of promises.

However, we may take this even further, since Hume proposes examples of conventions that clearly have no basis in individual behaviour, like the conventions of language and the standard of money (Hume, [1739] 1983, p. 608). According to Hume, the use of gold or silver as "common exchange measures" does not involve a promise. Also, in a more convincing manner, he recalls that there is absolutely no need for a promise in order to enter into a language-based relationship with others. Evidently, unless one enters into futile considerations, the question of knowing whether one language is more apt than another for providing the means for communication between people is without any object. This does not mean, of course, that if language systems are not subject to any particular finality, or do not conform to any physiological norm, that they are thus given over to arbitrariness and chance. Grammar can be studied, its history can be described, but its *genesis*, as an initiating act beyond which language would not exist, cannot be a subject of study.

For Hume, it is therefore no longer a matter of describing the evolution of the right of ownership by relying on a state of nature, as Locke had done with the theory of natural right, which Hume now considers to be an illusion, with, at best, pedagogical virtues, but which cannot be endowed with the slightest heuristic interest. On the contrary, it is important to write about its "natural history", in the sense that one must describe the rules that were progressively established to stabilise ownership. This history is certainly not the random record of legal accidents, since it is organised within itself around general rules:

These rules of attribution of ownership are simple, because they are identical to those governing judgement in general. Hume strives to recover the five rules of acquisition of ownership (possession, occupation, prescription, accession and succession) that follow the schemas of Roman law inscribed in the Scottish jurisprudence of his era. But the justification that is proposed is entirely founded on the general rules of understanding, that is, resemblance, contiguity and the relationship between cause and effect.

We know that the point of departure for Locke, in the famous chapter 5 of the *Second Treatise of Civil Government*, is the *collective ownership* of land and items of property and individual ownership of the body. The work that allows the private appropriation of goods is the original title of any *private* ownership. However, in the THN, there is a shift from *absence of ownership* (game belongs to no one, not to everyone) to ownership. Labour carried out in order to acquire (in Locke's sense of the word) an object may certainly confer the possession of an object, but under the conditions that are established by the rules of understanding. Hence, Hume emphasises that:

> A person, who has hunted a hare to the last degree of weariness, would look upon it as an injustice for another to rush in before him, and seize his prey. But the same person, advancing to pluck an apple that hangs within his reach has no reason to complain, if another, more alert, passes him, and takes possession. What is the reason of this difference, but that immobility, not being natural to the hare, but the effect of industry, forms in that case a strong relation with the hunter, which is wanting in the other? (Hume, [1739] 1983, pp. 506–507)

Therefore, while work may be—in the hunter's case—one factor in creating the right of ownership, it is not because labour or "industry" finds itself naturally (and hence theologically) invested in this mission. Quite to the contrary, it is only insofar as the qualified imagination (the understanding) implements general rules that it is possible to infer the right of ownership for a specific task *in general terms*. Since in this case it is both possible and easy to pass from effect to cause, the rule of accession to ownership through industry is therefore accepted.

The first artifice allowing the passion for acquisition to withdraw within itself is therefore the convention regarding the establishment of rules to stabilise ownership. But this artifice is insufficient. In its turn, the stability of possessions must be rectified by the exchange, which is a conventional one.

The Miracle of the Promises

While the rules that determine ownership are general rules, fixing its content and stabilising it, the accession to ownership is circumstantial in itself. Consequently, an adjustment is required (Hume, [1739–1740] 1983, p. 504). This remedy is the transfer of ownership through consent, that is, by donation or exchange. Hume does not preoccupy himself greatly with the rules governing exchanges, since exchanges are "limited", and in order to cross these limits, instituting the obligation to keep one's promises is required (but not sufficient):

> The invention of the law of nature, concerning the *stability* of possession, has already render'd men tolerable to each other; that of the *transference* of property and possession by consent has begun to render them mutually advantageous: But still these laws of nature, however strictly observ'd, are not sufficient to render them so serviceable to each other, as by nature they are fitted to become. Tho' possession be *stable*, men may often reap but small advantage from it, while they are possess'd of a greater quantity of any species of goods than they have occasion for, and at the same time suffer by the want of others. The *transference* of property, which is the proper remedy for this inconvenience, cannot remedy it entirely; because it can only take place with regard to such objects as are *present* and *individual*, but not to such as are *absent* or *general*. One cannot transfer the property of a particular house, twenty leagues distant; because the consent cannot be attended with delivery, which is a requisite circumstance. Neither can one transfer the property of ten bushels of corn, or five hogsheads of wine, by the mere expression and consent; because these are only general terms, and have no direct relation to any particular heap of corn, or barrels of wine. Besides, the commerce of mankind is not confin'd to the barter of commodities, but may extend to services and actions, which we may exchange to our mutual interest and advantage. Your corn is ripe to-day; mine will be so to-morrow. 'Tis profitable for us both, that I shou'd labour with you to-day, and that you shou'd aid me to-morrow. I have no kindness for you, and know you have as little for me. I will not, therefore, take any pains upon your account; and should I labour with you upon my own

> account, in expectation of a return, I know I shou'd be disappointed, and that I shou'd in vain depend upon your gratitude. Here then I leave you to labour alone: You treat me in the same manner. The seasons change; and both of us lose our harvests for want of mutual confidence and security. (Hume, [1739] 1983, p. 520)

This citation sheds light on the opposition between the transfer and the promise, and merits further comment.

The aim of barter exchange (I shall leave aside the donation) is to permit the adjustment of ownership, and, since Hume specifies the rules governing the establishment of the rights of ownership in a rather long passage, we could expect him to specify the general rules governing trade. However, he does not do so.

We may believe that if this is so, it is simply because Hume, like all of his contemporaries, considers bartering as an exceptional and hence *accidental* form of exchange, which is therefore not governed by any law. To understand this, it is first necessary to note that in an economy where more than two agents and more than two items of property coexist, barter transactions must therefore be centralised, since they must be *immediate*. This kind of economy is thus hardly any different from a patriarchal economy in which all goods are taken to a centre, which ensures that they are shared out: this is the domain of distributive justice. The *centralisation* of the transactions therefore constitutes the first limitation of an economy without money.

Hume highlights another limitation of such an economy in the previous citation: inter-temporal exchange is impossible. Since this economy is confined by its immediacy, it has no means at its disposal for connecting present to future, or near to far (which amounts to the same thing).

The final limitation is even more difficult. As we have just seen, Hume points out that bartering allows me to exchange *my* 10 bushels of wheat for *your* 5 hogsheads of wine, which are specific objects, because they belong to us who are particular agents but it prohibits me from exchanging my 10 bushels of wheat for 5 hogsheads of wine "in general terms", that is, stripped of any individual or personal dimension.

In a manner that is perfectly coherent with Hume's philosophy of knowledge, this requirement for generality signifies that the value of a commodity cannot be a *quality* of it, that is perceptible (or, by extension, conceivable) outside of the exchange. If we take the famous example (Marx, *The Capital*, Book I, 1) of two individuals exchanging 10 yards of linen for one coat, there is nothing in this statement that can allow us to consider that this exchange relationship is a balanced one. Only a long repetition of the experience would prompt us, out of habit, to declare that in *general*—that is, in *practice*—a coat is worth 20 yards of linen. But unfortunately, for Hume, as for all of his predecessors, such a repeated experience is inconceivable, since barter exchanges can only be *accidental*.

I can provisionally conclude that barter exchanges certainly allow for adjustments to the stability of possessions, but its limits are identical to those of sympathy: it does not allow access to a level of generality. It is remarkable to note that for Hume, the disadvantages of bartering are not only those that economic analysis would come to consider: bartering is not only limited because it can engender the traditional problem of the "double coincidence of wants", but because there is no way that it can be governed by any general rule.

However, from this point on, we thus understand the very ambitious programme that was forming in Hume's mind. It would be necessary to: (i) release the temporal constraint that impedes barter exchanges, this would be provided by the function of an exchange of an item of property today for the *promise* of another tomorrow (private credit), and, (ii) pass from the private promise to the general promise, that is, money. This second part of the programme is not broached in the THN.[4] The first is already complicated enough and I will stop at that. It is a question of demonstrating how the feeling of obligation is engendered, no less.[5]

According to Hume, the convention instigating the obligation of the promise is necessary (but not sufficient) for generalised exchange to be possible. This is what we shall now examine.

It is the experience that allows us to learn the advantages of the promise. But how is this learning achieved? How can I predict that the other party will do me a favour in exchange for the favour that I am doing for them? It is clear that while Hume assumed that this question was

[4] I have attempted to deal with this difficult question cf. Diatkine (1989). See also: C. Wennerlind (2001).

[5] The artificial character of the feeling of loyalty and honour is obviously a profoundly subversive proposition (meaning, in the eighteenth century). Hume, spurning all the values deemed essential in an aristocratic society, quite simply affirms that the respect of promises has nothing to do with a transcendental value (honour or faith) and is nothing other than a means of service for the "interests of society".

resolved, he would not need to distinguish the transfer of the promise. However, Hume poses the question and answers it by affirming that it is a mystery.

Hume defines the promise as follows: in interested commerce (obviously the only kind under consideration here), a certain verbal formula exists whereby we commit to accomplishing an action.

More precisely:

> This form of words constitutes what we call a *promise*, which is the sanction of the interested commerce of mankind. When a man says *he promises any thing*, he in effect expresses a *resolution* of performing it; and along with that, by making use of this *form of words*, subjects himself to the penalty of never being trusted again in case of failure. A resolution is the natural act of the mind, which promises express: But were there no more than a resolution in the case, promises would only declare our former motives, and would not create any new motive or obligation. They are the conventions of men, which create a new motive, when experience has taught us, that human affairs would be conducted much more for mutual advantage, were there certain *symbols* or *signs* instituted, by which we might give each other security of our conduct in any particular incident. (Hume, [1739] 1983, p. 522)

Hume evokes here the effect of reputation, which may prompt an agent to keep his or her engagements. But it is clear that this effect is insufficient, for two reasons: the first lies in the fact that the effect of reputation only works in small economies, where anonymity is not the norm (we covered this earlier: Hume is evoking the secret of the loan); secondly and most importantly, because the feeling of obligation is generally felt independently of any calculation of utility. The main point regarding this major difficulty lies in the last sentence of the previous citation: how can a symbol or a sign create a *new feeling*, that of obligation?

> The difficulties, that occur to us, in supposing a moral obligation to attend promises, we either surmount or elude. For instance; the expression of a resolution is not commonly suppos'd to be obligatory; and we cannot readily conceive how the making use of a certain form of words shou'd be able to cause any material difference. Here, therefore, we *feign* a new act of the mind, which we call the *willing* an obligation. (Hume, [1739] 1983, p. 523)

K. Haakonssen (1978) used this passage to resolve the problem posed by the existence of the feeling of obligation. He interprets this "ruse" as an illusion engendered by the repetition of the experience of the useful character of loyalty, following which, we imagine that loyalty is a natural ground for action. Therefore, if we experience guilt feelings when we do not fulfil our engagements, if we come to hate one another because of this, it is the result of an error produced by our imagination. J. L. Mackie (1980) even deduces from this that Hume is a theorist of errors.

D. Gauthier (1992) corrects Hume on this point. To explain that subjects are inclined to keep their promises, it is not necessary to suppose this "ruse" as Hume does. It is enough to assume that each agent has an interest in keeping his or her promises if (s)he knows that all of the others also have an interest in keeping theirs. But this argument is fragile and Gauthier suggests that Hume knows this well, since in *An Enquiry Concerning the Principles of Morals*, Hume presents the "sensible knave" who knows that, with a little cunning, it can be profitable to be disloyal. Hence Hume's ultimate message would be that human society has no moral fundament.

For my part, I believe that what Hume is suggesting here, by underlining the verb "to feign", is that when we make promises, we are acting out a *drama* to ourselves, and that the effect of this drama is to create the sentiment of willingness to enter into obligation, exactly like any theatrical experience can produce rich and varied sentiments. However, play-acting does not necessarily mean fooling oneself, although Hume does not develop his analysis any further in this direction, which Smith would follow when developing his theory of the impartial spectator.

The obligation engendered by the promise thus seems to be a pure artifice, to which we adhere by way of the same game used to adhere to a theatrical representation. Invoking play-acting only allows us to postpone the difficulty, by showing that it is not only in the case of promises that language games engender feelings. The main question still remains to be answered: how can it be explained that words can be effective, in both cases? With the added difficulty that in the case of the theatre, the feelings produced by the verbal expressions of the actors are not durable, whereas promises are indelible. The dramatic illusion is an illusion that is resolved, sooner or later. The promise is central to the notion of justice, and is not an illusion.

Hume thus poses an essential question: how can a simple verbal expression engender this kind of feeling? In the notion of the promise, it is easy to recognise the moral form of the relationship of causality, and it is therefore unsurprising to find the initial question of the theory of knowledge posed here again in a particularly urgent form: how are we able to place our trust in the laws? Once again, what Hume finds incredible is not that laws exist, but that we obey them. What is incredible is not that promises exist, but that we trust one another. We are thus faced with a "miracle".

This is because, indeed, Hume does not seek to resolve the difficulty, and he is led to conclude in a very impressive way that in the end, we are faced with a "miraculous" operation:

> I shall farther observe, that since every new promise imposes a new obligation of morality on the person who promises, and since this new obligation arises from his will; 'tis one of the most mysterious and incomprehensible operations that can possibly be imagin'd, and may even be compar'd to *transubstantiation*, or *holy orders*, where a certain form of words, along with a certain intention, changes entirely the nature of an external object, and even of a human creature. (Hume [1739] 1983, p. 524)

This passage, as surprising as it is, seems to have virtually gone unnoticed. A meticulous commentator such as Harrison (1981, p. 137) regrets that "Hume does not fully realize that all promising is saying that the words 'I promise' in suitable circumstances". It is quite possible that Harrison is thinking of Austin here, and of the *Speech Acts*. This position is close to the one supported by A. E. Pitson (1988), who also highlights the performative character of the promise but it is precisely this "active speech" that Austin studies as a linguist and sociologist that seems to be a pure miracle to Hume, since Hume is faced with this difficult question: Feelings are the results of our perceptions, and we perceives things. Here feelings are the results of signs: how can a sign produce the same degree of effectiveness as a thing? As he says himself, there is a choice to be made. Society imposes that we believe in the obligation of promises in exactly the same way as the Catholic religion imposes our belief in transubstantiation, with the following essential difference, which he emphasises: transubstantiation has no social utility, whereas loyalty is indispensable to society. This is why this miracle of faith in ourselves and in others must be accepted.

It is important to understand that, basically, the problem is not that of finding out what constitutes the rules of justice (Hume pays little attention to whether or not laws determine exchange relationships, for instance), nor is it concerned with why certain people (or most; this is beside the point) do not respect it, since he (and we) is (are) certain of the existence of *sensible knaves*. The main issue is why the latter generally experience a feeling of guilt, or—and this amounts to the same thing—why these ancestors of the rational agent are not *always* perverse.

The problem poses considerable difficulty; Kant (and Rawls) would also take it up. Classical Benthamian utilitarianism would erase it by supposing that we are all (except probably Bentham himself) *sensible knaves* who may sometimes experience regret but never remorse. On the other hand, Hume takes this experience into account, which every individual may feel, provided that (s)he is not perverse—it is not only the fear of punishment that encourages people to respect their promise. Kant would seek to demonstrate that we obey moral law because this is the law, not because an individual's infraction would be punished, but because their infraction would result in guilt feelings, which is the flipside to the feeling of obligation. We all know a specific and very common type of promise: the ones that we make to ourselves. Here, there is no effect of reputation nor, it seems, any Leviathan to fear. Yet being capable of respecting these, being autonomous, is the most basic and most eloquent definition of freedom. Don Juan did not keep any of the thousand and three promises made to his mistresses, but he kept the one that he addressed to this other self, the statue of the commander. Just a few words thus provoke his downfall.

References

Diatkine, D. (1989). Hume et le libéralisme économique. *Cahiers d'Economie Politique*, n°17.

Ege, R., & Iggersheim, H. (Eds.). (2011). *Freedom and happiness in economic thought and philosophy*. Routledge.

Forbes, D. (1976). Sceptical whiggism, commerce and liberty. In A. Skinner & T. Wilson (Eds.), *Essays on Adam Smith*. Oxford University Press.

Gauthier, D. (1992). Artificial virtues and the sensible knave. *Hume Studies, 18*(2), 401–427.

Haakonssen, K. (1981). *The science of a lagislator, the natural jurisprudence of David Hume and Adam Smith*. Cambridge University Press.

Harrison, J. (1981). *Hume's theory of justice*. Oxford University Press.

Hume, D. ([1739–1740] 1983). *A treatise of human nature* (2nd éd., L. A. Selby-Bigge, ed.) with text revised and notes by P. H. Nidditch. Clarendon Press.

Pitson, A. E. (1988). Hume on promises and their obligation. *Hume Studies*, XIV, n°1.

Wennerlind, C. (2001). The link between David Hume's a treatise of human nature and his fiduciary theory of money. *History of Political Economy, 33*(1), 136–160.

Winch, D. (1978). *Adam Smith's politics*. Cambridge University Press.

CHAPTER 3

The Rules of the Game

An important part of The *Theory of Moral Sentiments* tries to solve the problem raised by Hume, which lies at the heart of his theory of justice, and which seeks an explanation for the feeling of ***obligation***. Smith's solution was remarkable in many ways.

First, Smith showed that the explanation may be found in the same process which is at work in the shaping of moral judgement, concerning good and evil or just and unjust. Smith rehabilitated the "sympathy" put forward by Hutcheson, and which was criticised for its inherent partiality by Hume. At the heart of Smith's analysis is his theory of the ***impartial spectator***, who makes moral judgements concerning what is just and unjust, as well as about good and evil. I will show how Smith assumed that moral conscience could result from the *theatrical game*, the prototype of the political game.

Second, another important novelty by Smith concerns greed. For Hume, this passion was "destructive of any society". Yet it was deeply transformed in The *Theory of Moral Sentiments*, as Smith perceived it as a ***modality*** of the desire for unlimited enrichment. Surprisingly enough, he saw greed as an important manifestation of *love of the system*. This arose when a person or subject, faced with a relationship between means and

D. Diatkine, *Adam Smith and the Wealth of Nations*, Palgrave Studies in the History of Economic Thought, https://doi.org/10.1007/978-3-030-81600-1_3

ends, was more interested in the *aesthetics*[1] of this relationship than in the end itself. I will show that this love of the system, which seems at first to be a *game*, is transposed into the field of economics to explain capital accumulation as an effect of this passion. More generally, greed then ceased for Smith to be an anti-social passion, as Hume had argued. The incompatibility of greed and the general interest, which was the starting point of Hume's theory of justice, was then transformed by Smith to become a question of the compatibility of capital accumulation with the general interest. This question is no more trivial than that raised by Hume, but it ceases to be an ethical question to become an economic question, while at the same time being a political question: how and under what conditions is the accumulation of capital compatible with the common good?

I will start here by showing how Smith constructed the concept of impartial spectator, as his answer to the question of moral and political obligation (Section 1). He fully used the theatrical game hypothesis which was the germ of his notion of sympathy.

We shall see that the "desire for distinction", which is close but different to vanity, was an important driving force in the shaping of moral judgement, but was not sufficient to explain it. Indeed, in Section 2, I then set out the important debate sparked by Smith's position concerning the desire for unlimited enrichment. For commentators, this desire for limitless enrichment as expressed by Smith was due to vanity. Yet we shall see that this was not the case. The accumulation of wealth was an effect Smith was proud to have discovered, namely the *love of the system*. This explained not only what was largely attributed to greed (including by Hume), but also to the taste for power and even to scientific *curiosity*. Surprisingly, the same passion drives the lover of trinkets and baubles, the builder of empires (economic and political) and the philosopher. And that was not all. Whoever experienced this passion was not always aware that they were experiencing it, and the passion could also disappear as soon as it reached the consciousness of the person driven by it. This was the case of the builder of an economic empire, who believes to be seeking luxury and yet does not *know* that he is driven by a love of the system, which differentiates him from the philosopher (or the lover of trinkets)

[1] The moral judgement concerns here judgements about the beautiful.

who knows well enough that the object he pursues is a well-constructed theoretical model (or a well-made bauble).

Viewed like this, the love of the system makes it possible to highlight how the accumulation of capital actually connects logically The *Theory of Moral Sentiments* to the *Wealth of Nations*, instead of opposing the two works, as was long assumed, and what was commonly called the *Das Adam Smith Problem.*

The Theatrical Game/Play and the Construction of the Impartial Spectator: Taking Distance and Politics

David Raphael and A. L. Macfie (TMS, p. 15) had emphasised that the name of Adam Smith, in the history of ethics, is mainly associated with the concept of the impartial spectator. Indeed, it is easy to check that this concept has a central place in The *Theory of Moral Sentiments.* As I showed previously, Hume, following both Shaftesbury and Hutcheson used sympathy (the capacity of every human being to identify with another) to explain how moral judgements were formed. But, in contrast to these theorists of moral sentiment, Hume asserted that sympathy does not allow judgements to be made on what is just or unjust, because it is partial. This is exactly where Smith comes in. He highlighted a practical procedure by which sympathy could free itself from the limits of partiality. The result of this procedure was the construction of the impartial spectator.

Indignation is the starting point of Smith's theory of the impartial spectator.

Smith set out this issue in terms very similar to those used by Hume. Moreover, they were very traditional and were often put forward to highlight the partiality of sympathy.[2] This can be found almost identically in Hume, who famously wrote that "'Tis not contrary to reason to prefer the destruction of the whole world to the scratching of my finger" (*THN*, p. 416).

For his part, Smith introduced a sentiment of injustice as follows:

[2] Popular questionnaires which test participants' sympathy, using experimental psychology, are just as fashionable today as they were in the eighteenth century.

"Let us suppose that the great empire of China, with all its myriads of inhabitants, was suddenly swallowed up by an earthquake, and let us consider how a man of humanity in Europe, who had no sort of connection with that part of the world, would be affected upon receiving intelligence of this dreadful calamity. He would, I imagine, first of all express very strongly his sorrow for the misfortune of that unhappy people" … "when all this fine philosophy was over, when all these humane sentiments had been once fairly expressed, he would pursue his business or his pleasure, take his repose or his diversion, with the same ease and tranquillity as if no such accident had happened. The most frivolous disaster which could befall himself would occasion a more real disturbance. If he was to lose his little finger tomorrow, he would not sleep to-night; but, provided he never saw them, he will snore with the most profound security over the ruin of a hundred millions of his brethren, and the destruction of that immense multitude seems plainly an object less interesting to him than this paltry misfortune of his own. To prevent, therefore, this paltry misfortune to himself, would a man of humanity be willing to sacrifice the lives of a hundred millions of his brethren, provided he had never seen them? Human nature startles with horror at the thought, and the world, in its greatest depravity and corruption, never produced such a villain as could be capable of entertaining it. But what makes this difference? When our passive feelings are almost always so sordid and so selfish, how comes it that our active principles should often be so generous and so noble?" (TMS, III, p. 3)

Smith refers here to the sentiment of *indignation*. While sympathy is partial, it is impossible to deny the sentiment of injustice. Where does it come from? Why do we find it scandalous to prefer the destruction of the Chinese Empire to the loss of our little finger?[3]

"It is not the soft power of humanity, it is not that feeble spark of benevolence which Nature has lighted up in the human heart, that is thus capable of counteracting the strongest impulses of self-love. It is a stronger power, a more forcible motive, which exerts itself upon such occasions. It is reason, principle, conscience, the inhabitant of the breast, the man within, the great judge and arbiter of our conduct. It is he who,

[3] For Smith, the point was to explain a sentiment and not to set standards. This seems to have astonished his contemporaries. Thus, General Clerk (or Ferguson) vehemently reproached Hume and Smith for not answering "the most first and most important question that arises in the life of a man: What good can men derive from happiness or by avoiding misery?". See Campbell Mossner, E., 1960, pp. 222–232.

whenever we are about to act so as to affect the happiness of others, calls to us, with a voice capable of astonishing the most presumptuous of our passions, that we are but one of the multitude"... "when we prefer ourselves so shamefully and so blindly to others, we become the proper objects of resentment, abhorrence, and execration"... "the natural misrepresentations of self-love can be corrected only by the eye of this impartial spectator" (TMS, III, p. 3).

We have seen that for Hume, partiality stems from the preference for what is near over what is far away. This leads to a preference for the particular over the general. The tendency towards impartiality therefore requires taking *distance*, which Hume said was produced by the rules of understanding. For Hume, such a taking of distance leads a "violent passion" to become a "calm passion" and is thus constructed exactly as the rules of understanding: it is the frequency and so eases of normal social relationships, brought about by their proximity, which is the driver of familiarisation. And it is the progressive extension of these relationships that allows "irregular and inconvenient" feelings to be suppressed in "affections", just as this extension broadens the scope of sympathy. However, as we have seen, sympathy alone is not able to accede to impartiality. For this to occur, Smith introduced the judgement of the *impartial spectator* which here substitutes itself for the rules of understanding. And this is the result of a wholly new relationship, which an actor creates with his spectator(s). As Raphael (*op. cit.*) had shown, Smith completed this shift by moving from the actor to the spectator. At this point, two subjects find themselves face-to-face, the actor and the spectator. The former imagined the sentiments which spectator could feel by looking at him, as in a mirror. And according to Smith, moral judgement is the result of this relationship, which I qualify as theatrical, and to which we now turn.

According to Smith, this reversal of the spectator and actor relationship was necessary because one of our most treasured desires is "[t]o be observed, to be attended to, to be taken notice of with sympathy".[4]

[4] "From whence, then, arises that emulation which runs through all the different ranks of men, and what are the advantages which we propose by that great purpose of human life which we call bettering our condition? To be observed, to be attended to, to be taken notice of with sympathy, complacency, and approbation, are all the advantages which we can propose to derive from it. It is the vanity, not the ease, or the pleasure, which interests us. But vanity is always founded upon the belief of our being the object of attention and approbation". (*TMS, I, iii. 2. 2*). We will see that "the bettering [of] condition" takes

This desire is ambiguous as there are two ways to obtain such consideration. The display of riches attracts the attention of spectators who do not have them. The search for such admiration is an expression of vanity, which did not solicit Smith's indignation, but rather his irony.[5] This insistence on the place of the desire of recognition by others, of the sympathy of others is characteristic in Smith's thought. While Hume mentioned it, Smith used this fully. For Hume, the Gordian knot of the theory of justice was the theory of obligation. This was the "miraculous" effect of the power or performance (as we may see today) of certain signs. Smith sought to explain this "miracle". The fact that signs may touch or provoke sentiments follows from the way the theatrical expression renews each representation.[6] Smith moreover took into account the views of the spectator by the actor: this opens up a new way for understanding how the actor's sentiments (and not those of the spectator) may be affected. The transitory nature of the theatrical illusion then in fact fades away as it concerns the actor. The latter's judgement about his "performance" is no longer fleeting.

Immediately after having restated the traditional definition of sympathy as the principle which allows a spectator to share, albeit weakly, the sentiments of the actor, Smith adopts the point of view of the actor who *needs* the sympathy of the spectator.

For sentiments between the spectator and the actor to correspond, the former has to adopt the situation of the latter, as much as possible. Yet that is not enough, because as Smith adds:

> The emotions of *the* spectator will still be very apt to fall short of the violence of what is felt by the sufferer. Mankind, though naturally sympathetic, never conceive, for what has befallen another, that degree of passion which naturally animates the person principally concerned. That imaginary change of situation, upon which *their* sympathy is founded, is but momentary. The thought of *their* own safety, the thought that they themselves are not really the sufferers, continually intrudes itself upon them; and though

on a very different meaning in the *Wealth of Nations*, referring to savings (see Chapter 4 below).

[5] We know that this was nothing exceptional in the eighteenth century, and we shall find it again soon.

[6] The previous chapter showed how close Hume was to this approach, although he did not extend it.

> it does not hinder them from conceiving a passion somewhat analogous to what is felt by the sufferer, hinders them from conceiving anything that approaches to the same degree of violence. The person principally concerned is sensible of this, and at the same time passionately desires a more complete sympathy. He longs for that relief which nothing can afford him but the entire concord of the affections of the spectators with his own. To see the emotions of their hearts in every respect beat time to his own, in the violent and disagreeable passions, constitutes his sole consolation. But he can only hope to obtain this by lowering his passion to that pitch, in which the spectators are capable of going along with him. He must flatten, if I may be allowed to say so, the sharpness of its natural tone, in order to reduce it to harmony and concord with the emotions of those who are about him. What they feel will, indeed, always be in some respects different from what he feels, and compassion can never be exactly the same with original sorrow; because the secret consciousness that the change of situations, from which the sympathetic sentiment arises, is but imaginary, not only lowers it in degree, but in some measure varies it in kind, and gives it a quite different modification. These two sentiments, however, may, it is evident, have such a correspondence with one another, as is sufficient for the harmony of society. Though they will never be unisons, they may be concords, and this is all that is wanted or required. (TSM, I, iii, 2.1: italics are mine)

It is important to notice the shift made here by Smith, almost surreptitiously. Up to this point, Smith's text contrasted *an* actor and *a* spectator, but now the actor plays before *the spectators*. The plural here is important because the spectator becomes *an* audience, a public. The spectator/actor relationship, which mobilised sympathy for Smith's predecessors, was a private relationship, between one individual and another. Here the relationship is between the actor and the spectators, linking the actor to a *public*, which changes the nature of the problem. The design of the sympathy requires the actor to make an effort which is not self-evident. It requires self-control which can only be acquired from experience in theatre, or more generally in public speaking. Faced with another person, as an actor I can (I must) make an effort to show the necessary sympathy for me to be seen and judged by the other person's eyes. By contrast, with a public, I cannot identify with each individual spectator. I need to *construct* a spectator who I hope will be representative, and it is from this point of view, that I will seek the esteem and approval of this "representative spectator". In this way, the public becomes the actor's public, and will be the first to appreciate the actor's performance.

In this way too, the respective sentiments of the actor and the spectators may agree, without being "in unison". Sympathy may therefore lead to social harmony, as long as the actor and spectators consent to making the necessary effort. But it must be noted here that this is not the situation of a *natural identity of interests* (to use Halévy's [1926] terminology in the), but indeed a *harmony of identities*: i.e. the mutual recognition of the roles played. Smith took aim at these identity conflicts, and this scenic practice made it possible to reduce their violence as felt by the actor.

Yet to appreciate is not judge. How can the actor judge himself impartially? Smith's *The Theory of Moral Sentiments* does not answer this crucial question. However, we have some elements to help us do so, without having to turn to the deism Smith sometimes put forward: it is possible to assume that a second abstraction was at work. If a profession allows the actor to adjust the expression of his sentiments so that they agree with those of the representative spectator, then the proven profession of the actor also allows him to judge himself from the standpoint of another spectator, the *critical* spectator who is capable of impartiality and whose views have no reason to coincide with the views of the representative spectator. Indeed, the ability to adopt the point of view of the impartial spectator (to be *well* informed and hence *critical*) seems to assume a confrontation of points of view and hence an internal *deliberation* needed to judge the quality of this criticism.

The experience of the actor's profession allows such a taking of distance, both with respect to himself and with respect to the representative spectator. We can see therefore that Smith transforms the partiality of sympathy by this process of *taking distance*, which was very different from that used by Hume. The latter contrasted phenomena which are nearby and far away, as the opposition between the partiality of sympathy with the impartiality of justice. Hume resorted to rules of understanding to construct the necessary devices of the latter. By stressing the importance of the actor in the sympathy relationship, Smith is able to emphasise the importance of real or symbolic staging in the art of making moral judgements. Smith called on us to seek the *adequate* distance between an actor and his public: if it is too close, the actor cannot ensure sufficient control over his passions; if it is too distant, he cannot mobilise his sentiments nor those of the public. Smith therefore used the practice of the scenic relationship to show how the actor manages to take distance from himself, in order to *control his passions* that is required to *move* the representative spectator, and in order to achieve such self-control that would allow him to judge himself with the impartiality of the critical spectator. It is clear that it is impossible to break away from the theatrical metaphor, and to view the relationship between the actor/spectators as characteristic of the relationship to the public: i.e. in a certain way, as a political relationship,[7] in which the actor may be a tribune, a teacher or a lawyer facing his audience.

Indeed, The *Theory of Moral Sentiments* does not just pursue a theatrical dimension. It also mobilises a second dimension, namely that of the *courtroom*. If we are able to be our own judges, then we are also able to experience the sentiment of what is just and unjust. It is quite typical of this work by Smith to move its reader from the theatrical dimension (and the adjustment of the actor to his role) to the court (and justice) dimension. Smith even mixed these two dimensions, as if there were no continuity solution between these two areas of public life. This is shown by the following quotation in which the impartial spectator comes onstage: "But though man has, in this manner, been rendered the immediate judge of mankind, he has been rendered so only in the first instance; and an appeal lies from his sentence to a much higher tribunal, to the tribunal of their own consciences, to that of the supposed impartial and well-informed spectator, to that of the man within the breast, the great judge and arbiter of their conduct" (TMS, III, ii, p. 32).

Smith did not therefore challenge the idea that sympathy may *spontaneously* be incapable of making us feel obligation. But he explained the extension of the power of sympathy by this practice of the actor, who absolutely has to identify himself with the spectators and (if possible), with the critical spectator, who also has his "trade" or "profession". The theatrical experience can of course be extended, as we have just seen, to all forms of public speech. In any case, this construction mobilises the experience of the actors and is never assured. The theatrical model of social relationships is therefore not metaphorical, and Smith here possibly anticipated more Diderot and Pirandello than Freud.[8]

[7] In his stimulating book, Vivienne Brown (1994) stresses the role of stoicism in Smith's morality, as we shall see. Stoicism emphasises self-control as an expression of virtue, and is much present in the *Theory of Moral Sentiments*. I will return to this a little later, I would like to underline the fact here that self-control is not the result of a choice of values by a well-brought-up individual. Instead, it follows from the practical necessity *experienced* as soon as one enters the public arena.

[8] In their "Introduction" to the *Theory of Moral Sentiments* in the 1976, D. D. Raphael and A. L. Macfie suggest there is a certain convergence here with Freud's idea of the

Indeed, the scenic game does not always succeed and even when it succeeds, the impartial spectator is not infallible. He does not necessarily manage to create a sentiment of obligation and even make it operational. It is accordingly the adjustment of these "situations" which determine the happy combination of humanity's virtues and its self-control. This adjustment follows from the distance separating the actor, the real spectators (the representative impartial spectator) and the impartial spectator. If the real spectators are too close to the actor and if the impartial spectator is too distant, then sentiments are "corrupted". In Chapter 5 of this book, we shall find once more the political importance of the idea of optimal distance in the formulation of judgement by the impartial spectator. But at this point, Smith gave the example of war:

> When two nations are at variance, the citizen of each pays little regard to the sentiments which foreign nations may entertain concerning his conduct. His whole ambition is to obtain the approbation of his own fellow-citizens; and as they are all animated by the same hostile passions which animate himself, he can [218] never please them so much as by enraging and offending their enemies. The partial spectator is at hand: the impartial one at a great distance. (TMS, III, pp. 3, 42)

In this case, "truth and fair dealing are almost totally disregarded". And sentiments are never more corrupted than during civil or religious wars. In these situations, the sentiment of obligation disappears almost entirely: "Whether faith ought to be kept with rebels; whether faith ought to be kept with heretics; are questions which have been often furiously agitated by celebrated doctors, both civil and ecclesiastical" (TMS, III, iii, p. 43).

Thus, if the impartial spectator and the representative spectator are not placed at a suitable distance from the actor, if the staging is defective, then the theatrical game may lead to the violence of identity conflicts rather than to the harmony of sentiments.

This fragility in the forming of moral sentiment is accentuated when we take into account the important modifications Smith made to the last edition of The *Theory of Moral Sentiments*, published in 1790. The first editions of the book suggested that it was the practice of judgement by

superego. In my opinion, there is however an essential difference between the impartial spectator and the superego: the latter is unconscious, whereas the former speaks clearly to conscience. By contrast, Smith does not deny that an agent may act for reasons he is not aware of, as we shall see later.

others which progressively permitted the shift from a "real judge" (who I have called the representative spectator here) to the impartial spectator. However, in the sixth edition, Smith underlines strikingly to what extent the impartial spectator may practically succumb, "as a half-god", to the sentencing of the "real judge", as the real spectators may not only applaud out of context, but may also blame the actor unfairly and lead to a sentiment of a false awareness of guilt by the actor:

> But in this, and in some other cases, the man within seems sometimes, as it were, astonished and confounded by the vehemence and clamour of the man without. The violence and loudness with which blame is sometimes poured out upon us, seems to stupify and benumb our natural sense of praiseworthiness and blameworthiness; and the judgments of the man within, though not, perhaps, absolutely altered or perverted, are, however, so much shaken in the steadiness and firmness of their decision, that their natural effect, in securing the tranquillity of the mind, is frequently, in a great measure, destroyed. (TMS, III, ii. p. 33)

As we can see, the forming of a moral judgement and more especially a sentiment of obligation is possible, but it is neither universal nor compulsory. That is why it is possible to see, following Raphael (*op. cit.*), that Smith studies moral sentiments more as a psychologist than as a moralist. This psychological dimension in the theory of moral sentiments is strongly highlighted by the fact that Smith, again in the sixth and last addition of the work, adds a new chapter in which he describes a new cause for the "corruption of moral sentiments". This new cause is our tendency to admire the rich and despise the poor (TMS, I, iii).

Having recalled the commonplace view that wealth and greatness are more appreciated than wisdom and virtue, Smith stated that ambitious persons may follow two paths: both the study of wisdom and the practice of virtue, or the acquisition of wealth and greatness. This leaves us with the impression that these two paths are the traditional opposition between virtue and vice, and that the latter is immediately assimilated to the search for wealth and greatness. However, it must be said that while the first path can be immediately identified with virtue, the second is not qualified as vicious without any conditions. Smith indeed starts by telling us that: "in the middling and inferior station of life" the way to virtue is spontaneously open to ambitious people, even people looking for wealth. He goes on to add that: "[i]n the superior stations of life the case is unhappily not always the same. In the courts of princes, in the drawing-rooms of the great, where success and preferment depend, not upon the esteem of intelligent and well-informed equals, but upon the fanciful and foolish favour of ignorant, presumptuous, and proud superiors; flattery and falsehood too often prevail over merit and abilities. In such societies, the abilities to please are more regarded than the abilities to serve" (TMS, I, iii, p. 6).

The corruption of moral sentiments then is measured here by the yardstick of classical virtue. Indeed, the legitimate search for respect and admiration by human beings may follow the path to wealth and greatness in some societies, but not in others. In the former, where the highest ranks are obtained by favour and not by merits, moral sentiments are corrupted.

The *TMS* thus moves away from morality towards psychology. The result of this shift is a very detached attitude to the vices *par excellence* of vanity (or pride) and greed. Smith's critique of Mandeville is very clear from this point of view. If vanity does indeed conform to the common good as claimed in the *Fable of the Bees*, then it is a virtue and it would be absurd to rail against as a supposed private vice. Smith's general tone concerning luxury spending, characterising expenditure by "the great", is neither that of Rousseau's indignation nor Mandeville's apology. Instead he uses humour. Smith deployed his irony concerning spending he judged as childish. He thus broke with a certain moralising judgement, because his notion of enrichment takes on a wholly new dimension—of progress—and in The *Wealth of Nations* of the accumulation of capital. It is this latter concept which will substitute itself for greed and, at the same time, the issue will no longer be one of making moral judgements about behaviour. Instead, it will concern the political conditions that make the accumulation of capital and the general interest compatible.

So what happened to the theory of justice? As Haakonssen (1981) has shown, it became part of a much broader project, namely that of the science of legislation. Smith tried to lay the foundations for this, and his point of departure was the theory of the impartial spectator who Smith used in his lectures at the University of Glasgow, which were transcribed in his *Lectures on Jurisprudence*.[9]

[9] Smith, *Lectures on jurisprudence*, R. L. Meek, D. D. Raphael and P. G. Stein (Ed.), (1978). *The Glasgow editions of the works and correspondence of Adam Smith*. Oxford University Press. There are two versions of these courses. The first stems from Smith's classes in 1762–1763, and was relocated by Edwin Cannan in 1896, and is referred to

The impartial spectator is invoked in the *Lecturers on Jurisprudence* (*LJ(A)*) to explain how picking up of an apple may be judged as legitimising the private appropriation of a good with no ownership.[10] The difference in Smith's approach to Hume is clear. As we have seen, Hume tried to explain such legitimacy using rules of understanding.[11] The impartial spectator allowed Smith therefore to rediscover certain results of natural law theory without appealing to the rules of understanding, as Hume had done, and by avoiding (or staying clear of) the considerable problems Hume encountered in his THN. The rules of justice are in the final analysis of legal and political institutions which are very much constructed by humans. And these rules are deduced from the rules governing the material life of human beings, namely the economy. This has been called the theory of stages, to which I shall return later.

Similarly, the impartial spectator, evoked by Smith to explain the sentiments of obligation to respect one's promises, which seemed so mysterious to Hume. As we have seen, the impartial spectator is meant to be able to generate the sentiments of obligation in general. More challenging still, the impartial spectator must also be capable of judging the sincerity of promises made by third parties.

We can check here how the notion of the impartial spectator and the theatrical metaphor takes the place of the construct put forward by Hume and results from the application of the rules of understanding (see Chapter 2 here).

In this way, if a moral judgement is formed, if it is not corrupted: i.e. if the *right distance* is found, then as we have seen, it may be hoped (possibly) to alleviate the most formidable conflicts, like religious conflicts, or civil and foreign wars. This of course requires being able to answer to the question of which types of human institutions are necessary to ensure the *universality* of this political judgement. In any case, it

here as *LJ(A)*. The second version was found by John Lothian in 1958. It is shorter and dates to 1766. It is referenced as *LJ(B)*.

[10] LJ(A), i, pp. 42–43. We may note here that if the judgement by the impartial spectator may be invoked to explain the legitimacy of property stemming from an initial occupation, the same can obviously not be said in the case of trade: here we come up against the universality of impartial judgement.

[11] This discussion may appear abstruse. But if we replace the words "game" or "apple" with the words "country" or "island" and the word "owner" with "colonial power", then the stakes involved in the classical discussion of the time become clearer, as the first colonial system was being established.

must be stressed that Smith here has left the field of morality to move on to what Hume wanted so much to explore, namely the field of political science. Both The *Theory of Moral Sentiments* and Hume's *THN* refused to state what is "good" or "just". The philosopher is not a religious person and is no substitute for the legislator.

I will now show how Smith created a new break between morality and politics, by making greed a form of very general behaviour: the love of the system.

The Modelling Game, the Love of the System and the Unlimited Desire for Wealth[12]

Nowadays, the assumption that consumers will always seek more of any given good is rarely questioned in consumer theory. So too, challenging capital accumulation without limit, in other words, the pursuit of wealth in general, seems meaningless.

Yet Smith provides an explanation for such behaviour, which is often referred to as greed. For him, love of systems, essentially an *aesthetic* principle, may explain the accumulation of riches, independently of their utility. This explanation is all the more remarkable, as Smith stressed it is an illusion, in as far as the person experiencing such a love of systems is ignorant of it. In particular, the love of systems concerns not only limitless enrichment. Its field of application is vast, as it also covers political practices and scientific activity. In Chapter 4 of this book, I show how this love of systems is used, according to Smith, by the proponents of the mercantile system to seduce its victims.

The assertion of the love of systems as a principle of action is especially remarkable in the *Wealth of Nations*, and Smith attaches importance to what he considers to be one of his original contributions (TMS, p. 180), contrary to what an abundant recent literature assumes.[13] This contrasts two principles of action: the desire to improve one's condition (which is very important in the *Wealth of Nations*), and vanity (which the TMS roundly denounces). This once again raises the question of the consistency between Smith's two major works. We need therefore

[12] On this debate see Tribe (1999) and Montes (2004).

[13] See Hont and Ignatieff (1981, pp. 1–44), Brown (1994), Griswold (1999), and Fleischacker (2004).

to examine the different versions of this old problem (*Das Adam Smith Problem*), before showing that taking into account a third principle of action—namely what Smith calls love of the system—removes this old, false problem.

Since the publication of the *Glasgow Edition of the Works and Correspondence of Adam Smith,* a considerable effort has been made to reassess the place of moral philosophy in Smith's work.[14] Much of this research has been done on the role and place of vanity in The *Theory of Moral Sentiments* and the *Wealth of Nations.*

Today, we judge vanity first and foremost from a moral point of view. This however has not always been the case. The former discussion focussed on the apparent contradiction between the central place given to sympathy in The *Theory of Moral Sentiments* and to egoism underlying the behaviour of economic agents in The *Wealth of Nations.* This is what has become known as *Das Adam Smith's problem.* Economists of the "first German historical school" (Wilhem Roscher [1817–1894], Karl Knies [1821–1898] and Bruno Hildebrand [1812–1878]) raised the issue of compatibility between Smith's two works. In fact, the *Wealth of Nations* was subject to increasingly violent criticism as of its first translations into German. Starting with a relatively benign position that limited the pertinence of its analysis to the particular case of Great Britain, attacks on the English classical school—with Smith deemed its founder—became more and more violent. Smith's criticism of the mercantile system, as well as a defence of free trade by the Manchester School that seemed to follow from it, were both interpreted as expressions of British desire to "pull up the ladder" of protectionism that had allowed the British economy to take its lead in global economic competition. The English classical school, then drawing on Ricardo, was thus seen as promoting "abstract cosmopolitanism", to the detriment of "national values".

As Leonidas Montes (2004) has shown, Lujo Brentano[15] in this context, shed light on Smith's break with The *Theory of Moral Sentiments* on the one hand, which puts sympathy at the heart of its approach

[14] This is variously borne out in the works of Haakonssen (Ed.) (2006). *The Cambridge companion to Adam Smith.* Cambridge University Press; Berry, Paganelli and Smith (Eds.). (2013). *The Oxford handbook of Adam Smith.* Oxford University Press and Evensky. (2015). *Adam Smith's wealth of nations, a reader guide.* Cambridge University Press.

[15] Brentano, L. (1877). *Das Arbeit verhhältniss Gemäss dem Heutigen Recht.* Duncker & Humblot quoted in Montes (*op. cit.*).

to social relations, and the *Wealth of Nations* on the other hand, which stresses interest and hence egoism. As expected, as soon as this opposition between Smith's two works was identified, an interpretation was put forward. It turns out that between 1759 (when The *Theory of Moral Sentiments* was published) and 1776 (when the *Wealth of Nations* came out), Smith had resided in Paris (between 1765 and 1766), where he met Helvetius and d'Holbach. These meetings led to a break pushing Smith away from his idealism in moral philosophy towards the "sordid materialism" of his economics.

Yet it is easy to show that this interpretation is wrong. We may question the observation by Dugald Stewart that the essence (of what is being discussed here) of the *Wealth of Nations* was already put forward by Smith in his lectures at the University of Glasgow.[16] However, the subsequent publication by Edwin Cannan in 1896 of Smith's first series of *Lectures on Jurisprudence* provided startling confirmation of this. Smith's ideas about the division of labour and commodity exchange were already clearly set out in his notes for a lecture given *before* his stay in France. Lastly, it is clear that Smith, who re-published The *Theory of Moral Sentiments* and the *Wealth of Nations* up until the end of his life, never denied what he wrote in his first work.

The publication of Smith's complete works in 1976 brought this debate to a close, when the editors of *The Theory of Moral Sentiments*—D. D. Raphaël and A. A. Macfie—emphasised in their "Introduction" that sympathy is not benevolence, any more than self-love or egoism.

The contradiction revealed by the German historical school is thus a highly dated interpretation of Smith's work. This however does not mean that the question of the relationship between moral philosophy and economic theory in Smith is no longer relevant. On the contrary, it remains one of the most active areas of research into Smith's work. The linkages between Smith's two works today take two forms:

1) The question of moral judgement concerning enrichment and vanity in The *Theory of Moral Sentiments* and the *Wealth of Nations*;
2) The status of sympathy, which, according to numerous researchers, is not only found at the heart of The *Theory of Moral Sentiments*,

[16] *Account of the Life and Writings of Adam Smith.* 1793, reproduced in Smith, A. (1980). *Essays on philosophical subjects*, edited by W. P. D. Wightman and J. C. Bryce.

but also in the background to Smith's analysis of commerce put forward in the *Wealth of Nations*.

Here, I will look at the first of these questions, and I will address the second question in Chapter 6 of this book.

I shall start by looking at the role played by *vanity*. The point is to understand the desire for riches and wealth. The most common explanation put forward today is to explain this as a result of vanity. In Smith's terms, as well as those of Hunt and Ignatieff (*op. cit.*), it has long been shown that the aim is to render compatible Smith's stated contempt for the search for wealth, which lies in the taste for acquiring frivolous "baubles and trinkets", and his demonstration of generalised enrichment, which is the subject of the *Wealth of Nations*. Hunt and Ignatieff readily admit that this is no easy task.[17]

This is why Vivienne Brown (*op. cit.* Chapter 4) went further by dedicating part of her book in trying to meet the challenge set out by Hunt and Ignatieff: Smith would thus assimilate *Wealth and Power* with "frivolous baubles", in a context of Stoic discourse, which implies the hierarchy of virtues established by the "impartial spectator". Yet Smith considered that "the great mob of mankind" did not share this hierarchy of virtues and did not totally (or even not at all) obey the injunctions of the impartial spectator, as we have seen. Having pointed out Smith's position, Brown then draws on Chapter 1 of Book IV which appears to assert that wealth and power are merely baubles and deduces that Smith despised wealth and power. She sees this chapter as expressing Stoic concepts according to which material wealth does not contribute to moral good (*summum bonum*).

Brown's analysis generated much interest, and Griswold (*op. cit.* p. 222) drew on it to support his idea that Smith supported the following theses: (1) the search for wealth by certain agents does not generally lead to happiness, but instead to moral corruption; and (2) this misfortune for some agents nevertheless leads to happiness for humanity. More recently, however, Samuel Fleischacker returned to the question raised by Hunt and Ignatieff by repeating that the position leads to an evident contradiction: How is it possible to agree that the search for wealth implies

[17] At first sight, it is not an easy task to reconcile his evident distaste for the vulgar materialism of "the great scramble" of commercial society with his clear endorsement of economic growth" (Hunt and Ignatieff, *op. cit.*, p. 298).

moral corruption and approve of an economic system which encourages the desire for wealth, as it applies to the whole system?[18] More generally, how is it possible to make the Stoic discourse of The *Theory of Moral Sentiments* compatible with the constant assertion in the *Wealth of Nations* that the desire for wealth is universal and permanent for everyone? Fleischacker raises these questions, but does not answer them.

Yet I will now show that the question raised by these commentators does not necessarily need asking. For this, I too need to comment on Chapter 1 of Book IV of The *Theory of Moral Sentiments*.

It has perhaps not been emphasised enough that this chapter is above all focussed on *aesthetics*, as clearly indicated in its title: "Of the beauty which the appearance of Utility bestows upon all the productions of art, and of the extensive influence of this species of Beauty". Indeed, the point of departure of the text is a critique of Hume's theory of aesthetics. Having paid homage to Hume ("an ingenious and agreeable philosopher, who joins the greatest depth of thought to the greatest elegance of expression"), Smith immediately goes on to state:

> The utility of any object, according to him, pleases the master by perpetually suggesting to him the pleasure or conveniency which it is fitted to promote. Every time he looks at it, he is put in mind of this pleasure; and the object in this manner becomes a source of perpetual satisfaction and enjoyment. The spectator enters by sympathy into the sentiments of the master, and necessarily views the object under the same agreeable aspect. [...] But that this fitness, this happy contrivance of any production of art, should often be more valued, than the very end for which it was intended; and that the exact adjustment of the means for attaining any conveniency or pleasure, should frequently be more regarded, than that very conveniency or pleasure, in the attainment of which their whole merit would seem to consist, has not, so far as I know, been yet taken notice of by anybody. That this however is very frequently the case, may be observed in a thousand instances, both in the most frivolous and in the most important concerns of human life. (*TMS*, p. 180)

[18] "If Griswold is right, Smith urges us throughout *Theory of Moral Sentiments* to see the pursuit of wealth as morally corrupting and conductive to unhappiness, but also applauds a social system that depends upon, and encourages, that very pursuit" (Fleischacker, *op. cit.*, 104).

To justify that utility is not the only motivation that guides our aesthetic judgements, Smith gives the following example (borrowed from Hume himself):

> When a person comes into his chamber, and finds the chairs all standing in the middle of the room, he is angry with his servant, and rather than see them continue in that disorder, perhaps takes the trouble himself to set them all in their places with their backs to the wall. (Ibid.)

At first sight, Smith seems to be relying on a kind of objective conception of utility with a lot of naiveté (chairs are made to sit on and not for anything else), thus rejecting utility as an aesthetic principle, and so asserting that aesthetic judgement is based on a *principle other* than utility.

This contrast between frivolous goods or "baubles" and what seems *really* useful would disconcert a contemporary economist. It is thus clear why the use of a Stoic reference, which attempts to establish a hierarchy of values, could be used by Hunt and Ignatieff, and then by Brown, to save Smith from the accusation of naiveté. However, I will show that this is not necessary, and above all that it can lead to a misunderstanding.

It should be noted that these amateurs of "baubles" play a game that was curiously forgotten by Roger Caillois (1958) in his book on the issue. This type of game is a puzzle or good detective story that sometimes captures our imagination. These games share the goal of creating order from disorder. To be sure, people who do not like detective stories, puzzles, model building or Conan Doyle novels may look on with dismay at anyone engaged in such activities which they may find both obsessive and futile. But we need only continue reading to ensure that Smith's position goes beyond this banal and superficial denunciation. For he immediately adds:

> Nor is it only with regard to such frivolous objects that our conduct is influenced by this principle; it is often the secret motive of the most serious and important pursuits of both private and public life. (*TMS*, p. 181)

Here we come to the crucial passage of the chapter in which Smith invites us to shift from "games", and "frivolous objects" to *serious* business. But how exactly should "*this principle*", this "*secret motive*", which is at work in the most important cases, be named?

We need to wait until the passage following the preceding quote (the passage containing the poor man's parable and the metaphor of the invisible hand, to which I shall return) to find out how Smith calls this principle:

> The same principle, the same love of system, the same regard to the beauty of order, of art and contrivance, frequently serves to recommend those institutions which tend to promote the public welfare. (TMS, p. 185)

So what is this principle, this love of the system, which Smith contrasts with utility as the principle of aesthetic judgement? It is the love of order that makes us view a house as "beautiful", if it is well-adapted to its purposes, even if we do not see ourselves living in it. Smith explicitly opposed Hume on this point, who believed that aesthetic judgement proceeds directly from the utility of an object, by the way, its owner can identify enjoyment of the object. Smith countered that such sympathy for the utility an owner gets from possessing a good is not required to make an aesthetic judgement, and Smith gave the above-mentioned example of a watch amateur who may admire the beauty of a *mechanism* that tells time so accurately, even if he is not himself especially precise. For Smith, love of the system is *disinterested*, and he makes an aesthetic judgement on the way means relate to ends. It is this love that justifies the taste of "trinkets", but also concerns "the most serious" economic or political undertakings. The field of aesthetics is thus surprisingly broad, reaching areas where it is not usually found. Smith equates the love of the system with the love of machines or models. Systems, machines and models share the fact that they are sets of *interdependent* elements.[19] Therefore, a system can also be a theoretical model. In this case, love of the system is very close to love of theory, of rational knowledge. In another context, this would be neither more nor less than philosophy. We are thus faced with an astonishing but not so unlikely proposition: whoever builds the model of a machine with a complicated mechanism derives an aesthetic pleasure that is not very different in nature from what a mathematician

[19] Mr. Biziou (2003) devoted an important part of his book to showing the importance of the concept of systems in Adam Smith's work. However, he does not seem to me to have given the importance it deserves to the concept of love of the system, which he translates as the "system spirit" (pp. 197 and sqq.) by then giving it a connotation close to that given by the encyclopaedists, which brings it closer to dogmatism.

experiences when *elegantly* demonstrating a theorem. And, of course, this pleasure is totally detached from the final causes of these activities, which are lacking, by definition. That is why Smith contrasts the love of the system with the search for utility.

This aesthetic of the system concerns at least three areas: economics, politics and science. I will start by looking at the first of these, and show that an ambitious person (the "poor man's son") can become rich if he shares the love of the system, and it can be shown that love of the system may substitute for greed to explain the desire for limitless enrichment. So the "parable of the poor man's son" thus deserves to be read carefully. It starts with:

> The poor man's son, whom heaven in its anger has visited with ambition, when he begins to look around him, admires the condition of the rich. He finds the cottage of his father too small for his accommodation, and fancies he should be lodged more at his ease in a palace. (*TMS*, p. 181)

So who are the "rich" whose condition the son of the poor man admires? They are the vain rich who *show off* their wealth. They live in palaces and ride in coaches. In eighteenth-century literature, the landlords spent their rent ostentatiously on luxury goods. Mandeville's idea of the pride of the rich expresses this cliché in a very classical way. Vanity thus plays an important role in this story, because without the vanity of the rich, the poor man's son could not *see* the carriages and castles that rich are so proud of that they display them for all to see.

The reader may therefore understand that the ambitious "poor man's son" does not strive for enrichment in the same way as his father. The latter seeks to improve his lot through work and savings. But laborious activity is, as it should be, limited by needs: he works to acquire the *necessaries* and *conveniences* he *needs*. When he acquired these, he stops working. On the other hand, his son, while he thinks he is looking for *luxuries*, is above all passionate about the clever and elegant combination of the means necessary to obtain them, *without his knowing it*. Certainly, Fleischacker sees clearly that the ambitious person does not simply seek to improve his lot, but actually wants "very great" enrichment: i.e. according to Fleischacker, he wishes to be sufficiently rich to stop working.[20] Yet

[20] "It is a desire for great wealth, for sufficient wealth that one would no longer need to work at all" (Fleischacker, *op. cit.*, p. 105).

one can easily object that seeking to be sheltered from want, that is to say, and by definition, to be sheltered from work, seeking no longer to work but to live on rent, is not really looking for "very great wealth". This was the dream generally achieved by all the petty-bourgeois in realist nineteenth-century novels who, when the time came, would sell their shops, lend their capital to the state and thus live by spending their annuities. But for Smith, this is not the ambition of the poor man's son, who does not seek such a happy and quick retirement. Indeed, Smith stressed the *insatiable*—limitless—nature of his activity. The wealth aimed for by the son, without him actually knowing it, is not even "very great", but limitless.

As immediately becomes clear:

> He is enchanted with the *distant* idea of this felicity. It appears in his fancy like the life of some superior rank of beings, and, in order to arrive at it, he devotes himself *for ever* to the pursuit of wealth and greatness. (*TMS*, p. 181, author's italics)

Thus, the idea that happiness remains "forever" distant, so that the poor man's son will search ceaselessly (or at least as long as love of the system drives him) and that "he submits in the first year, nay in the first month of his application, to more fatigue of body and more uneasiness of mind than he could have suffered through the whole of his life from the want of them" (Ibid.).

After listing in an impressive passage the sum of trials and humiliations the poor man's son inflicts upon himself, Smith concludes:

> Through the whole of his life he pursues the idea of a certain artificial and elegant repose *which he may never arrive* at, for which he sacrifices a real tranquillity that is at all times in his power, and which, if in *the extremity of old age* he should at last attain to it, he will find to be in no respect preferable to that humble security and contentment which he had abandoned for it. (Ibid., author's italics)

Two ideas are expressed here. On the one hand, this "artificial repose" is therefore hardly ever achieved; on the other hand, if by misfortune the poor man's son actually does reach it, it will seem less preferable than his initial condition. Let us look at this.

1. Why is the intended end almost never reached?

Brown believes that the aim of the hero of this parable is the happiness brought about by the enjoyment of palaces and coaches and by the esteem which the display of wealth brings. According to her, vanity is the driver of the poor man's son. If the end is therefore not reached according to these authors, it is because the happiness coming from vanity is illusory. Smith however insists that it is only when the love of the system quits the ambitious person, when he has sold his business and finally enjoys his painfully acquired palace and coach, or worse when he is ill, that he regrets not having been satisfied with his father's fate. By contrast, when he is possessed by love of the system, he will push away happiness. It is a distant horizon that is never reached. That is why Smith stressed the insatiable character and limitless desire of the poor man's son. But normally, vanity is not limitless. Limitless vanity (or pride) is the hallmark of excessiveness of someone who feels himself to be god. In the eighteenth century, such an attitude was already considered a symptom of megalomania.

In contrast, cupidity is always insatiable. Traditionally it is seen as the desire for money for money's sake.[21] Indeed, as we have seen in Chapter 1 above, because money satisfies no private need, the desire for money for money's sake, if it is conceivable at all, is insatiable. In my opinion, Smith's novelty lies in this[22]: the desire for endless enrichment does not, according to Smith, have money as its object. Instead, it seeks what he designates in the *Wealth of Nations* by the term capital, i.e. accumulated stocks aimed at providing the highest possible rate of profit, as we will see in Chapter 7 below. In the classical tradition which began here, capital was not a stock of tools and various raw materials, but a *general* stock regardless of any particular consideration about the techniques employed and the goods produced. The highest possible rate of profit then testifies to most the efficient, but also the most *elegant* use of the means of production, because a higher rate of profit relative to another expresses not only a faster enrichment, but also a more perfect match of means to ends. Capital is thus invested with certain properties previously associated with money: as a system and general form of wealth, it does not satisfy any particular need. Instead, it provides a particular and *unconscious* enjoyment to the

[21] See Berthoud (1981).

[22] See Diatkine (2010), Diatkine and Waelrevens (2019).

person employing it. Thus, love of the system and of machines replaces love of money. This change should not be underestimated.

2. So why is "the poor man's son" unhappy?

When expressed in today's economic analysis, the "poor man's son" imagines that he is making an inter-temporal allocation of utility. However, Smith asserts that this ambitious person is fooling himself. Here, the *Theory of Moral Sentiments* puts forward an astonishing proposition, because according to Smith, this error is *normal*. In fact, its correction is the symptom of a *pathology*, both physical and mental, as borne out by the following extract:

> It is then, in the last dregs of life, his body wasted with toil and diseases, his mind galled and ruffled by the memory of a thousand injuries and disappointments which he imagines he has met with from the injustice of his enemies, or from the perfidy and ingratitude of his friends, that he begins at last to find that wealth and greatness are mere trinkets of frivolous utility. (*TMS*, p. 181)

The rational calculation of costs and benefits is therefore only carried out at the moment when the love of the system disappears, due to old age or illness. Then, immediately, the calculation of utility takes over, and wealth and greatness are finally correctly evaluated. This is why, from the new point of view which is now that of the poor man's son, wealth and greatness are worth no more than "the tweezer-cases of the lover of toys". And Smith even adds that, after all, on a desert island, the latter would undoubtedly be more useful than the former. But once again, it is not utility that matters to the poor man's son, as a spectator of greatness and wealth.

"If we examine, however, why the spectator distinguishes with such admiration the condition of the rich and the great, we shall find that is not so much upon account of the superior ease or pleasure which they are supposed to enjoy, as of the numberless artificial and elegant contrivances for promoting this ease or pleasure. He does not even imagine that they are really happier than other people: but he imagines that they possess more means of happiness. And it is the ingenious and artful adjustment of those means to the end for which they were intended, that is the principal source of his admiration" (Ibid., p. 182).

Moreover, a few lines later Smith returns to the ambitious person who "in the languor of disease and the weariness of old age" *is no longer* a lover of the system. At this point, Smith's own voice can be heard:

> Power and riches appear then to be, what they are, enormous and aperose machines contrived to produce a few trifling conveniences to the body, consisting of springs the most nice and delicate, which must be kept in order with the most anxious attention, and which, in spite of all our care, are ready every moment to burst into pieces, and to crush in their ruins their unfortunate possessor. They are immense fabrics which it requires the labour of a life to raise, which threaten every moment to overwhelm the person that dwells in them, and which, while they stand, though they may save him from some smaller inconveniencies, can protect him from none of the severer inclemencies of the season. (*TMS*, p. 182)

Seen from this depressive state (called "splenetic philosophy" [TMS, p. 183]), power and wealth appear for what they *really* are in terms of consumer rationality. In comparison to the trouble, it takes to own machines that provide such pleasures, the pleasures actually to be derived from them are very slim. Is this a Stoic judgement? No, because the objectivity acquired as death approaches does not follow from a value judgement about "real" happiness: it is merely the result of rational calculation. The remarkable particularity of this text lies in stating that in general, when the poor man's son is in good health he does not act rationally, simply because *he is not utilitarian*. His father, as a worker, probably was. But the son loves systems, and is not.

That is why this depressive calculation does not last, as either the poor man's son dies or he is healed. In any case, he quickly abandons this "melancholic philosophy".

"But though this splenetic philosophy, which in time of sickness or low spirits is familiar to every man, thus entirely depreciates those great objects of human desire, when in better health and in better humour, we never fail to regard them under a more agreeable aspect" (Ibid.).

It should be noted that Smith generalises his argument, as it no longer applies only to "the poor man's son", but to *us all*, in our attitude to "great objects of human desire". And in fact, Smith drops the figure of the poor man's son and assigns to us all the *splenetic* philosophy we adopt when we are sick. For it is only when we are ill that we associate power and wealth with frivolous baubles. Yet following Brown, I find it hard to support Smith's view of a philosophy which he judges to be symptomatic of a disease, even if it is quite frequent.

That is not all, as it must be asked what these "enormous and aperose machines" are which the poor man's son spends his lifetime acquiring. If they would be are castles and coaches it would be hard to see what danger they would present to their possessors. It would even be quite comical to consider here the poor man's son being overwhelmed by domestic worries, on having become a squire. A stately home or manor surely requires upkeep, but a well-selected steward avoids any concern of such kind to the owner. Obviously, this is not what Smith had in mind. The poor man's son is a *self-made man*, who dedicates his entire life to his business. He will no doubt wish to sell it later and buy a castle, but only after having given up his love of the system. This is because the lover of the system, as long as he remains in good health, will never stop building systems: i.e. being an entrepreneur. The risk of bankruptcy of the "immense fabrics"—i.e. companies—is far higher than the risks of ruin of a castle. Neither Brown nor Fleischacker even considered it. The latter even finds such a "boy [to be] fantastically ambitious" (*op. cit.*, p. 106). It may be thought that ambition is in no way fantastic and that the poor man's son is quite usual, even if success remains rare.

We therefore find in this chapter the contrast between two types of desire for wealth, that of the father and that of his son: one is involved in laborious activity (limited by the needs he wishes to satisfy), and the other is driven by love of the system whose economic expression is the accumulation of capital. The father seeks to improve his lot through work and savings: the son too seeks to improve his lot, but actually fools himself. The former gets rich within the limits of his needs (whatever they may be), whereas the desire for wealth by the latter is limitless. Such then will be the general framework of one of the central issues of the *Wealth of Nations*, as we shall see later. This chapter of the *Theory of Moral Sentiments* emphasises two forms of enrichment. Yet instead of generating a new Adam Smith problem, in fact allows new linkages in Smith's works to emerge. Griswold (1999) understood this partially. Yet he entirely bases his demonstration on the idea that "the poor man's son" seeks happiness, fools himself and does not find it. That is why according to Griswold, the unhappiness of some contributes to the happiness of humanity. This is not exactly true, as "the poor man's son" also seeks happiness. He likes machines. But he does not know this, which is why he imagines he is seeking future happiness.

Returning to our chapter in The *Theory of Moral Sentiments*; as soon as "we" emerge from our depression, we forget the Stoic philosophy:

> If we consider the real satisfaction which all these things are capable of affording, by itself and separated from the beauty of that arrangement which is fitted to promote it, it will always appear in the highest degree contemptible and trifling. But we rarely view it in this abstract and philosophical light. We naturally confound it in our imagination with the order, the regular and harmonious movement of the system, the machine or economy by means of which it is produced. (*TMS*, p. 183)

If "we" were Stoic, we would despise "all these things". But indeed "we" are not. And, "we", Smith said, willingly confuse the purpose of the system with the system itself.

Finally, who exactly is this "we" staged here? The question must be asked, because Brown rightly taught us to pay attention to the "voices" that are expressed in Smith's text. Of course the "we" included Smith himself and his reader.[23] So Smith and his reader are also systems lovers. Indeed, if they were not, Smith would not have written and we would not have read The *Theory of Moral Sentiments*. By contrast, someone who uses knowledge as a means to acquire wealth and power is a Sophist, as we all know too.

It must be noted above all that the love of the system is therefore *sometimes unconscious*. The philosopher may imagine being published for the sake of humanity, but he then risks being a poor philosopher if love of knowledge is not his first motive. By contrast, the "poor man's son" *must* imagine accumulating to enjoy the future happiness of riding in a carriage to accumulate. He is necessarily the victim of *an illusion* that makes him confuse happiness with the systems that he accumulates endlessly. That is why he is *a real amateur*, not very different in the final analysis to the watch enthusiast who may imagine buying watches because he wants to be on time or to impress his neighbour, while he is actually most passionate about a mechanism that is hidden.

[23] C. Griswold (1999, p. 222, note 45) assumes that the first "we" refers to the philosopher, while the next two refer to ordinary moral actors. But this assumption is only deduced from the Stoic thesis that the values defended by philosophers are not those of the common man. I think Smith's text is quite clear: when we are depressed (and this can happen unfortunately to everyone!) we take the first point of view. And when we are healthy, we adopt the second.

However, there is a crucial difference between the entrepreneur (the poor man's son) and the watch enthusiast, because *the illusion* of the former has changed the face of the world:

> And it is well that nature imposes upon us in this manner. It is this deception which rouses and keeps in continual motion the industry of mankind. It is this which first prompted them to cultivate the ground, to build houses, to found cities and commonwealths, and to invent and improve all the sciences and arts, which ennoble and embellish human life; which have entirely changed the whole face of the globe, have turned the rude forests of nature into agreeable and fertile plains, and made the trackless and barren ocean a new fund of subsistence, and the great high road of communication to the different nations of the earth. The earth, by these labours of mankind, has been obliged to redouble her natural fertility, and to maintain a greater multitude of inhabitants. (Ibid.)

What is this illusion? I recalled above that many commentators on the latest avatar of the "Das Adam Smith problem" claim that the poor man's son is, according to Smith, the victim of the confusion between wealth (knick-knacks/baubles) and independence. We can now see that this reading is wrong. In fact, Smith's words are much more subversive. This is the illusion that Smith is proud to be the first to describe, and that, without us being aware of it, makes us believe *that we are looking for wealth* and glory when what we really like are the machines, models or systems that buy them. In short, it is capital—an abstract form of means to wealth—that the poor man's son loves, while believing he is seeking the enjoyment of luxury goods.

Love of the system is an endless activity, because it is of no private utility. Yet it also escapes the person pursuing such love, and so is socially useful. This is the meaning of the metaphor of the "invisible hand": it refers here, as it also does in the *Wealth of Nations*, to the unintended beneficial consequences of human actions.[24]

Immediately after this paragraph, Smith states the following thesis:

[24] The metaphor of the invisible hand is used three times in Smith's work. In *The History of Astronomy*, (Smith, 1980, p. 49) "the invisible hand of Jupiter" is evoked (in the "origins of philosophy", i.e. science) by the first philosophers to explain the irregularities of nature. It is found in the TMS in the passage that I comment here. Finally, the invisible hand is mentioned in the WON. It is this latter occurrence which is supposed to represent competition in markets. It can be shown that in any case the use of this metaphor has a strong ironic dimension. See Emma Rothschild (2002).

> It is to no purpose that the proud and unfeeling landlord views his extensive fields, and without a thought for the wants of his brethren, in imagination consumes himself the whole harvest that grows upon them. The homely and vulgar proverb, that the eye is larger than the belly, never was more fully verified than with regard to him. The capacity of his stomach bears no proportion to the immensity of his desires, and will receive no more than that of the meanest peasant. The rest he is obliged to distribute among those who prepare, in the nicest manner, that little which he himself makes use of, among those who fit up the palace in which this little is to be consumed, among those who provide and keep in order all the different baubles and trinkets which are employed in the economy of greatness; all of whom thus derive from his luxury and caprice that share of the necessaries of life which they would in vain have expected from his humanity or his justice. The produce of the soil maintains at all times nearly that number of inhabitants which it is capable of maintaining. The rich only select from the heap what is most precious and agreeable. They consume little more than the poor; and in spite of their natural selfishness and rapacity, though they mean only their own conveniency, though the sole end which they propose from the labours of all the thousands whom they employ be the gratification of their own vain and insatiable desires, they divide with the poor the produce of all their improvements. They are led by an invisible hand to make nearly the same distribution of the necessaries of life which would have been made had the earth been divided into equal portions among all its inhabitants; and thus, without intending it, without knowing it, advance the interest of the society, and afford means to the multiplication of the species. (*TMS*, p. 184)

This text was published in 1756. Smith makes a point in pitting the rich (nonworking) against the poor (working), and it is in this opposition in which he argues that the insatiable desire for wealth by the former creates employment and thus an improvement in the conditions of the poor.

In 1776, in the WON, he contrasted two types of nonworkers: landlords and manufacturers (whom Turgot had called capitalists). Typically (but not exclusively), some of the former are motivated by vanity, while some of the latter are driven by love of the system. Ostentatious expenditure is therefore the reason why landlords spend their rent, whereas capitalists use their profits for investment.

The WON will later present three types of relationships to wealth, defining three social classes:

1. Labour, as a means of acquiring wealth within the limit of needs. The wealth of workers consists of *necessaries* and *conveniences*, which constitute wage property.
2. Land ownership, which allows the acquisition of *luxuries* for ostentatious reasons.
3. The accumulation of capital, i.e. stocks considered from the point of view of the merchant manufacturer, who combines them as well as possible, in order to maximise his profit rate.

Workers' desire for enrichment is thus limited by need. The landlords' desire is to be much admired by their neighbours. Only the accumulation of capital is insatiable and thus without any limits.

The introduction of this distinction between capitalists and landowners, it seems to me, helps us to understand the TMS today. It tells us that the poor man's son thinks he wants to live like a vain landowner. But to get rich in this way, he must first be a capitalist (a merchant manufacturer). To succeed (in becoming rich), he must be driven, albeit without his knowledge, by some form of love of the system, love of machines, or capital. Thus, the unintended result of the love of the system by the "poor man's son" and his like is general enrichment, just as the vanity of the landlord compels him to trade his surplus wheat for luxury goods. The poor man's son is driven (without knowing it) by the love of the system, the landlord is by vanity (and he knows it very well). Both contribute unwittingly to the (limited) enrichment of the poor. In order for the son of a worker to achieve his goal of living like a landlord, he must experience the love of the system. However, as long as he feels love for the system he does not become a landlord and remains a merchant manufacturer (a capitalist entrepreneur).

The landlord is certainly motivated by vanity. He shows off his *luxuries* for all to see. But the poor man's son, the "budding" entrepreneur, is unwittingly motivated by his love of the system. He remains hidden behind the walls of his austere factory and his office. The capitalist entrepreneur does not expose himself to sight, he does not live in a castle on the top of a hill. Lurking at the back of "the secret workshop of production", as Marx would say, he remains silent in his being. The search for profit for profit's sake expresses successful greed, and Smith later describes this insatiable activity in the *Wealth of Nations* as an *endless* activity. Because its object remains hidden from the person who experiences it, accumulation can be analysed as a process that is not the result of a decision by *a given individual.*

Moreover, at the end of the paragraph mentioning the invisible hand, Smith seems to take a cynical view. After assuming that inequality in landholdings does not challenge the allocation of goods through redistribution as carried out by landlords whose stomachs are restricted, Smith evokes "the beggar, who suns himself by the side of the highway", and who "possesses that security which kings are fighting for" … "In ease of body and peace of mind, all the different ranks of life are nearly upon a level" (TMS 185).

It is possible to read this cynical proposal as merely being ironic. But it is difficult to read it as actually expressing Smith's point of view, as Brown does (*op. cit.*, p. 90), who still uses it at the heart of her demonstration. Whether a king can envy the security (an important component of happiness, it is true) of a beggar who has nothing to lose is possible, but it only shows that a king may also adopt a "melancholic" philosophy. But surely not Smith, who readily compares a beggar to a dog in the WON. Griswold (*op. cit.*, p. 226, n. 55) rightly points out, it seems, that this difficult to follow Brown in making the beggar "the paragon of virtue we would wish to emulate"!

After publication of the *Wealth of Nations*, which puts the accumulation of capital at the forefront of its analysis, Smith does not need to specify that the poor man's son is a debutant manufacturer, in the subsequent editions of the *Theory of Moral Sentiments*. It seems to me that such detailed precision would be unnecessary because not all system lovers are merchants. They also include leading politicians and scholars, whose encounter produced the mercantile system, which, we shall see, was the target of the *Wealth of Nations*. The last paragraphs of the chapter in the *Theory of Moral Sentiments* I am commenting here are particularly enlightening from this point of view. Indeed, in the sentence that finally names love of the system, Smith writes:

> The same principle, the same love of system, the same regard to the beauty of order, of art and contrivance, frequently serves to recommend those institutions which tend to promote the public welfare. When a patriot exerts himself for the improvement of any part of the public police, his conduct does not always arise from pure sympathy with the happiness of

> those who are to reap the benefit of it. It is not commonly from a fellow-feeling with carriers and waggoners that a public-spirited man encourages the mending of high roads. When the Legislature establishes premiums and other encouragements to advance the linen or woolen manufactures, its conduct seldom proceeds from pure sympathy with the wearer of cheap or fine cloth, and much less from that with the manufacturer or merchant. The perfection of police, the extension of trade and manufactures, are noble and magnificent objects. The contemplation of them pleases us, and we are interested in whatever can tend to advance them. They make part of the great system of government, and the wheels of the political machine seem to move with more harmony and ease by means of them. We take pleasure in beholding the perfection of so beautiful and so grand a system, and we are uneasy till we remove any obstruction that can in the least disturb or encumber the regularity of its motions. All constitutions of government, however, are valued only in proportion as they tend to promote the happiness of those who live under them. This is their sole use and end. From a certain spirit of system, however, from a certain love of art and contrivance, we sometimes seem to value the means more than the end, and to be eager to promote the happiness of our fellow-creatures, rather from a view to perfect and improve a certain beautiful and orderly system than from any immediate sense or feeling of what they either suffer or enjoy. (*TMS*, p. 185)

Thus, love of the system also animates great politicians as it animates the merchants who submit their plans to them. This shared love is at the origin of the mercantile system which is the subject of criticism in *Wealth of Nations*, and which I will study in the following chapters. Finally, Smith takes a backhanded swipe at overly consensual rhetoric about corruption, which he replaces by mutual *seduction*. The importance of this aesthetic relationship in Smith's work cannot be over-emphasised.

In a few lines, this paragraph offers us a striking picture of an aspect of the mercantile system that is the target of the *Wealth of Nations*: the meeting of two enthusiasts of systems, that of entrepreneurs and politicians. They have little difficulty seducing one another, which is why their conjunction is so formidable. Against them, the chances of Adam Smith (an amateur of the system of natural liberty) appear to be slim. Nevertheless, Smith wrote the WON to this end. This is the project that Smith sets out in conclusion of this chapter:

> In the same manner, if you would implant public virtue in the breast of him who seems heedless of the interest of his country, it will often be to

> no purpose to tell him what superior advantages the subjects of a well-governed state enjoy; that they are better lodged, that they are better clothed, that they are better fed. These considerations will commonly make no great impression. You will be more likely to persuade, if you describe the great system of public police which procures these advantages,—if you explain the connections and dependencies of its several parts, their mutual subordination to one another, and their general subserviency to the happiness of the society; if you shew how this system might be introduced into his own country, what it is that hinders it from taking place there at present, how those obstructions might be removed, and all the several wheels of the machine of government be made to move with more harmony and smoothness, without grating upon one another, or mutually retarding one another's motions. It is scarce possible that a man should listen to a discourse of this kind, and not feel himself animated to some degree of public spirit. He will, at least for the moment, feel some desire to remove those obstructions, and to put into motion so beautiful and so orderly a machine. Nothing tends so much to promote public spirit as the study of politics,—of the several systems of civil government, their advantages and disadvantages,—of the constitution of our own country, its situation, and interest with regard to foreign nations, its commerce, its defense, the disadvantages it labours under, the dangers to which it may be exposed, how to remove the one, and how to guard against the other. Upon this account political disquisitions, if just, and reasonable, and practicable, are of all the works of speculation the most useful. Even the weakest and the worst of them are not altogether without their utility. They serve at least to animate the public passions of men, and rouse them to seek out the means of promoting the happiness of the society. (*TMS*, p. 86)

The WON completed this programme—at least in part. So it is time to address this fragment of a still-to-be-written general political theory that will require an understanding of capital accumulation. Thereafter, the shift in Smith's ideas takes place, which needs to be measured at its fair value. The question is then no longer whether the search for wealth is a vice or a virtue. Instead, it is necessary to understand to what extent the accumulation of capital, which allows the enrichment of all, constitutes a threat to the polis.

References

Berry, P., & Smith, C. (Eds.). (2013). *The Oxford handbook of Adam Smith*. Oxford University Press.

Berthoud A. (1981). *Aristote et l'argent*. PUG Maspero.

Biziou M. (2003). *Adam Smith et l'origine du libéralisme*. P.U.F.

Brown, V. (1994). *Adam Smith's discourse*. Routledge.

Caillois, R. (1958). *Les jeux et les hommes*. Gallimard.

Campbell Mossner, C. (1960). Of the principle of moral estimation: A discourse between David Hume, Robert Clerk, and Adam Smith, An unpublished MS by Adam Ferguson. *Journal of the History of Ideas*, 21(2).

Diatkine, D. (2010). Vanity and the love of system in theory of moral sentiments. *The European Journal of the History of Economic Thought, 17*(3).

Diatkine, D., & Waelrevens, B. (2019). From vanity to the love of systems …. In R. Ege & H. Iggersheim (Eds.) (2011). *Freedom and happiness in economic thought and philosophy*. Routledge.

Evensky, J. (2015). *Adam Smith's wealth of nations*. Cambridge University Press.

Fleischaker, S. (2004). *On Adam Smith's wealth of nations*. Princeton University Press.

Griswold, C. L. (1999). *Adam Smith and the virtues of enlightenment*. Cambridge University Press.

Haakonssen, K. (1981). *The science of a lagislator, the natural jurisprudence of David Hume and Adam Smith*. Cambridge University Press.

Halévy, E. (1926). *The growth of philosophic radicalism*. The Macmillan Company.

Hont, I., & Ignatieff, M. (Eds.) (1981). *Wealth and virtue. The shaping of political economy in the Scottish enlightenment*. Cambridge University Press.

Montes, L. (2004). *Adam Smith in context*. Palgrave Macmillan.

Rothschild E. (2002). *Economic sentiments. Adam Smith, condorcet and the enlightment*. Harvard University Press.

Smith A. (1980). *Essays on philosophical subjects, with Dugald Stewart's 'account of Adam Smith'* (Edited by W. P. D. Wightman, J. C. Bryce and I. S. Ross).

Tribe K. (1999). Adam Smith, critical theorist ? *Journal of Economic Literature, 37*(2).

PART II

"The Very Violent Attack I Made Upon the Whole Commercial System of Great Britain"

CHAPTER 4

The (Benign) Economic Consequences of the Mercantile System

To my knowledge, few commentators (Coats [1975] is an exception) of the *Wealth of Nations* have focused their study on Smith's main adversary, the mercantile system. This shortcoming may explain why Smith's position with regard to the economy and society of his day appears so ambiguous. Smith did indeed seem to be indifferent to most of the oppressions he denounced, as if injustice and scandal were the price to pay for improving the condition of the greatest number (see Cropsey, 1957) they indeed shed light on some of the most characteristic positions (or the most glaring errors, as the reader wishes) of Smith's economic analysis.

To this end, it is first necessary to examine the set of propositions which constituted, according to Smith, the founding "principle" of the mercantile system (section "Of the "Principle of the Commercial, or Mercantile System""). Smith acknowledged this to be set out by the Physiocrats. However, Smith differed from the latter in a very characteristic way on an important point. For Quesnay, the mercantile system resulted from prejudices that science could undoubtedly dispel. By contrast, Smith sought to show that the mercantile system was *the product of European history*. Yet, far from expressing the triumph of capitalism, the mercantile system was, according to Smith, nothing, other than the expression of the medieval deadweight of which it is the product (section "The Mercantile System

D. Diatkine, *Adam Smith and the Wealth of Nations*, Palgrave Studies in the History of Economic Thought, https://doi.org/10.1007/978-3-030-81600-1_4

as an Unintended Result of Human Action"). I will then study how the inefficiency induced by the mercantile system was largely compensated in Great Britain by "the incessant desire to improve one's lot"—i.e. by saving (section "The "Frugality and Good Conduct" as a Temporary Remedy for the Mercantile System"). Yet, this was not the case of the colonies when they were governed by privileged companies, such as the (English or Dutch) East India Companies. Moreover these savings were not enough, as evidenced by the growth in public debt. This in turn led to the crucial question of Empire reform (section "The Public Debt and the System of Natural Liberty").

Of the "Principle of the Commercial, or Mercantile System"

This is the title of Chapter 1, Book IV of the *Wealth of Nations*. This principle is simple, namely that the legislator *must ensure a surplus or balance on foreign trade*. Preclassical authors or "mercantilists"[1] maintained that the legislator had to *favour* a surplus on foreign trade. This was because gold and silver—the standards for currencies—were imported, and so a trade surplus was necessary to ensure the replacement of used coins, and to support domestic growth. Precious metals were indeed the only goods which it seemed impossible to do without (to pay for troops in the first place), and which are not produced locally. Yet how was it possible to know whether foreign trade was in surplus or deficit? The traditional answer was simple: foreign exchange was the only indicator available. This was why the *main* issue in the controversy opposing Smith to Thomas Mun and John Locke (the two authors Smith quoted in this context)[2] was also the question of whether the monetary authorities had to ensure the value (external, but also internal) of precious metals, via monetary policy. Smith's position on this was brutal. It spans the whole of the *Wealth of Nations*: monetary policy, *in terms of watching over the price of gold*, was quite simply irrelevant. This was all the more so since bank credit was (and remains) a substitute for gold. In this case, the situation was quite

[1] This expression was used in the nineteenth century, and so justifies the use of quotation marks.

[2] As will all his contemporaries, Smith seldom used citations, so their occasional use is remarkable.

different, and we shall return to this essential point in Chapter 8 of this book.

After having swept aside the confusion of money and wealth, Smith tackled the assertion according to which "we" find it more difficult to acquire money than to "get rid of it". This Smithian criticism was the foundation on which he formulated the notion of real wealth.

According to Smith, this "illusion" of the asymmetry between buying and selling was shared by both legislators and individuals. It was based on the following principle: in an open economy, what is true for an individual also holds for an economy, and the only measure of a country's economic efficiency is the positive balance on foreign trade, and therefore the inflow of precious metals. Smith then described Spain and Portugal, which tried unsuccessfully to ban the outflow of precious metals and the importation of foreign goods. Moreover, the merchants argued that if, for example, trade with the East Indies was in deficit, then the re-exports of goods imported from these regions made it possible to rebalance trade with the Far East in favour of England. This was the opinion defended by Thomas Mun (1571–1641), one of the Directors of the East India Company, in his posthumous book *England's Treasure by Forraign Trade or the Balance of Forraign Trade is the Rule of Our Treasure* published in 1664.

Smith argued that while Mun's opinion prevailed, "the only way to keep gold from flowing out" was to avoid a deficit in foreign trade.[3]

This "fundamental maxim" expressed the idea that the interests of the East India Company (directly at issue here), and more generally the interests of exporting merchants, were identical to the general interest. This was because, in the final analysis, they were responsible for importing precious metals essential to all of England's economic activity and which were therefore resources with no possible substitute as England did not produce them. Smith firmly opposed his adversaries, arguing that gold was a commodity like any other whose quantity "naturally regulates itself in every country according to the effectual demand, or according to the demand of those who are willing to pay the whole rent, labour,

[3] "The attention of government was turned away from guarding against the exportation of gold and silver to watch over the balance of trade as the only cause which could occasion any augmentation or diminution of those metals. From one fruitless care it was turned away to another care much more intricate, much more embarrassing, and just equally fruitless. The title of Mun's book, *England's Treasure in ForeignTrade*, became a fundamental maxim in the political economy, not of England only, but of all other commercial countries" (WON 434).

and profits which must be paid in order to prepare and bring it to market"... "no commodities regulate themselves more easily or more exactly according to this effectual demand than gold and silver" (WON 435).

As I will show in Chapter 8, Smith was very close to holding the view that money is not a commodity: gold therefore, which is a commodity like all others, was not a money.

I will return to the important notion of *effectual demand* in Chapter 7. For now, it should be noted that this text raises a delicate problem which we will often find in the economic analysis of money. To be sure, there are certainly buyers of gold and silver, willing to pay the wages, profits and rents necessary to bring these metals to the market, provided these metals have some private uses. In this case, precious metals are indeed commodities like any other; and in this case, the principle that goods are bought by goods holds for precious metals too. This applied all the more so as the cost of transport of precious metals was relatively low (without insurance, no doubt). Yet, if goldsmiths, for example, were willing to pay the price necessary to attract to the market the quantities of precious metals they needed, it was much less easy to explain the "demand for money" more generally, since:

> In all countries where there is tolerable security, every man of common understanding will endeavour to employ whatever stock he can command in procuring either present enjoyment or future profit. If it is employed in procuring present enjoyment, it is a stock reserved for immediate consumption. If it is employed in procuring future profit, it must procure this profit either staying with him, or by going from him. In the one case it is fixed, in the other it is a circulating capital. A man must be perfectly crazy who, where there is tolerable security, does not employ all the stock which he commands, whether be his own or borrowed of other people, in some one or other of those three ways. (WON 235)

Thanks to the remarkable simplification of the assumption that it *is not* easier to buy than to sell, because monetary exchange is an exchange of commodities by means of commodities, Smith removed with one stroke of the pen the difficulties his predecessors had encountered. As can be seen, this "simplification" found its full meaning in Smith's struggle against the mercantile system. Characteristically, Smith considered that there is no need to pay attention to the foreign exchange. The passage from the *Wealth of Nations* devoted to the foreign exchange market

(Book IV, Chapter 3) is moreover intended to show that little relevant information can be drawn from it concerning the balance of foreign trade:

> There is no certain criterion by which we can determine on which side what is called the balance between any two countries lies, or which of them exports to the greatest value. National prejudice and animosity, prompted always by the private interest of particular traders, are the principles which generally direct our judgment upon all questions concerning it. There are two criterions, however, which have frequently been appealed to upon such occasions, the customhouse books and the course of exchange. (WON 475)

And Smith, although he was *Commissioner of Customs* in Edinburgh from 1778 to 1790, immediately added: "The custom-house books, I think, it is now generally acknowledged, are a very uncertain criterion, on account of the inaccuracy of the valuation at which the greater part of goods are rated in them. The course of exchange is, perhaps, almost equally so".

Indeed, he argued that a variation in the exchange rate of one currency against another could often be caused by the variation in the value of a third currency, which is difficult to dispute.

So to conclude this point: the economic principle on which the mercantile system was based was therefore simple. By asserting the asymmetry between buying and selling, the mercantile system postulated that exchange was necessarily monetary. This principle put monetary theory at the heart of economic analysis. Smith however pushed it to the periphery. As we shall see in Chapter 6, *real* wealth was the concept Smith used to oppose this principle. His notion argued that the fundamental symmetry of exchange was a relationship of equivalence, which granted all commodities generalised purchasing power, which until then had been considered the privilege of money. As all goods had the essential properties of money, the difference between barter and monetary exchange lost most of its meaning.

Yet the principle on which the mercantile system was based was not just an illusion that science alone would be enough to dispel. It was above all the product of European history, which I shall study now. It was European history which generated this partial system that confused the interest of a part with that of the whole: that mixed up the interest of the capitalist class with the general interest. This confusion was not the product of ignorance, but resulted from the historically necessary encounter of the large manufacturing merchants and the legislators.

The Mercantile System as an Unintended Result of Human Action

The mercantile system was very different to the future alternative models to economic liberalism like socialism, the planned economy or the welfare economy. These latter concepts describing systems were not coined by Fréderic Bastiat or Friedrich Hayek. By contrast, we do owe to Smith (and to Mirabeau) the *invention* of the concept of mercantile system. No one has ever claimed to be its defender as such. The adversaries that Smith set up for himself (the foremost being Sir James Steuart, who Smith never actually cited),[4] had studied *political economy*.

As a matter of fact, Smith provided a seductive *explanation* of how his adversary came into being, a fact that is exceptional enough to be emphasised. For Smith, the mercantile system was the result of history, and was indeed a historical *necessity*.

Smith reached this conclusion in Book III of the *Wealth of Nations*, in which he shows how the barbarian invasions, by destroying the Roman Empire, destroyed at the same time all urban civilisation and plunged Europe's countryside into autarky. The conquerors went on to occupy land, not to make it a "means of subsistence", but a means "of power and protection" (WON 383).

According to Smith, this difference then produced a substantial modification in the "natural law of succession". Instead of land being divided between each heir, as would be "natural" when land is a "means of subsistence", land inheritance was subjected to the law of primogeniture to maintain its integrity as a "means of power". Now, "it seldom happens, however, that a great proprietor is a great improver" (WON 385). Indeed,

[4] In a letter dated 3 September 1772 and addressed to W. Pulteney, Smith wrote that he held the same negative opinion as his correspondent concerning Sir James Steuart's book, and that "*Without once mentioning it, I flatter myself, that every false principle in it, will meet a clear and distinct confutation in mine*" (Adam Smith, *Correspondence*, *op. cit.* p. 163-164). Steuart's book was probably his *Inquiry into the Principles of Political Economy* published by Millar in 1767. This book was one of the most important contributions to economic analysis in the pre-classical literature: see for example, P. Chamley (1963); and more recently R. Tortajada (1999).

his savings were often zero or negative.[5] This under-exploitation of land was not only due to the policy of the aristocratic owners, but also followed from the status of their tenants. Smith insists that the serf, like the slave, had no incentive to increase production since he was not interested in selling the product.

The evolution of land tenure (i.e. the disappearance of serfdom) led to the establishment of farm rental contracts. These were certainly more effective as farmers had an interest in the development of their capital, but they were penalised by the shortness of leases. For Smith, and unlike Quesnay, direct tenure was, without doubt, the most efficient mode of land use.

The first consequence of the plunge into the barbarity of Western Europe after the fall of the Roman Empire was therefore the stagnation of agriculture. It persisted as long as Europe remained hampered by the struggle to survive during such "dark" times. The same was not true for the cities: the last inhabitants of the cities were reduced to serfdom, as testified by the charters of emancipation granted later by the sovereigns. The reason for these emancipations was simple: it was necessary to build an alliance between city burghers and monarchs, against the local lords.[6]

I will return to the importance given by Smith to the political conditions of capital accumulation in the next chapter. It seemed quite obvious to him that freedom—i.e. political autonomy—was the necessary condition for the stabilisation of property rights. Moreover, it was because the

[5] "If the expense of his house and person either equalled or exceeded his revenue, as it did very frequently, he had no stock to employ in this manner. If he was an economist, he generally found it more profitable to employ his annual savings in new purchases than in the improvement of his old estate. To improve land with profit, like all other commercial projects, requires an exact attention to small savings and small gains, of which a man born to a great fortune, even though naturally frugal, is very seldom capable. The situation of such a person naturally disposes him to attend rather to ornament which pleases his fancy than to profit for which he has so little occasion" (ibid.).

[6] "The lords despised the burghers, whom they considered not only as of a different order, but as a parcel of emancipated slaves, almost of a different species from themselves. The wealth of the burghers never failed to provoke their envy and indignation, and they plundered them upon every occasion without mercy or remorse. The burghers naturally hated and feared the lords. The king hated and feared them too; but though perhaps he might despise, he had no reason either to hate or fear the burghers. Mutual interest, therefore, disposed them to support the king, and the king to support them against the lords. They were the enemies of his enemies, and it was his interest to render them as secure and independent of those enemies as he could" (WON 402).

norm in the countryside was for possessions to be insecure, subject to lordly whims, that rural areas remained miserable and the land was under-exploited "because to acquire more might only tempt the injustice of their oppressors" (WON 405). By contrast, "the inhabitants of trading cities, by importing the improved manufactures and expensive luxuries of richer countries, afforded some food to the vanity of the great proprietors, who eagerly purchased them with great quantities of the rude produce of their own lands" (WON 406–407).

The importation of luxury goods by city merchants then encouraged the development of factories, whose output substituted for imports: and Smith cited the silk factories that developed in Italian cities, in Lyon and in London. Finally, the countryside was put to better use, which Smith studied in the last chapter of Book III.

According to Smith, urban growth had three happy consequences for the countryside: first, it offered a market and therefore allowed rural areas to enrich themselves. Second, the city merchants invested in the land and developed it. Third, the most important effect of urban development was the pacification of rural areas.[7]

The *Wealth of Nations* then follows with a startling description of how the market economy literally ended the feudal lords' capacity to cause trouble. The barbarian times of the High Middle Ages are now evoked, supported by contemporary examples drawn from the Scottish *highlands*. In the countries that were models of ancient times without foreign trade or important manufactures, the surplus product of land was left without purchasing power, as it, in turn, had no effective demand. These goods with no purchasing power could be used to feed friends or menial servants.[8]

[7] "Commerce and manufactures gradually introduced order and good government, and with them, the liberty and security of individuals, among the inhabitants of the country, who had before lived almost in a continual state of war with their neighbours and of servile dependency upon their superiors. This, though it has been the least observed, is by far the most important of all their effects. Mr. Hume is the only writer who, so far as I know, has hitherto taken notice of it" (WON 412).

[8] Smith then cited famous examples of extravagance, like the Earl of Warwick who fed some thirty thousand people in his various stately homes: "A hospitality nearly of the same kind was exercised not many years ago in many different parts of the highlands of Scotland. It seems to be common in all nations to whom commerce and manufactures are little known" (WON 413).

The development of the cities implied that the income of landowners contributed to the livelihoods not just of thousands of retainers, but of an even greater number of workers directly or indirectly producing the luxury goods henceforth bought by landowners.[9] Increased spending by workers prompted landowners to expand their farms. At the same time, farmers were able to obtain more favourable terms from landowners, thereby helping to improve agricultural productivity. But above all:

> The tenants having in this manner become independent, and the retainers being dismissed, the great proprietors were no longer capable of interrupting the regular execution of justice or of disturbing the peace of the country. Having sold their birthright, not like Esau for a mess of pottage in time of hunger and necessity, but in the wantonness of plenty, for trinkets and baubles, fitter to be the playthings of children than the serious pursuits of men, they became as insignificant as any substantial burgher or tradesman in a city. A regular government was established in the country as well as in the city, nobody having sufficient power to disturb its operations in the one any more than in the other. (WON 421)

This subordination of the nobility was therefore the result of an alliance forged by the monarchy with the merchants and the manufacturers, an alliance which was then expressed by the identification of the interests of merchants and the interest of the monarch, and subsequently of the identification of these two interests with the general interest. It was this twofold identification that constituted the mercantile system: "A revolution of the greatest importance to the public happiness was in this manner brought about by two different orders of people who had not the least intention to serve the public. To gratify the most childish vanity was the sole motive of the great proprietors. The merchants and artificers, much less ridiculous, acted merely from a view to their own interest, and in pursuit of their own pedlar principle of turning a penny wherever a penny was to be got. Neither of them had either knowledge or foresight of that great revolution which the folly of the one, and the industry of the other, was gradually bringing about" (WON 422).

The economic consequences of this collusion were then immediately stated by Smith: "It is thus that through the greater part of Europe the

[9] We may find here Smith's own historical illustration of the invisible hand metaphor, used in the *Theory of Moral Sentiments*, see Chapter 3 above.

commerce and manufactures of cities, instead of being the effect, have been the cause and occasion of the improvement and cultivation of the country".

> This order, however, *being contrary to the natural course of things*, is necessarily both slow and uncertain. Compare the slow progress of those European countries of which the wealth depends very much upon their commerce and manufactures with the rapid advances of our North American colonies, of which the wealth is founded altogether in agriculture. (Ibid., italics are mine)

I will return to the important case of the American colonies in the next chapter and to the "natural course of things" in Chapter 7 of this book. In the meantime, it should be noted that the meaning of Smith's historical study was twofold. It was, on the one hand, to show that the mercantile system, which sealed the coming together of the interests of monarchs with those of merchants and manufacturers, was ultimately the result of the fall of the Roman Empire. On the other hand, it was necessary to describe the sequence of investments which followed as a consequence. First, the merchants invested in "distant trade" to exchange the rent from "wheat" of the big landowners for imported luxury goods; then, in a second phase, they invested in "factories" and finally in agriculture.

We will see in Chapter 7 how Smith tried to show that this European "march" of accumulation was "retrograde", and "contrary to the natural course of things". This inversion resulted in lower and more uncertain rates of enrichment than that which would be established under the system of natural freedom. Within the latter, the sequence of investments take place in accordance with the "natural course of the progress of opulence", as was the case in the English colonies of North America. We can assume that this natural course, which would occur under a regime of natural freedom, was *constructed* by Smith as the *reverse image* of the historical order described here.

In the meantime, what were the economic effects of the mercantile system? I will show that they were benign in Great Britain, at least as long the country still escaped from the government of the merchants. However, I will show in the next chapter that these effects were catastrophic, when a single, exclusive company of merchants governed, as was the case in Bengal which was ruled by the British East India Company.

The "Frugality and Good Conduct" as a Temporary Remedy for the Mercantile System

If the mercantile system was the target of the *Wealth of Nations*, it is however interesting to emphasise that the economic damages which this system caused in Great Britain were easily compensated. To show how, I will rely on Smith's criticism of Quesnay,[10] in the last chapter of Book IV. It will allow us to see better the scope of Smith's critique of the mercantile system, and at the same time, certain specificities of the economic construction of the *Wealth of Nations*.

We know that Smith's critique of the agricultural system was twofold: firstly, Smith seemed to criticise Dr Quesnay's "speculative" method, and secondly, Smith only broached what he called the "capital error" of the agricultural system, which consisted in asserting the sterility of the sterile class.

I want to show here that the critique of method, which appears to be secondary, is in fact a political criticism, which is quite devastating and that the "capital error" could be easily accepted by Physiocracy, provided only that it was formulated slightly differently. I will start with this last point, by showing that it was enough to simply integrate the profit alongside rent in the net product, an operation that does not involve any deep transformation of the system, since we had known (since Vaggi, 1987) to what extent the hypothesis whereby the agricultural sector was deemed to be characterised by the physical homogeneity of its input and output is false (section "Interdependence and Sterility"). On the other hand, I will show Section '"Colbert's Dazzlement"' that the mercantile system, as the target of an intellectual struggle, is an important notion borrowed by Smith from Physiocracy. However, its treatment in the *Wealth of Nations* was very specific: the mercantile system is the result of history, as we have seen before, and not the effect of an error, an "*éblouissement*" (dazzlement) as Quesnay note. Finally I will show (section "A Speculative Physician") that the critique of Physiocracy's method targets its utopian character of above all. Here, it is Smith's refusal of a utopia and his use of history as a science of politics that he employs to oppose Quesnay.

[10] According to Smith's biographer, Dugald Stewart (*Account of the Life and Writings of Adam Smith*, 1793, in Smith A. 1980),Smith admired Quesnay to the point of wanting to dedicate the WON to him.

Interdependence and Sterility

According to Smith, Quesnay's capital error is to assert the sterility of the sterile or unproductive class. However, I will show that Smith's critique is not the one we can expect. This critique takes place on three levels.

The first is semantic: it is absurd to assert that the sterile class is sterile when it reproduces its annual advances. A couple that raises only two children is not sterile. Smith interprets this clumsiness of expression in the following way: in fact, Quesnay means that the net product is not attributable to the class of manufacturers, artisans and merchants.

The critique thus develops on this second level. In Smith's eyes, the sterile class is synonymous with the unproductive class. If Quesnay affirms that merchants, manufacturers and artisans are sterile, he is also asserting that they are similar to the *menial servants*, which is entirely "improper". The inherent difficulties with the Smithian distinction between productive and unproductive labour[11] complicate the Smith's critique.

Finally, Smith states his central proposition: the real revenue of the society can only be raised through "parsimony" (savings), and, from this point of view, the farmers are not particularly better off than the manufacturers and merchants, since it is the savings on profits that constitutes the better part of the savings.

This is the main part of the critique of Quesnay's *capital error*. It is therefore curious to note that Smith does not use an argument that he nonetheless outlined *before*, when he presented the Physiocratic theory. What he told us at the time was that the sterile class indirectly contributes to the formation of the net product. But this contribution is presented in a typically Smithian manner. It is because the specialisation between productive class and sterile class increases the productivity of the agricultural work that the activity of the non-agricultural sectors contributes to the growth of the net product.[12]

[11] See Chapter 8.

[12] "The unproductive class, however, is not only useful, but greatly useful to the other two classes." [...] "By means of the unproductive class, the cultivators are delivered from many cares which would otherwise distract their attention from the cultivation of land. The superiority of produce, which, in consequence of this undivided attention, they are enabled to raise, is fully sufficient to pay the whole expense which the maintenance and employment of the unproductive class costs either the proprietors or themselves. The industry of merchants, artificers, and manufacturers, though in its own nature altogether unproductive, yet contributes in this manner indirectly to increase the produce of the

However, what Smith does not mention here is even more important than what he does say: it is obvious that farmers have just as much need for the clothes and tools provided by the unproductive class as they do for their seeds. He doesn't develop this line of argumentation which would use the central properties of the Economical Table, showing the technical interdependences between the productive and sterile classes.

This technical interdependence between the sectors implies that it is not possible to attribute the net product to one or the other of the two sectors. This is the result of economic interdependence. Taking this technical argument into account is all that is required to affirm the productive character of the "sterile class". However *it is no*t this argument that is used here by Smith. We are to face a curious gap in his argumentation.

I will return to this important aspect, but I would simply like to point out that—even incomplete—Smith's critique called into question one of the definitions of the physiocratic model, the definition of the net income. The latter, as we know, consists solely of the profits of farmers and land owners, of the rent of the land owners, the revenue of *décimateurs* (clergy income) and the revenue of the king. From this point of view, it is necessary to replace the definition of the net income proposed by Quesnay by another one, in which the net income consists of the rent and the profit, from which the taxes and the tithe are deducted. Obviously this change of definition is not politically neutral, but in fact it reinforces the physiocratic model. It is then a matter of distinguishing the economic deduction from rent from the political deduction of taxes and tithe to form the classic economic model.

Quesnay's capital error is therefore not capital, precisely because it is not very hard to rectify, provided that we manage to escape from the dogmatism that characterises Quesnay's approach, perceptible with the definition of the net revenue. This is the first weakness in Dr. Quesnay's analysis. We must examine this now.

land. It increases the productive powers of productive labour by leaving it at liberty to confine itself to its proper employment, the cultivation of land; and the plough goes frequently the easier and the better by means of the labour of the man whose business is most remote from the plough" (WON 669).

"Colbert's Dazzlement"

Among Smith's acquisitions following his visit to Paris, there is one that strikes me as truly remarkable. It is the notion of the *mercantile system*. We know that it is probably in Mirabeau (1763) that one of the most ancient occurrences of this term is to be found. However, the mercantile system attacked in the *Wealth of Nations* is a very different notion from that of commercial jealousy, already denounced by Smith in the *Lectures on Jurisprudence* or by Hume in the *Political Discourses*.

Let us first examine the notion of "commercial jealousy", as found in the *Lectures* and in Hume.

This is how, for example, the 1760 Essay "Of the Jealousy of Trade" came to have no ambition other than that of completing the demonstration accomplished in Hume's *Political Discourses* in 1752. Above all, Hume denounced in its pages the *spirit of jealous emulation* that reigned in Britain. This spirit led them to undertake and perpetuate wars more frequently and for longer than political prudence required. Since these wars could not be financed by taxes, they were financed by borrowing, in anticipation of a growth in future fiscal returns owing to an excess in the balance of trade. The *Political Essays* are in large part dedicated to debunking this illusion. The consequence of this spirit *of jealous emulation* is therefore that of creating a disproportionate increase in public debt, which can only lead to the collapse of British institutions. According to Hume, *Jealousy of Trade* is therefore the result of a specifically British passion.

It gives rise to two kinds of misconceptions: the first is the belief that the cost of wars may be covered by the export surplus, and the second is the idea that the prosperity of the nation involves the poverty of one's neighbours. The criticism of the first theme is thus a criticism of Thomas Mun's famous proposition: *English Treasure by Foreign Trade*. Hume argues against it through his conception of the neutrality of the currency and the Price Specie Flow mechanism in order to show the futility of this thesis and hence the illusory character of this so-called "treasure". The second theme is important in that it attempts to highlight the interdependence of economies. This idea is magnificently formulated, right in the middle of the Seven-Year War (often described by historians as the "first world war" since it opposed France and Great Britain from Canada to India), by this concluding sentence of the Essay "Of the Jealousy of Trade":

> "I shall therefore venture to acknowledge, that, not only as a man, but as a British subject, I pray for the flourishing commerce of Germany, Spain, Italy, and even France itself". The "spirit of jealous emulation" thus pushes "narrows and malignant politics" into commercial jealousy. As Winch [1978] and Hont [2005] have shown long ago, this denunciation is found again in the *Lectures on Jurisprudence*, which insist on the disastrous character of a system, supported by Mun and Locke, seeking to avoid the export and encourage the import of precious metals, a system that led to the ruin of Spain and Portugal.

It was in the *Wealth of Nations* that Smith made the Mercantile System his main target. But the question here is not just a semantic one. The encounter between Smith and Quesnay allowed us to think of the mercantile system in a way that was surely not the way that Mirabeau saw it. One of the innovations in the *Wealth of Nations* consists of *forming a trio between the mercantile system, the agricultural system and the system of natural liberty*. The remarkable character of this trio resides in its historic nature. Smith is one of the rare authors who attempts to *explain* his adversaries. The latter are not ignoramuses who must be enlightened, but solidly established interests who defend their positions skilfully. Smith considers physiocracy, then, within this framework of intellectual combat. This is what the start of the chapter dedicated to it testifies to:

> "Mr. Colbert, the famous minister of Louis XIV, was a man of probity, of great industry and knowledge of detail, of great experience and acuteness in the examination of public accounts, and of abilities, in short, every way fitted for introducing method and good order into the collection and expenditure of the public revenue. That minister had unfortunately embraced all the prejudices of the mercantile system, in its nature and essence a system of restraint and regulation", [...] "The industry and commerce of a great country he endeavoured to regulate upon the same model as the departments of a public office; and instead of allowing every man to pursue his own interest in his own way, upon the liberal plan of equality, liberty, and justice, he bestowed upon certain branches of industry extraordinary privileges, while he laid others under as extraordinary restraints. He was not only disposed, like other European ministers, to encourage more the industry of the towns than that of the country; but, in order to support the industry of the towns, he was willing even to depress and keep down that of the country" (WON 664).

The reference to Colbert is found in Quesnay's writings to characterise the mercantile system. Quite a good idea of the Physiocratic view of Colbertism is present in *Le tableau économique considéré dans ses déprédations relativement au commerce*:

> Aduram, Comptroller General of the late King Solomon's finances, was dazzled by the trade of the Tyrians, and the brilliance of luxury factories. *He threw his country into such a delirium, that there was nothing more to talk about than trade and money, without thinking about the real trade of the country*. (Quesnay, 2005, I, 508)[13]

We also find this variant, in note [5] on maxim VIII:

> A large state must not leave the plow to become a valet. I will never forget that a minister of the last century, dazzled by the trade of the Dutch, and the brilliance of luxury factories, *threw his homeland into a greater delirium more than commerce and money, without thinking of the real use of money or the real trade of the country*.
>
> "This minister was much esteemed by his good intentions, but too attached to his ideas, and wanted to give birth to riches from the labour of fingers, to the detriment of the very source of wealth, and so disturbed the entire economic constitution of an agricultural nation"... "Everything tended to destroy the income from land, from factories and trade, which in an agricultural nation can only be sustained by the products of the earth". (Quesnay, 2005, I, 579–580, emphasis added)[14]

For Quesnay, Colbert was an honest but dazzled minister. For Smith also, Colbert "was a man of probity", he "embraced all the prejudices of the mercantile system". However "he was a man of great experience

[13] "Aduram, Contrôleur général des finances du feu roi Salomon, ébloui du commerce des Tyriens, et de l'éclat des manufactures de luxe, *jeta sa patrie dans un tel délire, que l'on n'y parlait plus que de commerce et argent, sans penser au véritable commerce du pays*".

[14] "Un grand Etat ne doit pas quitter la charrue pour devenir voiturier. On n'oubliera jamais qu'un ministre du dernier siècle, ébloui du commerce des Hollandais, et de l'éclat des manufactures de luxe, *a jeté sa patrie dans un tel délire plus que commerce et argent, sans penser au véritable emploi de l'argent ni au véritable commerce du pays*".

"Ce ministre si estimable par ses bonnes intentions, mais trop attaché à ses idées, voulut faire naître les richesses du travail des doigts, au préjudice de la source même des richesses et dérangea toute la constitution économique d'une nation agricole "... "Tout tendait à la destruction des revenus des bien-fonds, des manufactures, du commerce, qui dans une nation agricole ne peuvent se soutenir que par les produits du sol".

and acuteness". He was not dazzled. It was not the lack of knowledge which could explain his politics. Thus, the essential difference between Smith and Quesnay, in my opinion, resides in the *comprehension* of the mercantile system. Where Quesnay sees a minister "dazzled" by Holland's trade, and thus projecting the French economy into a "delirious state"; Smith described the mercantile system as the product of European *history*.

Understanding how the mercantile system is the effect of the inversion of the *Natural Progress of Opulence* that resulted from European History is the subject of Book III of the *Wealth of Nations*. The agricultural system itself appears as a *necessary* reaction to Colbertism:

> If the rod be bent too much one way, says the proverb, in order to make it straight you must bend it as much the other. The French philosophers, who have proposed the system which represents agriculture as the sole source of the revenue and wealth of every country, seem to have adopted this proverbial maxim; and as in the plan of Mr. Colbert the industry of the towns was certainly overvalued in comparison with that of the country; so in their system it seems to be as certainly undervalued. (WON 664)

Quesnay's *capital error* was therefore that of favouring agriculture to the detriment of manufacturing. The agricultural system introduced a bias in favour of agriculture in order to be able to correct the bias in favour of the factories that characterised Colbertism. Its *partiality* was therefore the *necessary consequence* of its struggle against the partiality of the mercantile system. Quesnay's "capital error" was therefore not the result of flawed thinking, and still less so of flawed knowledge.

The mercantile system was not a synonym of "Jealousy of Trade". It was no longer, as in Hume's *Essays*, or in Smith's *Lectures* and in Quesnay's writings, the product of national passions—or, what amounts to the same thing, a delirious state. Instead, according to Smith, it was the result of the close collusion between merchant and manufacturers and legislators, a complicity which was itself a product of European history, as we have seen before.

This is why the first critique put forward by Smith with respect to the agricultural system was no doubt more devastating than the denunciation of the capital error. Let us examine it now.

A Speculative Physician

Smith starts by recalling the purpose of Quesnay's *Tableau économique* (Economical Table):

> In what manner, according to this system, the sum total of the annual produce of the land is distributed among the three classes above mentioned, and in what manner the labour of the unproductive class does no more than replace the value of its own consumption, without increasing in any respect the value of that sum total, is represented by Mr. Quesnai, the very ingenious and profound author of this system, in some arithmetical formularies. The first of these formularies, which by way of eminence he peculiarly distinguishes by the name of the Economical Table, represents the manner in which he supposes the distribution takes place in a state of the most perfect liberty and therefore of the highest prosperity- in a state where the annual produce is such as to afford the greatest possible net produce, and where each class enjoys its proper share of the whole annual produce. (WON 672–673)

Smith stresses the fact that the *Economical Table* is based on the hypothesis of the full use of resources. For a given set of techniques, there is only one single system of prices that ensures the reproduction of the body politic:

> Some subsequent formularies represent the manner in which he supposes this distribution is made in different states of restraint and regulation; in which either the class of proprietors or the barren and unproductive class is more favoured than the class of cultivators, and in which either the one or the other encroaches more or less upon the share which ought properly to belong to this productive class. Every such encroachment, every violation of that natural distribution, which the most perfect liberty would establish, must, according to this system, necessarily degrade more or less, from one year to another, the value and sum total of the annual produce, and must necessarily occasion a gradual declension in the real wealth and revenue of the society; […]

The bearers of the net produce were the only agents likely to make economic decisions (to distribute the expenses of the net revenue between the productive and sterile classes). Yet there was only one form of distribution that is compatible with reproduction. Where did Smith read this? It is not too difficult to answer this question. It seems very clear that the *formularies* evoked here are the second part of the *Tableau économique avec ses explications* (in the 1760 version of the Table) where the Economical "table is considered in terms of its private depredations".[15]

This is how Quesnay describes these "depredations":

> "Let us now examine the *Economical table* when affected by these damages" (Quesnay, 2005, I, 479).[16] What are these disturbances? The first is private ("excessive luxury") the six others are public damages: they concern taxation, the population and its wealth, the currency, the police, trade and finally "destructive tax".

Quesnay imagines modifications in the distribution of wealth through decisions emanating either from the proprietors or the king and that all cause a decrease in income, except in one case: if the existence of available lands allows for a rise in the "faste de subsistance" to the detriment of the "luxe of decoration" causes a rise in the net product.

In other words the availability of this land would allow a modification of expenses in favour of the productive classes to be put in place.

Yet we know that Quesnay assumes what we could call today the full employment of resources. The only positive modification is therefore excluded in a "royaume qui a atteint le comble de l'opulence". Once we have understood Smith's critique: under the hypothesis of full use of the land, according to Quesnay only one form of distribution of wealth exists that does not lead to a negative growth rate.

In other words, since this distribution of wealth involves a system of prices, this system of prices that allows the reproduction of the body politic must be unique.

We are therefore in a somewhat paradoxical situation: Smith reproaches Quesnay for seeking to demonstrate that only one situation of equilibrium prices exists (or a single system of natural prices, which means the same thing here) having the required properties of optimality.

Today, an economist would surely find Quesnay's approach incomplete, poorly demonstrated, but would apparently not have much to criticise in terms of its objective.

Yet Smith continues his critique in a totally ironic mode, since a somewhat obvious medical metaphor then ensues, whereby certain doctors

[15] "tableau est considéré dans ses déprédations privées".

[16] "Etudions maintenant le Tableau économique sous ses dérangements".

wrongly claim that a single regimen of living is compatible with survival, thus suggesting that Quesnay, a doctor, must share this dogmatism:

> [...] Mr. Quesnai, who was himself a physician, and a very speculative physician, seems to have entertained a notion of the same kind concerning the political body, and to have imagined that it would thrive and prosper only under a certain precise regimen, the exact regimen of perfect liberty and perfect justice.

Smith opposes to this thesis the idea whereby it is savings that sustain the net income:

> He seems not to have considered that, in the political body, the natural effort which every man is continually making to better his own condition is a principle of preservation capable of preventing and correcting, in many respects, the bad effects of a political economy, in some degree, both partial and oppressive. Such a political economy, though it no doubt retards more or less, is not always capable of stopping altogether the natural progress of a nation towards wealth and prosperity, and still less of making it go backwards.

The "natural effort" produces the flow of annual saving. The "bad effects" of "a partial political economy" are to waste saving, and those effects are the same as to use income in employment of unproductive labour. We may accept Smith's intuition that there exists a plurality of rate of growth, which depends on the weight of productive employment in the total employment. However this argument is unrelated to the "regimen of perfect liberty and perfect justice". Bracketing the theoretical question of growth together with that of justice and liberty does not go without saying. In other words, we see here that it is not only the uniqueness of the system of prices ensuring the reproduction of the body politic that is at stake, but Quesnay's dogmatism in particular. In what ways does Smith see Quesnay as dogmatic?

Smith opposes to Quesnay savings, as one of the source of economic progress. The latter refutes the idea that "perfect liberty and perfect justice" are conditions for a positive rate of growth. For Quesnay those conditions are conditions of the intelligibility of the economic system, and history doesn't matter. For Smith, this lack of interest for history is also a lack of interest for the *political conditions* of opulence. Of course to build the "perfect liberty and perfect justice" and to reach the "comble de l'opulence" is an attractive goal for any legislator. However the important issue is: how to do it?

If we attempt to answer this issue, it would appear that the target of Smith's mocking criticism is perhaps the very idea of *physiocracy*. What separates Smith from Quesnay here is more profound than a disagreement about a hypothesis serving as the basis for a theoretical model. Quesnay wishes to enlighten the Sovereign, and believes that the latter, once educated in due form by economists, will be in a position to correct the errors of Colbertism. For Quesnay, the partiality of the latter is the consequence of a blindness that must be dissipated. Quesnay is not only a doctor, but also a schoolmaster. To describe something completely new, without any reference to the historical process which makes it possible. In other words to substitute teachings for politics is a good definition of utopia (Moreau, 1992).

As Quesnay, Smith combats the mercantile system. But according to him, the latter is not the result of ignorance, but of the self-interested collusion between the merchants and the legislators. While pedagogy is useful, it does not suffice for the establishment of the system of natural liberty.

The Public Debt and the System of Natural Liberty

Smith opposed Thomas Mun and probably to Steuart the same argument by putting forward the thesis according to which the treasure of England was not the surplus on trade, but its savings. As wage earners savings were very low, and those of landlords were often negative, it was obvious that capitalists were the most important savers. However, that was not all. The relentless desire to improve one's lot allowed Smith to alleviate Hume's concern about the growth of public debt in Britain.[17]

[17] Some data about UK public debts:

	UK GDP (£ billions)	*UK population (millions)*	*Public debt as a percentage of GDP*
1692	0.05885	9.100	5.61
1721	0.06536	9.733	84.00
1763	0.08433	11.617	157.24
1776	0.12347	12.467	106.26
1784	0.15611	13.131	155.60
1820	0.32318	20.736	259.95

Source ukpublicspending.co.uk

In the first two essays, “Of Commerce” and “Of Refinement in the Arts”, Hume takes a stand in the debate concerning the relationship between increasing wealth and virtue. He opposes the classical tradition that associates wealth with political decadence and which interprets the history of Rome as the story of an interminable abandonment of the virtues—especially martial virtues—of the earlier Romans, following the rise in luxury consumption. Hume’s thesis is moderate: of course “excessive” luxury may corrupt morals, but under reasonable conditions, commerce promotes both civilisation and “the martial spirit” (Hume 1777–1994).

What are those conditions?

After arguing that the politics of the balance of power between cities was practised in ancient Greece, Hume expressed surprise at the fact that this maxim had been discarded both by Rome (thus enabling it to build its empire) and by its adversaries (thus allowing the construction of the Roman Empire that caused their downfall). Yet the situation of Great Britain was comparable to that of Rome. The “excess” committed by Great Britain in its struggle against France (initiated in the days following the Glorious Revolution of 1688) led to an imminent catastrophe. Under the pretext of implementing the maxim of the balance of power in Europe, the British, animated by “jealous emulation” (Hume 1777–1994), undertook an entirely different policy that aimed not to preserve the balance of power in Europe, but to establish British domination on the continent. From then on, the maxim of the balance of power was modified and became a maxim of imperial expansion. This was very dangerous. “Enormous monarchies are, probably, destructive to human Edition: current; Page: nature; in their progress, in their continuance, and even in their downfall, which never can be very distant from their establishment” (Hume 1777–1994). This essay echoes the proposition in “Of Refinement on Arts” that imputes the decadence of Rome not to an increase in wealth but to the extension of their empire (Hume 1777–1994).

This policy could not be financed by taxes, and Hume showed that it could not be financed by the external trade surplus either, since this was inevitably ephemeral.[18] The external trade surplus could not therefore constitute the “English Treasure” evoked by Thomas Mun, for instance.

[18] The price specie flow mechanism was nothing but an attempt to demonstrate this important point.

The wars could therefore only be financed by public credit, Hume tells us in "Of Public Credit", the essay that concludes the series of *Political Discourses*, the content of which is essentially economic: "It must, indeed, be one of these two events; either the nation must destroy public credit, or public credit will destroy the nation" (Hume 1777–1994).

The last chapter of the *Wealth of Nations* is specifically devoted to public debt. Smith describes its growth since the beginning of the conflicts with France; i.e. since the Glorious Revolution of 1688. Like Hume, he assumed that this debt would probably never be paid. But he was very intrigued by the fact that the growth in the debt he described (rising from £20 million in 1697 to almost £80 million in 1748, then to £140 million in 1764, before dropping slightly £130 million in 1775) in no way hindered economic growth (as we shall verify in the next chapter):

> To the honour of our present system of taxation, indeed, it has hitherto given so little embarrassment to industry that, during the course even of the most expensive wars, the frugality and good conduct of individuals seem to have been able, by saving and accumulation, to repair all the breaches which the waste and extravagance of government had made in the general capital of the society. At the conclusion of the late war, the most expensive that Great Britain ever waged, her agriculture was as flourishing, her manufacturers as numerous and as fully employed, and her commerce as extensive as they had ever been before. The capital, therefore, which supported all those different branches of industry must have been equal to what it had ever been before. Since the peace, agriculture has been still further improved, the rents of houses have risen in every town and village of the country- a proof of the increasing wealth and revenue of the people; and the annual amount the greater part of the old taxes, of the principal branches of the excise and customs in particular, has been continually increasing- an equally clear proof of an increasing consumption, and consequently of an increasing produce which could alone support that consumption. Great Britain seems to support with ease a burden which, half a century ago, nobody believed her capable of supporting. Let us not, however, upon this account rashly conclude that she is capable of supporting any burden, nor even be too confident that she could support, without great distress, a burden a little greater than what has already been laid upon her. (WON 929)

Savings and economic growth had therefore not been affected up to that point.

However, Smith thought that if public bankruptcy was still possible (or even probable) it would not lead to the transformation of the nation into an absolute monarchy, which was what Hume *wanted*, for lack of better alternatives.

Smith set out what could be "better": yet this came at the cost of an impressive change in scale. It was no longer a question of thinking in terms of the "nation", but of the *empire*. Smith argued that it was just and possible to make the colonies pay tax, but at the cost of necessary *reforms* to empire.

It is here that we can gauge the distance between the Hume's *Essays* and the *Wealth of Nations*. Smith's emphasis on progress resulting from the division of labour and savings as the causes of enrichment contrasted decisively with Hume's catastrophic outlook. On the other hand, the discovery of the mercantile system and its partiality radically altered the political horizon. According to Smith, there was a profound confusion of the private interests of merchants and the general interest that characterised the partiality of the mercantile system. It was thus necessary to examine what a system of natural liberty could be, as it alone was capable of guaranteeing the impartiality of the laws.

References

Chamley, P. (1963). *Économie politique et philosophie chez Steuart et Hegel*. Dalloz.

Coats A. W. (1975). Adam Smith and the mercantile system. In A. Skinner & T. Wilson, *Essays on Adam Smith*. Clarendon Press

Cropsey, J. (1957). *Polity and economy: An interpretation of the principles of Adam Smith*. Martinus Nijhoff.

Hont, I. (2005). *Jealousy of trade*. Harvard University Press.

Hume, D. (1777–1994). *Political essays* (K. Haakonssen, Ed.). Cambridge University Press.

Mirabeau, V. R. (1763). *Philosophie rurale ou Economie générale et politique de l'agriculture*. Libraires associés.

Moreau P. F. (1992). *Le récit utopique*. Paris, Presses Universitaires de France.

Quesnay, F. (2005). *Œuvres économiques complètes et autres textes* (C. Théré, L. Charles, & J. C. Perrot, Eds.). INED.

Tortajada, R. (Ed.). (1999). *The economics of James Steuart*. Routledge.

Vaggi, G. (1987). *The economics of François Quesnay*. Palgrave MacMillan.

Winch, D. (1978). *Adam Smith's politics*. Cambridge University Press.

CHAPTER 5

The Malignant Effects of the Mercantile System

The core of the mercantile system is, according to Smith, the "monopoly of colony trade". As we know, colonial trade was typical of capitalism before the "industrial revolution". In other words, the building of the first Colonial Empire was also the building of capitalism. The *Wealth of Nations* studies this story very accurately, in the long Chapter VII of Book IV.

The intriguing question here is that Smith approved of *free* colonial trade. Yet, what does free colonial trade mean? Why was Smith not simply an advocate of free trade? This chapter suggests an answer to these questions. It is because from Smith's point of view, a reformed British Empire (as a colonial empire) was necessary to transform the partial Mercantile System and to build the impartial System of Natural Liberty. To establish this point, this chapter shows how the *Wealth of Nations* is embedded in the British political debates of its time. After the Treaty of Paris (1763), the ruling British aristocracy progressively began confusing the interests of Empire and the interests of merchants. How to avoid this confusion was the ultimate issue the *Wealth of Nations* sought to address.

> We must carefully distinguish between the effects of the colony trade and those of the monopoly of that trade. The former are always and necessarily beneficial; the latter always and necessarily hurtful. (WON 607)

D. Diatkine, *Adam Smith and the Wealth of Nations*, Palgrave Studies in the History of Economic Thought, https://doi.org/10.1007/978-3-030-81600-1_5

This famous proposition is often seen as symptomatic of the lack of analytical rigour of the *Wealth of Nations*. Smith's target was the mercantile system; colonial trade was an essential part of the mercantile system[1]; and the monopoly of colonial trade (colonial monopoly) was the core of the colonial system. So, how was it possible to suppose colonial trade was "beneficial"? In other words, how was it possible to situate colonial trade outside the mercantile system? Or in what manner could colonial trade be consistent with the system of natural liberty?

Smith seemingly confuses colonial trade with foreign trade, for a colony trade without a monopoly seems to be a sort of oxymoron, since the existence of a colony involves, by definition, the *political domination* of a territory and a population, and this political domination involves commercial policy. Consequently, commentators are used to presuming that Smith is writing about foreign trade when he writes about colonial trade. I will show that these statements must be understood as just one part of Smith's subtle analysis of colonial phenomena. As we will see, free colony trade *is not* exactly free trade. In order to understand this puzzling point, I will return to the issue "Smith and colonies".

The abundant literature on "Smith and colonies" (see Diatkine, 1996; Skinner, 1996; Winch, 1965, 1996) generally focuses on the important issue of North American colonies. Here I will show that it is useful to broaden the scope of the study and to consider the British colonial Empire in its entirety, which is precisely the field covered by Chapter 7 of Book 4 of the *Wealth of Nations*.

I will concentrate on two points.

The first issue is that of understanding why colonial expansion seems "natural" to Smith. The answer is given by Smith's study of the "motives of colonisation". Smith finds "natural colonies" in Greek and Roman civilisations. Those references are perhaps surprising nowadays, but they were commonplace in the second part of the eighteenth century.

The second issue is more intricate. We have to understand why "colonial free trade" is not identical to foreign free trade. Or more precisely, we have to ask: why Smith *is not* in favour of the independence of colonies, which seems to be a necessary (although clearly insufficient) condition for transforming colonial trade into free trade? To answer this issue, I will

[1] "In the meantime one of the principal effects of those discoveries has been to raise the mercantile system to a degree of splendour and glory which it could never otherwise have attained to" (WON 627).

deal with the opposite issue: why is the colonial trade not simply a form of other mercantile policies?

Like all other mercantile policies, the *monopoly* of colonial trade is inefficient. However, all of these inefficiencies are compensated (in Great Britain) by "natural effort which every man is continually making to better his own condition" (see previous chapter). However, the monopoly of colonial trade is, according to Smith, far more dangerous, since the danger is not economic but political. This point is fascinating and may be explained because colonial trade is nothing but *imperial trade*. Free *colonial* trade could only be *free trade* inside a particular political structure: the transformed British colonial empire, for the reform of the British Empire is necessary to create *impartial* legislators. The issue is this: how can *imperial* trade fit into this particular system, the system of natural liberty?

In the first part, I will examine how Smith understands the grounds for colonial expansion (I). Then I will study the extreme case of colonial monopoly: colonies tyrannised by companies (II). I will go on to analyse the effects of colonial monopoly in Great Britain. I will show that, according to Smith, it is the *political* consequences of colonial monopoly in particular that should be feared (IV). This discussion allows me to conclude with a return to the question of *Adam Smith's Politics* (V). I will conclude, as Smith concludes the *Wealth of Nations*, by showing that the British Empire (duly amended) is the condition for the establishment of the system of natural liberty.

Why Establish Colonies?

Smith's position with respect to the colonies and colonial monopoly is complex, but I would like to show that it is not ambiguous. It is easily understood if we admit that, for him, the creation of colonies is the *normal* form of increasing real wealth, expressed by the growth of employment and real wages. This growth is therefore the natural consequence of the increase in population, when natural resources have become insufficient within a given geographical framework. This was the situation of ancient Greek colonies (WON 556).

In this, we encounter the thesis found throughout the *Wealth of Nations* whereby "food" (or "corn") is the *only* commodity whose natural supply always meets with an effective demand that is ready to pay the required revenues (including rent) in order to lead it to market. The supply of "corn" (and only "corn") creates its own effective demand; the gain in wealth is achieved through the progress of the division of labour, which "naturally" results in both an increase in the effective demand of the non-food (or non-agricultural) goods plus an increase in population. This is why, if the cultivable land of the city is limited, geographic expansion and therefore colonisation (the departure of part of the population) are the "natural" consequences of an increase in wealth.

It is important to note here that while the reason for ancient colonisations was the same, that is, lack of land, Smith stresses the fact that its modalities were very different in Greece and in Rome. According to Smith, it was the geography of the small Greek cities that explains this constraint, whereas in the Roman case, it was *specific institutions*, namely slavery and great property that created it. The increase in the ownership of large domains in Rome was carried out to the detriment of the small owners, who, as we know, were supposed to constitute the basis of the Roman republic in its traditional representation. These small owners who were chased from their land did not become salaried workers because they faced competition from slave workers. They therefore formed the Roman plebs, some of whom were sent to create the colonies. So, it was specific institutions (great property and slavery) that engendered the land shortage and the colonisation that resulted from this situation.

However, this expansion is being carried out *under Smith's eyes* in the political mercantile system. The rate of growth is therefore generally slowed down and sometimes even, *in certain cases*, *inverted* by "the monopoly spirit", that is, by the colonial monopoly. These last cases are therefore very interesting to study, since they are specific cases in which this "partial and oppressive state" that is the mercantile system, engenders a *negative* rate of growth.

The primary motive for the modern colonies was not the lack of land, but, Smith tells us, the search for *profit*. It was not the natural population growth in the face of land shortages that provoked the European expansion of the fifteenth century. Smith explains that "the great profits of the Venetians tempted the avidity of the Portuguese" (WON 558). The latter first sought to directly procure gold and ivory from Africa, which arrived in caravans from Black Africa to the ports of the Maghreb, and were then re-exported in the East. The Portuguese explored the African coasts to this end. They thus came to cross the Cape of Good Hope and enter into direct contact with the East Indies. In the case of the great voyages of discovery and the resulting colonisation, the profit motive therefore effectively "changed the face of the world".

Here, greed is expressed by the desire to share (at least) the profits of the Venetians by searching for African gold, a *commodity* exported to the Far East. However, the unexpected result was remarkable, since, thanks to their direct implantation in the Indies, the Portuguese were able to supplant the old spice and silk route that passed through Venice and Alexandria almost entirely.

However, there is a third reason that explains the behaviour of the colonisers. This reason is money illusion. Smith emphasises a crucial difference between the conquest of the East and West Indies. Like all of his contemporaries, Smith considers the former, particularly China (the case of Hindustan is very specific, as we shall see), to be highly developed societies,[2] whereas the latter (the Indian societies of America) offered the observer the spectacle of societies that have remained at the first stage of society, with the exception of the two kingdoms of the Incas and the Aztecs, which were, as Smith stresses, immediately destroyed by the conquest. So Europe was placed "halfway", as it were, between the two Indies, not only in geographical, but also in economic terms.

The essential point is as follows: the motive for the colonisation of the West Indies was not the same as that of the colonisation of the East Indies, since the actual profit was *almost nil if not negative*. The countries discovered by Columbus were, Smith tells us, *truly* miserable (WON 559). Since the grounds for the colonial expansion in the Americas was the search for precious metals.

The conquistadors were not alone in sharing this illusion:

> The dream of Sir Walter Raleigh concerning the golden city and country of Eldorado, may satisfy us that even wise men are not always exempt from such strange delusions. More than a hundred years after the death of that great man, the Jesuit Gumila was still convinced of the reality of that wonderful country, and expressed with great warmth, and I dare to say with great sincerity, how happy he should be to carry the light of the go€spel to a people who could so well reward the pious labours of their missionary. (WON 563)

[2] "China is a much richer country than any part of Europe" (WON 111).

It is therefore because he did not find any real wealth in America that he remained persuaded that he had discovered a land very near Asia, which, in order to mask what had been a mistake (the Earth was much bigger than Columbus had thought) and a failure (he was unable to find a prosperous economy, but only a poverty-stricken country, at best), Columbus came to imagine Eldorado, represented during a grandiose spectacle given at the Spanish court upon his return. It was therefore in this "spectacular" register that Smith staged the "sacred thirst of gold" (WON 562), which was the primary reason for the conquest of America.

The implicit reference to Virgil is the *cliché* that allows Smith to closely associate the discovery of America with that of an *imaginary* treasure. It is no accident that the *Wealth of Nations*, concludes with the evocation of this very same *imaginary* treasure on the other side of the Atlantic Ocean (WON 947).

What we are dealing with here is Smith's denunciation of two illusions. The first concerns the confusion between money and wealth; the second concerns the illusion that precious metals were abundant all over America. However, and fortunately so, this was not the case in North America.

The unexpected result of this discovery was the prosperity (which Smith deemed remarkable) of the English colonies of North America. These colonies prospered because no gold was to be found there, and above all, because they were English. In order to understand this point, which may seem strange, Smith studied the nature of the political ties that associated the colonies with the mainland in order to complete his analysis of the colonial system.

For Smith, the most basic connection (but not always the best one) that could link the colony to the mother city was quite simply independence. This was the case in Ancient Greece. Greek colonies did not consider themselves to be dominated by their mother country, even though they could be allied in times of war. They were thus independent.[3] On the other hand, Rome sent colonies of Roman citizens to the conquered provinces, who could thus never attain independence. The

[3] "The mother city, though she considered the colony as a child, at all times entitled to great favour and assistance, and owing in return much gratitude and respect, yet considered it as an emancipated child over whom she pretended to claim no direct authority or jurisdiction" (WON 556). Smith seems to have been unaware that the colonies of Greek cities were not always independent cities, and that, for instance, the Athenian cleruchies resembled Roman colonies in many respects.

Roman citizens that populated the colonies were thus excluded from political deliberations.

This distinction between Greek and Roman colonies may seem irrelevant today, but it was most likely pertinent for Smith's readers, as it was easy for them to read in this description of Roman colonies—which remained under the authority of Rome, without the citizens who populated them being able to enjoy their political rights—a prefiguration of the situation inflicted on British colonial settlers within the British Empire. We know that Smith insisted on the fact that North America offered vacant land, while Europe, subject to the regime of primogeniture inherited from the "Dark Ages", had an abundance of land that had been monopolised by the aristocracy, who left it uncultivated. However, Smith is more discreet as regards the second cause of the settlement of New England: religious intolerance. Nonetheless, the proximity of the institutional situation of the Roman and English colonies of North America must be noted and we will see their importance a little further on.

In any case, colonial expansion thus "naturally" engenders an extension of the scope of markets, and it thereby contributes to the increase in wealth associated with this extension. However, according to Smith, the Greek and Roman colonies knew nothing of the colonial monopoly that characterises the colonies of the mercantile system.

Smith (WON 564–590) minutely studies the forms that colonial monopoly can assume. Monopoly can either confer the monopoly on trade with the colony to the merchants of the mother city, or it can confer this monopoly on one chartered merchant company from the mother city. We shall see that this distinction is laden with economic and political consequences. I will show that a relationship exists on the one hand between the *distance* (not only geographic) separating the merchants from legislators (both in the mother city and in the colonies) and, on the other, the mutual benefits engendered by the extension of the markets, which is one of the consequences of modern colonisation.

Was What Was Good for the East India Company Good for Bengal?

If the case of the ancient colonies seems to Smith to be a basic example of "natural" colonisation, since it is motivated by demographic expansion within an apolitical space (as it is populated by "barbarians"), and any notion of monopoly is absent within this context, how then does he describe the modern colonies characterised by monopoly?

Let us first examine the case in which this distance between the merchants and the legislators is very slight, and sometimes even annulled. This is what happened in colonies that were dominated by chartered companies. In this case (the worst case scenario) colonial monopoly does not favour all of the merchants from the mother city, but only one specific company. The legislator thus guarantees the Company's monopoly with respect to national merchants, but not with respect to foreign competitors. With respect to the latter, the company must conquer and protect its possessions on its own, with weapons in hand. They therefore have sovereign powers over their possessions. This is why these chartered companies are the most pure expression of colonial monopoly. Smith's assessment of their harmfulness is uncompromising:

> The government of an exclusive company of merchants is perhaps the worst of all governments for any country whatever. (WON 570)

This was the case in the East Indies. The East India Company, founded at the turn of the seventeenth century, on the heels of the creation in Amsterdam of the Vereenigde Oostindische Compagnie (VOC), began its conquest of the Indian sub-continent during the Seven Years War. In Smith's view, the action of these companies was *disastrous* for the colonies, *ruinous* for the companies themselves[4] and *costly* for the mother cities. This is precisely where the mercantile system can make a nation "go backwards", namely a colony that is dominated by a chartered company. Just as the system of colonial monopoly concentrates all the negative aspects of the mercantile system, so the chartered companies and the East India Company in particular, express the essence of the system of colonial monopoly. The regime that the East India Company imposes in Bengal and in its other possessions is precisely the model of what can occur

[4] "No two characters seem more inconsistent than those of trader and sovereign. If the trading spirit of the English East India Company renders them very bad sovereigns, the spirit of sovereignty seems to have rendered them equally bad traders. While they were traders only they managed their trade successfully, and were able to pay from their profits a moderate dividend to the proprietors of their stock. Since they became sovereigns, with a revenue which, it is said, was originally more than three millions sterling, they have been obliged to beg extraordinary assistance of government in order to avoid immediate bankruptcy" (WON 819).

in an economy that is entirely dominated by the interests of merchants and manufacturers, when the latter is totally ***identified*** with the general interest. In this, partiality and oppression find their purest expression.

According to Smith (WON 91) the rate of accumulation of capital is *negative* in Bengal, and this negative rate of growth is provoked by the predatory approach of the East India Company (like all of the chartered companies operating in Asia).

As monopolies, in Great Britain and Europe, the chartered companies hampered the mechanism of gravitation and sold at a market price higher than the natural price. But the interest of the chartered companies in Asia, since they are monopsonies, is to limit the scope of the market of the products that they buy, by ensuring that they eliminate any competitors on the local markets.

This asymmetry is what allows Smith to radically oppose the interest of the "merchant companies" to the general interest in the mother city and in the colonies. After having evoked the destruction of wealth (opium in Bengal, spices in Molucca) operated by the chartered companies, Smith adds:

> It is the interest of the East India Company, considered as sovereigns, that the European goods which are carried to their Indian dominions should be sold there as cheap as possible; and that the Indian goods which are brought from thence should bring there as good a price, or should be sold there as dear as possible. But the reverse of this is their interest as merchants. As sovereigns, their interest is exactly the same with that of the country which they govern. As merchants their interest is directly opposite to that interest. (WON 637)

Let us now conclude this study of monopoly taken to its extreme, that is, in the case of the chartered companies. It allows us to understand that the distance—less geographic than political—that Smith would later propose to establish between the legislator and the merchants, was not only the result of the denunciation of a government enacting protective regulations allowing merchants to use competition to their advantage, by hampering the mechanism of gravitation, instead of submitting to it. Here, Smith shows that the disastrous character of these companies is due to the fact that, acting as "tax collectors", the companies *are sovereigns. They have become the legislators.*

It was therefore this tendency to entirely identify the government with the interests of the merchants and manufacturers that brought the chartered companies in the East Indies to an end: it is precisely what defines the mercantile system and colonial monopoly in their purest and most tyrannical form.

The Economic Consequences of Colonial Monopoly

While colonial monopoly was fatal in Bengal, it was dangerous in the mother country.

The text of the *Wealth of Nations* carefully sets out the forms adopted by the colonial system in Europe. In Spain and Portugal, where the mercantile system had been developed on the grounds of *imaginary* gains in wealth, following the search for Eldorado, the effects of the mercantile system were particularly serious, and Smith (WON 609) thinks that these two countries became poorer because of this.

On the other hand, in his opinion, the French mercantile system did not develop for imaginary reasons, but was motivated by profit (WON 467).

Great Britain is another case, since the mercantile system was commercial and financial:

> To found a great empire for the sole purpose of raising up a people of customers may at first sight appear a project fit only for a nation of shopkeepers. It is, however, a project altogether unfit for a nation of shopkeepers; but extremely fit for a nation whose government is influenced by shopkeepers. (WON 613)[5]

The economic consequences of the mercantile system overall consisted of a large deduction being made in savings and thus a reduction in the rate of growth. As we know, Smith analyses these privileges (protective

[5] It is amusing to note that this famous expression is often considered typically French, as it was invented by Bonaparte. This is how Cobbett came to write, in a letter to Chateaubriand "*vous nous appelez une nation de boutiquiers*" (cited by Chateaubriand, *Congrès de Vérone, Guerre d'Espagne*, Paris, Delloye, 1838, p. 346). It is possible that Bonaparte had read this formulation in the *Wealth of Nations*.

measures, export subsidies) with precision, but it is not necessary to go into more detail here.

However, the direct economic effects of colonial monopoly were benign. For instance, the colonies of Virginia and Maryland can only sell their tobacco to Great Britain. The first effect of this monopoly is (perhaps) that the latter will pay its tobacco at a better price than if there was free trade, but it seems clear to Smith (WON 595) that this is not the case, because the monopoly maintains the profit rates of the planters above their natural level and prevents the price from falling as much as it could under the effect of competition. Monopoly is only to the advantage of American planters and British importers. It tends to maintain the profit rates of colonial trade at a higher level than its natural level. British prices are therefore much higher, and non-colonial markets are lost. According to Smith, the monopoly of the colonial market does not compensate this loss (ibid.). Therefore, in the British case, the positive effects (the colonies increase the effective demand for British products) and the negative effects (colonial monopoly makes the European competitors poorer and thereby lessens their effective demand in Europe for British products) are (perhaps) not far from cancelling each another out.

Furthermore, a rate of profit that is higher than the natural rate also causes an interest rate that is higher than its natural level, which tends to lower the price of assets, particularly that of land. But this is not dramatic, and the economic consequences of monopolies—which are certainly inadmissible on principle—do not possess any inherently lethal content with respect to the social body.

I will soon come back to the British situation. Before, I have to consider the case of colonies in North America. The contrast with the situation of Bengal is striking. According to Smith, the chartered companies can't prosper (for, as land is abundant, colonist compete easily the chartered companies); British Colonies *benefit* from colonial monopoly; finally the "manners" (of the colonists) "are more republican, and their governments, those of three of the provinces of New England in particular, have hitherto been more republican too" (WON 585).

So Smith affirms that the rate of growth is higher in British American colonies than the natural one. However, the political distance between colonists and legislators is *too great*. British colonies are victims of "those rancorous and virulent factions which are inseparable from small democracies, and which have so frequently divided the affections of their people, and disturbed the tranquillity of their governments, in their form so nearly democratical" (WON 945).

Clearly the American situation is perceived by Smith as *symmetrical* to the one of Bengal: the rate of growth is higher than the natural one when it is negative in Bengal; anarchy of little democracies prevails in America when Bengal is tyrannised by the East India Company. The political distance between legislators and merchants is too great in one case and nil in the other one. This intellectual building may lead to this conclusion: at least *one optimal distance must exist*, somewhere *between* the British and the American situation. At this optimal distance, legislators may control the commercial society (Table 5.1).

Table 5.1 Between West and East, between anarchy and tyranny, the system of natural liberty

	North American British colonies	*System of natural liberty (Utopia Island?)*	*Great Britain*	*Bengal*
Rate of growth g (g_n is the natural rate of growth)	$g > g_n$	$g = g_n$	$0 < g < g_n$	$g < 0$
Distance between legislators and merchants (d* is the optimal distance)	$d > d^*$	$d = d^*$	$d < d^*$	$d = 0$
System of government	Colonies, then anarchy of little independent republics	Impartial legislators	Polybian[a] Constitution	Tyranny of a company of merchants

[a]The political regime that resulted from the 1688 revolution was glorified by the Whig tradition under the name of the Polybian regime, because, like the Roman republic studied by Polybius, it combined instead of opposing the three traditional political forms: the democratic, aristocratic and monarchic regimes. Also, just as Polybius attributed the invincibility of the Roman republic to the equilibrium between these three political forms, which prevented them from degenerating into demagogy, oligarchy or tyranny, Whiggism attributed its "newfound" grandeur to Great Britain's Polybian constitution

Unfortunately, as we will see, the political context in Great Britain since the end of the Seven Years war *reduces the political distance* between legislators and merchants and manufacturers.

By identifying the interests of the merchants and manufacturers with the general interest, the partiality of the British mercantile system calls the Polybian regime into question, and threatens to bring Great Britain's situation (at least partially) closer to that of Bengal. The growth of the Roman republic led to the tyranny of the Prince; British Empire's growth could lead it to tyranny of the merchant companies.

This danger of this identification of the interests of the merchants and the interests of the empire is central to the political debates that lie at the heart of the *Wealth of Nations*.

This is what I must now examine.

The Malignant Consequences of Colonial Monopoly: The Apoplexy of the Political Body, a Psychosomatic Disease

According to Smith, the mercantile system was rendered particularly dangerous in Great Britain by the *illusion* that it engendered. It seems to me that the most impressive effect of colonial monopoly (and therefore the mercantile system as a whole) was to promote the *belief* that the exceptional rate of profit that it engendered *was* the natural rate. This *illusion* is laden with consequences, which I shall attempt to show, with reference to the text of the *Wealth of Nations*:

> The monopoly of the colony trade besides, by forcing towards it a much greater proportion of the capital of Great Britain than what would naturally have gone to it, seems to have broken altogether that natural balance which would otherwise have taken place among all the different branches of British industry. The industry of Great Britain, instead of being accommodated to a great number of small markets, has been principally suited to one great market. Her commerce, instead of running in a great number of small channels, has been taught to run principally in one great channel. But the whole system of her industry and commerce has thereby been rendered less secure, the whole state of her body politic less healthful than it otherwise would have been. (WON 604–605)

Colonial monopoly disrupts the balance of the economy by concentrating the risks on a single sector of activity. The text continues, now developing a medical metaphor, as follows:

> In her present condition, Great Britain resembles one of those unwholesome bodies in which some of the vital parts are overgrown, and which, upon that account, are liable to many dangerous disorders scarce incident to those in which all the parts are more properly proportioned. A *small stop in that great blood-vessel*, which has been artificially swelled beyond its natural dimensions, and through which an unnatural proportion of the industry and commerce of the country has been forced to circulate, *is very likely to bring on the most dangerous disorders upon the whole body politic*. (Ibid., my emphasis)

However, it is not the diagnostic of this disease that is important here, but rather its political extensions. Smith immediately continues:

> The *expectation* of a rupture with the colonies, accordingly, has struck the people of Great Britain with more terror than they ever felt for a Spanish armada, or a French invasion. It was this terror, *whether well or ill grounded*, which rendered the repeal of the Stamp Act, among the merchants at least, a popular measure. In the total exclusion from the colony market, was it to last only for a few years, the greater part of our merchants used to fancy that they foresaw an entire stop to their trade; the greater part of our master manufacturers, the entire ruin of their business; and the greater part of our workmen, an end of their employment. A rupture with any of our neighbours upon the continent, though likely, too, to occasion some stop or interruption in the employments of some of all these different orders of people, is foreseen, however, without any such general emotion. The blood, of which the circulation is stopped in some of the smaller vessels, easily disgorges itself into the greater without occasioning any dangerous disorder; but, when it is stopped in any of the greater vessels, convulsions, apoplexy, or death, are the immediate and unavoidable consequences. If but one of those overgrown manufactures, which, by means either of bounties or of the monopoly of the home and colony markets, have been artificially raised up to an unnatural height, finds some small stop or interruption in its employment, it frequently occasions *a mutiny and disorder* alarming to government, and embarrassing even to the *deliberations of the legislature*. How great, therefore, would be the disorder and confusion, it was thought, which must necessarily be

occasioned by a sudden and entire stop in the employment of so great a proportion of our principal manufacturers. (Ibid., my emphasis)

This passage is very important for the development of my argument, as it allows us to understand that it is not only the loss of the colonial markets, but, above all, the *political amplification* that results from the *anticipation* of this loss, that provokes the "apoplexy". So, what does the latter consist of? What are the "disorders", the "mutinies", provoked in Great Britain by the question of American independence, which Smith only alludes to (the "repeal of the Stamp Act") and which nonetheless require the (progressive) establishment of the system of natural freedom.

In order to answer these questions it is essential to examine the political context at the start of writing of the *Wealth of Nations*. Three points are worth mentioning:

a. The birth (or renaissance) of an opposition party in Great Britain. This one is a fraction of the ruling aristocracy who progressively will be induced to claim the identity of the interest of the Empire and of the interest of the merchants.
b. Then I will show how this evolution is provoked by the awareness of the new glory and the new problems engendered by colonial expansion following the British victory that ended the Seven Years War.
c. Finally how this evolution is amplified by the first economic crises following the decisive beginnings of "industrial revolution".

A Recent Fraction: The Rockinghamite Whigs

The political regime that was implanted in Great Britain by the 1688 revolution was first stabilised under the reign of Queen Anne (1702–1714), then under that of her successors, George I and George II.

One of the important characteristics of these first two reigns of the Hanover dynasty is that the Whig party occupied the British government practically without any open opposition. The Tory party was disqualified owing to the action of its leader, Henry Saint John, Viscount Bolingbroke, who declared himself in favour of the Pretender (the son of James Stuart, who had been overthrown in 1688), while paradoxically emphasising certain Neo Republican themes that, as Pocock (1975) has shown, served as an argument in support of the criticism of hegemonic Whiggism.

This anti-dynastic position prohibited the Tory party from attracting opposition to the Whig party in power. Quite to the contrary, the opposition's arguments consisted of systematically condemning the parties, which were ritually denounced as "factions". The objective proclaimed by the criticism of the Whig domination was destruction of the parties, the distinction between Whig and Tory being deemed fallacious.

Thus, the Whigs governed without any *organised* opposition until the death of George II in 1760.

The accession of George III has been the object of a good deal of study, all the more so for the fact that the memory of this reign has remained strongly divided.[6] One uncontested fact is certainly the political rupture that took place at the time of his accession. Historians (Brewer, 1989; Ditchfield, 2002; Koehn, 1994) have underlined the fact that the political scene changed considerably in the early 1760s, under the influence of two important factors, even if it is difficult to measure their respective importance.

The first factor resides in the personal position of George III, who was much closer with respect to British political life than his predecessors. He was hostile to the parties in general, and thus distrusted the Old Corps of Whigs represented by the leaders of his father's government, the Duke of Newcastle and William Pitt the Elder. In 1762, he decided to replace the Duke of Newcastle as principal minister by one of his friends, Lord Bute. It cannot be underestimated just how radically new this approach was. In thus affirming his prerogative (and by choosing a Scotsman), he exposed himself to attacks from his adversaries, who readily accused him—most paradoxically—of harbouring Tory sympathies.

The second factor of change is the end of the Seven Years War, three years after the accession of George III, under Bute's ministry, which negotiated the Treaty of Paris in 1763. The choice of Bute to replace the Old Corps of Whigs (William Pitt, the Duke of Newcastle) was also perceived to be the choice of a compromising peace with France, to the detriment of

[6] "The history of the present King of Great Britain is a history of repeated injuries and usurpations, all having in direct object the establishment of absolute Tyranny over these States" (*Declaration of Independence of the United States*), which greatly contrasted, apparently, with the memory left by this sovereign in Great Britain, where, despite his illness, he remained as the one who would represent the country during the wars of the Revolution and the Empire.

the prolongation of the victorious war, right through to France's definitive collapse. Great Britain came away from the Seven Years Wars largely victorious. However, this peace for France seemed far too generous in the eyes of a considerable portion of English public opinion.

It is undeniable that George III and Bute were the subject of very violent campaigns, the most famous of which was led by John Wilkes, who had supported William Pitt during the war. In his newspaper *North Briton* (the title itself is a transparent allusion to the fact that Bute is the first Scotsman to have been appointed by the king to head the British government) he unified in a single attack both the denunciation of the Treaty of Paris and the choice of Bute to lead the government. In the face of these attacks Bute had to be replaced by Grenville. This change of government was interpreted as a royal retreat, but Wilkes and his editors were arrested, and the battle was displaced to the realm of the freedom of the press.

Furthermore, the government's main concern was how to manage the public debt, which as we know had considerably increased during the Seven Years War.[7] Increasing the direct tax was deemed impossible and Bute's attempts to raise the indirect taxes was met with fierce opposition; there was nothing left to do but tax the colonial settlers, if only to finance the maintenance of a garrison designed to protect them from the natives. Grenville thus passed the Stamp Act[8] in March 1765. The innovation of the Stamp Act resided in the fact that it was no longer a customs duty (that is, a measure affirming and completing colonial monopoly), but a tax that fell well and truly on official documents and the press, and was thus directly linked to the *internal* activity of the colonies.

Agitation against this tax developed in the colonies of North America. The fragility of the Grenville government revealed itself in the spring of 1765 when the Spitalfield riots broke out among silk weavers, who accused the Duke of Bedford, one of the negotiators of the Treaty of Paris, of having accepted bribes to allow the importation of French silks. These riots continued almost every year, through to the most serious of them, which took place in 1769.

[7] It almost doubled, passing from nearly £70,000,000 to £130,000,000 (160% of GDP [ukpublicspending.co.uk]). See above p. 90.

[8] The *Stamp Act* cited by Smith, see above.

The fall of Grenville is a good illustration of the intricacies of royal attempts to impose a personal politics that was hostile to the Whigs, in terms of colonial issues, tax issues and, finally, social issues.

The fear of a return to absolutism was to continue under the government of the Marquess of Rockingham, from July 1765 to July 1766—this fear was crystallised in the figure of Bute and the tax policy that he inspired. From the start of autumn in 1765, the news concerning the American riots against the Stamp Act reached Great Britain. The settlers were becoming organised and threatening to boycott English products (Middlekauff, 1982). At the same time, Rockingham (powerfully aided by his secretary Burke) led a campaign that aimed to organise London's merchants so that they and their colleagues across the British territory could put pressure on their representatives to abolish the Stamp Act by emphasising the losses the American boycott threatened to make them suffer. The Stamp Act was thus repealed, after a stormy debate at the House of Commons that began in January 1766.

This is precisely the episode that Smith was alluding to, as we saw, when he evoked the "terror" provoked by the threat of a rupture with the colonies, that is, a rupture of colonial monopoly. It is this "terror" which provoked the repeal of the Stamp Act.

The internal dissensions of the Rockingham government led to his replacement by William Pitt, then by the Duke of Grafton. Rockingham's Whigs thus found themselves in opposition. This is an important point, since, as John Brewer (1989) has noted, the disbandment of the Old Corps of Whigs into diverse factions, who would thus succeed to government, gave rise to a real opposition party, forming alliances and criticising government policy with brio and stamina.

Since they had been stripped by the King of all their responsibilities, including local ones, the Rockingham Whigs were obliged, if only to recover their political influence, to take part in local politics, to pay court to those who had sullied their hands with mercantile wealth.[9] As a result, Rockingham Whigs assert the identity between interest of the Empire and the interest of the merchants which necessitates the conciliation with American settlers. The many conflicts that used to oppose the gentry and the aristocracy in rural areas, and corporations and the bourgeoisie in the city, remained limited to the local level during the long period of the Whig

[9] Burke had already entered into alliance with mercantile interests when he agreed to act as agent for the state of New York (I am grateful to D. Winch for that information).

party as the sole political party. Thenceforth, local conflicts were able to be heard nationally, since the same local quarrels were sometimes nourished by the major questions posed in the 1760s and 1770s: the Wilkes affair, parliamentary reform and above all, the colonial question.

An Empire as Glorious as It Was Costly

It is on this point that the change in political practices engendered by the start of the reign of George III seems important. Instead of denouncing the parties as factions, the opposition, that is, the Rockingham Whigs, fully assumed their legitimacy, and very precisely came to the latter's defence in the face of the monarchy—or, more cautiously, in the face of "the court"—the cornerstone of his politics. The Parties (which he named *connexion*) seemed to Burke to be both indispensable and threatened in their very existence by the "cabala" of the courtiers. Burke is sought to bring down the "tyranny" exercised by the courtiers on the country and on the King himself.

It was an open question as to how this new "party" was going to conduct itself with the extra-parliamentary groups with which it had to collaborate in opposition. The Rockingham Whigs supported a highly aristocratic conception of politics. According to them, only those who had "a natural and fixed influence" (Burke, in Brewer, 1989, p. 195) on society were capable of preserving the peace in society and the government. Preserving this aristocratic privilege was the *raison d'être* of this opposition party. The agitation, the riots caused by shortages (in 1766[10] and 1769, then at the start of the 1770s), the first waves of violence associated with industrialisation, and the consequences that disturbed the peace in 1763 were solely attributed to the disastrous influence of the "courtiers' cabala" (Bute and his supporters) who had sought to destroy the "connexion" required for the equilibrium of the political body. This denunciation of Bute's politics could only be effective by basing itself on public opinion and therefore on extra-parliamentary interests: those of merchants and manufacturers, but also of the first radicals, concerned with constitutional reforms that were in action at the time of the Wilkes affair and which called into question the freedoms of political expression.[11] This

[10] I evoked those of Spitalfields above.

[11] The radical agitation led by John Wilkes, which had therefore contributed to Bute's fall, continued through the late 1760s with the question of whether or not the Parliament

contradiction that was expressed between the aristocratic affirmation of the Rockingham Whigs on the one hand, and on the other, their alliance with the first radicals, was adopted in a rather strange way by Burke's thesis whereby this party was playing the role of "doctor" for the political body, relying on its disease in order to better cure the political body, and thus operating a kind of "inoculation" of the political body by treating the problem with the problem.

Whatever the case may be, the result of this curious and very new coalition was therefore the repeal of the Stamp Act, but also, and above all—thanks to this retreat inflicted on both the government and the Parliament—the calling into question of the constitutional order. Yet it is clear that this calling into question is the consequence of the new issues posed by the Treaty of Paris: how to adapt Great Britain's political regime to the management of an empire that has become both immense but also overly weak in terms of the French threat it faced, and a source of considerable revenues but which were nonetheless insufficient for maintaining it? Here, then, we find the expression of the crisis of the Polybian constitution.[12]

The repeal of the Stamp Act could only proceed in exchange for an increase in customs duties in the colonies. This rise in customs duties was voted by the Parliament in 1767 in a set of laws known as the Townshend Acts,[13] which created new taxes on paper and on the glass imported from Great Britain in the colonies.

Curiously, the governmental instability that had characterised Great Britain since George III's accession ended at that time and, against all odds, Lord North stayed in power from 1770 until the Battle of Yorktown in 1782. This can be at least partly explained by the fact that economic instability, then the war, forced the opposition to compromise with the government. The tension connected with the management of the colonial empire was coupled with the economic crisis of 1772 whose political consequences were significant. This "sacred union" led to an affirmation of the identity of the merchants' interests with those of the Empire. There was evidently no proclamation of the fusion of these interests (we have

could deprive an elected member of parliament (Wilkes) of his seat (Wilkes was the MP for Middlesex) and the debate was to continue into the 1770s, when Wilkes was elected Lord Mayor of London.

[12] Cf. footnote 8.

[13] Townshend was Chancellor of Exchequer in Lord Chatham's government. He was well known by Smith—I will come back to this.

already noted the elitism of the Rockingham Whigs, and this was shared by all of the British political factions) as in the case of the East India Company in Bengal, but they tended to band closer together.

The Economic Crisis: Was What Was Good for the East India Company Good for the Empire?

The economic growth in Great Britain in the 1760s was impressive. The East India Company participated even more strongly in this growth through the fact that, since 1765, it was the de facto ruler of Bengal, Bihar and Orissa, from which it directly took an estimated income of between £2 and 4 million per year, since it had acquired the *diwani*, that is, the right to deduct seigniorial and fiscal revenues. Certain "well informed" contemporaries even imagine that these revenues taken from Bengal could pay for all of the Company's expenditure purchases[14] both in India and in China. Considerable speculation on the Company's shares seems to have developed, with their dividend growing by 10% in 1766 and by 12.5% in 1767.

But it seems that these forecasts were disappointed, since, according to Bowen (1998), the agents of the Company had to draw on the Company in London (from £210,000 in 1768–1769 to almost £1,600,000 in 1771–1772). This perhaps indicates that these loans directly or indirectly supported the Company's share prices and undoubtedly that the net gains made from the *diwani* were largely overestimated; in fact, the Company had to enter into a costly conflict with the Raja of Mysore, Hyder Ali, which at least partially accounts for this brutal reversal of its financial situation. Finally, the terrible famine that ravaged Bengal, causing the deaths of possibly a third of the population (apparently this represented 10,000,000 fatalities), definitely weakened the Company. It is still under debate as to whether, as Smith affirms (1776–1976, I, viii, 26), the Company's commercial and fiscal policy caused this catastrophe. What is certain is that it at least aggravated the situation (Ray, 1998).

[14] "Letter from Lord Clive to the Directors", 30 September 1765, *Fort William—India House Correspondence*, iv, pp. 337–338, cited par H. V. Bowen (1998, p. 189). Indeed, this sum can be aligned with the value of importations from the East Indies: £1,101,000 in commodities were imported to England and Wales from 1750 to 1751. This amount doubled in 1772–1773, if we take into account the importation to Scotland.

We do not know whether speculation on the Company's shares and the growing indebtedness of its agents was the immediate cause of the 1772 crisis (Rockoff, 2009), but it was severe, because the East India Company was not the only one to have gone into debt: all of the colonies (the West Indies and North America) were also indebted. The most indebted of the thirteen colonies was Virginia, which traded its tobacco for manufactured products, especially in Glasgow. Since the trade balance was in deficit, the British merchants were thus creditors to the settlers. According to Julian Hoppit (1986), this credit extended to the settlers was unstable, poorly guaranteed, and not of inconsiderable size, since, following independence in 1783, £5,000,000 in debts issued before the war remained owing by English traders, which can be compared to the £1,300,000 invested in the canals at the start of the industrial revolution between 1761 and 1770.

These American drafts were included in all of the commercial papers that Scotland sent to be discounted or re-discounted in London. The economic boom of the 1760s in Scotland was brilliant. The growth that had started in the 1750s gained momentum. Not only were the linen industries undergoing a period of great expansion, but many investment projects were inaugurated in agriculture, but also in major infrastructural works such as roads and canals (such as the canal linking the Clyde to the Forth). The investments of the ruling classes (including and in particular the major landowners, the landlords) were so great that the expression "gentlemanly capitalists" could be used (Cain & Hopkins, 2016). These investments gave rise to speculative processes, which were added to those that affected the East India Company shares. The difficulties experienced by the latter preceded the 1772 crisis, as we have just seen. But the fall of the Neale, James, Fordyce & Down Bank (which had financed the speculation of the East India Company securities) in London in June 1772 precipitated that of the Ayr Bank of Douglas, Heron & Co[15] in Edinburgh, with which it had business relations. The other bankers in Edinburgh were also clients of the London banks. Panic broke out in the Scottish capital. The Bank of England's attempt to provide a lifeline failed, and the Ayr Bank suspended its payments. The economic consequences for the linen industry were serious, where unemployment brutally made its appearance (Hamilton, 1956, p. 413). The government set up an official investigation commission on the state of distress of the industry.

[15] See Henry Hamilton (1956). The Adam Smith protector, the Duke of Buccleugh, was one of the owner of the Ayr Bank.

Finally, a series of very bad harvests considerably aggravated the situation and riots broke out in the linen producing centres (Perth, Fife and Angus).

The economic crisis of 1772 was therefore very serious. First, as Fernand Braudel has stressed (1979, vol. III, p. 230), it was the first crisis in which London constituted the point of departure, since the previous financial crises had begun in Amsterdam. Above all, it was not limited to the economic domain. I must now return to the policy itself, because the economic crisis caused two essential questions posed by the political organisation of the British Empire (Cf. Marshall, 1998):

1. On the one hand, the question posed by this surprising event of a private company having conquered a vast territory (Bengal, Bihar and Orissa): how are the relations between the East India Company and the government of Great Britain to be envisaged?[16] Smith (WON 750) highlights the fact that the Company was in a state of distress, in the early 1770s, when it requested a loan from the government. Between 1769 and 1771, the Company borrowed £2,000,000 from the Bank of England and again, £1,500,000 during the 1772 crisis (Bowen, 1998).
2. On the other hand, and almost symmetrically, how was the empire to be financed without (literally) tyrannising the British subjects settled on the other side of the Atlantic? This was to incite the first radicals to pose the broader question of fairness in representation for all British citizens, and, broader still, the question of the relations between voters and the Parliament.

Finally, these two colonial questions were to coincide by way of a seemingly anodyne measure taken by Lord North's government. In order to allow the East India Company to repay its loan as quickly as possible, the latter passed the Tea Act[17] in 1773, whose importance, as we have seen,

[16] In 1757 the *opinion* voiced by Charles Patt and Charles Yorke limited the prerogatives of the crown on the lands that the East India Company (or other colonisers) had acquired by *Treaty, Grant or Conquest*. These lands were the full properties of the Company, which instigated a rupture with the (Norman) feudal tradition whereby the sovereign was the eminent owner of the land.

[17] The Tea Act authorised the Company to access the North American market, by directly delivering and selling tea, without paying any customs duties other than those

was primarily due to the fact that it sparked a series of decisions dotted throughout the Atlantic, which ineluctably led to the War of Independence. The British supporters of the settlers, such as the Rockingham Whigs, supported the rejection of the Stamp Act and Townshend's taxes only because these measures could result in a boycott that would harm the merchants' interests; they were not in favour of the abolition of colonial monopoly precisely for the *same reasons*. However, after the Tea Party, and the ensuing escalation, it was impossible for them to side with the "smugglers" who violently disputed this colonial monopoly, and they were thus incapable of opposing the repressive measures imposed by Lord North's government.

Adam Smith's Politics (Continued)

I may now conclude this excursion into the political context of the elaboration of the *Wealth of Nations*.

In the first instance, we know that Smith was involved in some of these events. Upon his return to London, in the autumn of 1766, Charles Townshend—the very man who had chosen him to become the Duke of Buccleuch's preceptor, in order to accompany him on his continental "tour"—consulted him (Ross, 1995, p. 222) with respect to the amortisation of the British public debt. Importantly, a letter that Townshend addressed to him in the autumn of 1766 has been conserved in which the Chancellor of the Exchequer not only discusses the burden of the public debt, but also presents his tax plan in particular (Smith, 1977, p. 302). However, Charles Townshend was close to William Pitt. He had refused the Chancellor of the Exchequer's office under the short-lived Rockingham government, but had accepted it when William Pitt succeeded the latter. Smith's political proximity to this trend is also attested by his correspondence with Lord Shelburne, who had also been a member of Pitt's temporary government, as Secretary of State, in charge of the Southern Department. We know that Lord Shelburne asked Smith for a report on the voyages of discovery in the South Pacific and the colonies (Smith, 1977, p. 101). This intellectual proximity does not signify that Smith

provided under Townshend's legislation. This law was thus combined with the latter to affirm the pre-eminence of the London parliament. Furthermore (and especially?) this law seriously harmed the interests of the smugglers who were active, as we have seen, in the port of Boston. The rejection of this law led to the famous Tea Party of Boston.

shared all of the political convictions of the Old Corps of Whigs. This tradition, as we have seen, had literally exploded after George III's accession, and Townshend and Shelburne seemed to be supporting moderate positions with respect to the American settlers: they considered it important and legitimate to be participating in the reimbursement of the public debt, but they accepted the compromise that while the Parliament could impose customs duties, it could not tax the settlers' activity.

Furthermore, in the *Wealth of Nations* (WON 313–315), Smith details the financial mechanisms that led the Ayr Bank to suspend its payments. Here again, Smith was well placed since the owners of this bank were all very wealthy Scottish lords, among them the Duke of Buccleuch.

Secondly, and above all, we now understand to which events Smith is referring when he describes the "apoplexy" of the British political body provoked by the mercantile system. As we have seen in the long reference cited earlier, he was explicitly referring to the campaign against the Stamp Act led by the Rockingham Whigs by relying on the merchants and manufacturers that feared the loss of the markets through the American boycott, just as he refers almost as openly to popular emotions such as those of Spitalfield, or those of the Scottish linen weavers. More profoundly, it is easy to show, as N. Koehn (1994) has done, that the supporters of the repression with regard to the colonies (from Lord Bute to Lord North), just as those who, on the contrary, support a conciliatory policy with regard to the settlers (like the Rockingham Whigs) *all* share the conviction that the commercial interests of the merchants and manufacturers *are* those of Great Britain and its empire. To convince oneself of this, it suffices to compare Smith's position here with that of Burke. In 1775, very shortly before the publication of the *Wealth of Nations*, the latter (secretary of Lord Rockingham) had presented this idea in his "Speech on Moving His Resolutions for Conciliation with the Colonies":

> But, it will be said, is not this American trade an *unnatural protuberance*, that has drawn the juices from the rest of the body? The reverse. It is the very food that has nourished every other part into its present magnitude. (Burke, 1999, 1, 173, my emphasis)

It is striking to note that the qualification of "unnatural protuberance" that here refers to the effect of colonial monopoly is almost the same metaphor as the one that will be used by Smith, which suggests that either it is already well known, or that Smith responded to Burke, since Burke draws a conclusion from this that is the opposite to that of Smith. For Burke, far from being a threat that renders the British economy more fragile, the monopoly of colonial commerce has stimulated it considerably. The merchants' interests thus appear to be perfectly aligned with the general interest. Burke, a defender of the established order, naturally defends the colonial monopoly that is Smith's target. Readers of Hayek will appreciate the irony of the situation.

The thesis whereby England's interests (or those of Great Britain) were identical to those of the merchants is obviously not a new one. This was affirmed by all supporters of the mercantile system since Thomas Mun, at least. However, the novelty of the 1760s resides in the fact that this common position was no longer restricted to the merchants' writings, but was resolutely affirmed by British *political* leaders, that is by the British aristocracy: by both the opposition and its spokesperson, Burke, and by Thomas Whately, Secretary of the Treasury in Grenville's government, then the Under Secretary of State of Lord North's government, and a firm supporter of the repression in the colonies of North America, or by Lord North himself (see Koehn, 1994).

Therefore, I shall risk the following hypothesis: the constitution of a real opposition party by Rockingham and Burke led them, as we have seen, to seek out an alliance with the business community. Consequently, they opened up a process of one-upmanship between them and the government, which led them to pose the colonial question on the grounds of the identification of the merchants' and manufacturers' interests with the interests of the empire, which was itself naturally assimilated to the general interest. This is why Grenville himself declared that his government's priorities were the commercial interests of Great Britain (Koehn, 1994, p. 123). The colonial question obviously brings the defence of the mercantile system to the fore, and each of its positions is justified in the name of the same defence of the interests of the merchants' and manufacturers' *class*.[18] The merchants' interests demand privileges (pricing protection, export subsidies), and the core of this arsenal is colonial monopoly. To call, as Smith did, for the abolition of these privileges, while

[18] A point that is often forgotten today: Smith, like most of his compatriots of the eighteenth-century reasons spontaneously in terms of social classes. These are not only characterised by their type of revenues, or by collusive behaviour on the market (which Smith evokes, naturally), but above all, by shared views. They are therefore truly political categories.

conserving the colonies, thus meant requesting and supporting free circulation within the Empire. Such measures could only be expected from *impartial* legislators, and not from Lord North or his opposition, who confused the interests of the merchants' class with that of the Empire. It was this growing proximity between the capitalists on the one hand and the legislators, that is, the British aristocracy, on the other, that deeply concerned Smith. As we have seen, it opposed with extreme assurance the colonies of North America protected by "the spirit of the British constitution" and Bengal, which was dominated by the spirit of a trading company.

Is it also necessary to recall the conclusion of Book I of the *Wealth of Nations*? After having affirmed that the owners' interests and those of the workers always conform to the general interest, Smith concludes with a few more home truths:

> The proposal of any new law or regulation of commerce which comes from this order ought always to be listened to with great precaution, and ought never to be adopted till after having been long and carefully examined, not only with the most scrupulous, but with the most suspicious attention. It comes from an order of men whose interest is never exactly the same with that of the public, who have generally an interest to deceive and even to oppress the public, and who accordingly have, upon many occasions, both deceived and oppressed it. (WON 267)

While Book I of the *Wealth of Nations* ends with this firm warning, the whole book itself concludes with a project for reform of the Empire in which the *General States* would draw together the representatives of all the components. The colonies, Smith tells us, would be the "impartial spectators" (WON 945) and thus allow the legislators to be kept at the *right distance* from the merchants. The reformed *British Empire would prevent Great Britain from falling into the tyranny of capitalists' domination*, which was still capable of seducing the legislators.

I have shown before (see Chapter 3) how Smith explained very clearly the deeply rooted connivance, founded on a shared love of systems, which united great men of state and entrepreneurs. As we can see, the mercantile system (the British capitalism of the eighteenth century) does not threaten British society by its inefficiency, which was dramatic in Bengal, but less so in the United Kingdom. The threat that colonial expansion brought to bear on its republican constitution was far worse. It was freedom that was at stake, and the mercantile system could transform this into tyranny, just as the extension of the Roman Empire had destroyed the Republic and placed monarchs in power who were constantly at risk of becoming tyrants. The reform of the Empire become urgent. What reform? Smith gives, very cautiously, some indications. First they concern taxation. However they concern also the more ancient colony, Ireland.

Indeed, it was obvious then that the colonies had the right to participate in voting taxes. This in turn implied a summoning of a *states general of the empire*, in which the colonies would all be represented, with all the provinces of the Empire. Smith insisted on the depth of these reforms, which he very carefully presented as a utopia, only intended to set out a hypothetical calculation of the tax it could be possible to collect from the colonies.[19]

Then Smith extended his study far beyond this examination of fiscal policy. In fact, a few pages later, he underlines how fair it would be to make Ireland and America contribute to the repayment of Great Britain's debt, part of which was occasioned to ensure their defence. This shift into the field of justice led Smith to emphasise the political importance of the union of Ireland and Great Britain:

> By a union with Great Britain, Ireland would gain, besides the freedom of trade, other advantages much more important, and which would much more than compensate any increase of taxes that might accompany that union. By the union with England the middling and inferior ranks of people in Scotland gained a complete deliverance from the power of an

[19] "By extending the British system of taxation to all the different provinces of the empire inhabited by people of either British or European extraction, a much greater augmentation of revenue might be expected. This, however, could scarce, perhaps, be done, consistently with the principles of the British constitution, without admitting into the British Parliament, or if you will into the states general of the British empire, a fair and equal representation of all those different provinces, that of each province bearing the same proportion to the produce of its taxes as the representation of Great Britain might bear to the produce of the taxes levied upon Great Britain"..."Without, however, pretending to determine whether such a union be practicable or impracticable, it may not, perhaps, be improper, in a speculative work of this kind, to consider how far the British system of taxation might be applicable to all the different provinces of the empire, what revenue might be expected from it if so applied, and in what manner a general union of this kind might be likely to affect the happiness and prosperity of the different provinces comprehended within it. Such a speculation can at worst be regarded but as a new Utopia, less amusing certainly, but not more useless and chimerical than the old one" (WON 933–934).

> aristocracy which had always before oppressed them. By a union with Great Britain the greater part of the people of all ranks in Ireland would gain an equally complete deliverance from a much more oppressive aristocracy; an aristocracy not founded, like that of Scotland, in the natural and respectable distinctions of birth and fortune, but in the most odious of all distinctions, those of religious and political prejudices; distinctions which, more than any other, animate both the insolence of the oppressors and the hatred and indignation of the oppressed, and which commonly render the inhabitants of the same country more hostile to one another than those of different countries ever are. Without a union with Great Britain the inhabitants of Ireland are not likely for many ages to consider themselves as one people. (WON 944)

I let the reader judge this impressive plea for religious tolerance in Ireland. However, Smith also extended the benefits of the representation of the colonies to America, which would deliver them from “rancorous and virulent factions”, that threatened the “tranquillity of their government, in their form so nearly democratical”, disorders which would increase tenfold should they became independent, which would surely happen if the reform of the empire Smith proposed were not adopted.

But Smith reckoned this proposed reform to be essential not only for the colonies, but also and above all for the empire itself:

> In all great countries which are united under one uniform government, the spirit of party commonly prevails less in the remote provinces than in the centre of the empire. The distance of those provinces from the capital, from the principal seat of the great scramble of faction and ambition, makes them enter less into the views of any of the contending parties, and renders them more indifferent and *impartial spectators* of the conduct of all. (WON 945, italics are mine)

Here we find again the question raised in Chapter 2 of this book about the optimal distance, which must separate the actor (the citizens), and the spectator (the legislators). This was a necessary condition (but undoubtedly not sufficient) to ensure impartial judgement, and therefore fair legislation. This unique occurrence of the impartial spectator in the

Wealth of Nations was noticed by not only its publishers, but also by its American readers.[20] Now Smith knew perfectly well that:

> The private interest of many powerful individuals, the confirmed prejudices of great bodies of people seem, indeed, at present, to oppose to so great a change such obstacles as it may be very difficult, perhaps altogether impossible, to surmount. (WON 933–934)

Before studying these "private interests" in the next chapters, it is useful to quote the last paragraph of the *Wealth of Nations*, which is quite desperate in tone:

> If it should be found impracticable for Great Britain to draw any considerable augmentation of revenue from any of the resources above mentioned, the only resource which can remain to her is a diminution of her expense.

Smith then showed that growth in public debt was not linked to spending on Britain's colonial policies. Spending therefore had to be reduced, and he continued to conclude the *Wealth of Nations*:

> If the colonies, notwithstanding their refusal to submit to British taxes, are still to be considered as provinces of the British empire, their defence in some future war may cost Great Britain as great an expense as it ever has done in any former war. The rulers of Great Britain have, for more than a century past, amused the people with the imagination that they possessed a great empire on the west side of the Atlantic. This empire, however, has hitherto existed in imagination only. It has hitherto been, not an empire, but the project of an empire; not a gold mine, but the project of a gold mine; a project which has cost, which continues to cost, and which, if pursued in the same way as it has been hitherto, is likely to cost, immense expense, without being likely to bring any profit; for the effects of the monopoly of the colony trade, it has been shown, are, to the great body of the people, mere loss instead of profit. It is surely now time that our rulers should either realize this golden dream, in which they have been indulging themselves, perhaps, as well as the people, or that they should awake from it themselves, and endeavour to awaken the people. If the project cannot be completed, it ought to be given up. If any of the

[20] Winch (1965, pp. 178–180) has recalled how this argument would be exactly that used shortly after by James Madison in No 10 of the *Federalist Papers*, in 1787, to convince the North American settlers to create a Federal State.

provinces of the British empire cannot be made to contribute towards the support of the whole empire, it is surely time that Great Britain should free herself from the expense of defending those provinces in time of war, and of supporting any part of their civil or military establishments in time of peace, and endeavour to accommodate her future views and designs to the real mediocrity of her circumstances. (WON 947)

References

Bowen, H. V. (1998). British India 1765–1813: The metropolitan context. In P. J. Marshall (Ed.), *Oxford history of the British Empire, the eighteenth century*. Oxford University Press.

Braudel, F. (1979). *Civilisation matérielle, Economie et Capitalisme, XV–XVIII siècle, t. III*. Armand Colin.

Brewer, J. (1989). *The sinews of power: War, money and the English state, 1688–1783*. Unwin Hyman.

Burke (1999). Speech of Edmund Burke on moving his resolution for conciliation with the colonies. In *Select works of Edmund Burke*. A New Imprint of the Payne Edition. Liberty Fund.

Cain, P. J., & Hopkins, A. G. (2016). *British imperialism, 1688–2015*. Routledge.

Diatkine, D. (1996). Smith et le projet colonial ou l'avenir d'une illusion. *Cahiers d'Economie Politique*, n° 27–28.

Ditchfield, G. (2002). *George III, an essay in Monarchy*. Palgrave.

Hamilton, H. (1956, April). The failure of the Ayr Bank, 1772. *The Economic History Review*, *8*(3), 405–417.

Hoppit, J. (1986). Financial crises in eighteenth-century England. *The Economic History Review, New Series*, *39*(1), 39–58.

Koehn, N. (1994). *The power of the commerce*. Cornell University Press.

Marshall, P. J. (1998). The British in Asia: Trade to dominion, 1700–1765. In P. J. Marshall (Ed.), *The Oxford history of British Empire* (Vol. III). Oxford University Press.

Middlekauff, R. (1982). *The glorious cause: The American revolution, 1763–1789*. Oxford University Press.

Pockock, J. G. A. (1975). *The Machiavellian moment: Florentine political thought and the Atlantic republican tradition*. Princeton University Press.

Ray, R. K. (1998). Indian society and the establishment of British supremacy, 1765–1819. In P. J. Marshall (Ed.), *The Oxford history of the British Empire, the eighteenth century*. Oxford University Press.

Rockoff, H. (2009). Adam Smith on money, banking, and the price. In C. J. Berry, M. P. Paganelli, & C. Smith (Eds.), *Oxford handbook of Adam Smith*. Oxford University Press

Ross, I. S. (1995). *The life of Adam Smith*. Oxford University Press.

Skinner, A. (1996). Adam Smith: The demise of the colonial relationship with America. *Cahiers d'Economie Politique*, n° 27–28.

Smith A. (1977). *Correspondence* (E. C. Mossner, Ed.). I. S. Ross.

Winch, D. (1965). *Adam Smith's politics*. Cambridge University Press.

Winch, D. (1996). *Adam Smith's Politique Coloniale*. Cahiers d'Economie Politique, n° 27–28.

PART III

The Market and Capital Accumulation

As we have seen, Smith wrote the *Wealth of Nations* to criticise the political dimension of commercial society as it existed in Britain in his day, that is to say, the mercantile system. It was during this attack that Smith discovered capitalism. This he studied in two different forms, which are not necessarily compatible. In Smith's first form, capitalism is a stage (perhaps the ultimate stage) of the historical development of economies. It is distinguished from all previous stages by the existence of a social class—that of manufacturing merchants (or capitalists)—which seeks profit for profit's sake, and which therefore accumulates capital for the sake of accumulation. It is this stage of capitalism that Smith often called the commercial society, and which succeeded the hunter-gather societies, as well as pastoral and agricultural societies. Smith's second form of capitalism no longer drew on reasoned history but on economic analysis. Here, the economics of capitalism is expressed by a norm concerning the natural rates of profit that competition is supposed to impose on prices. The (difficult) coexistence of these twofold dimensions of capitalism—historical and analytical—characterised the *Wealth of Nations*. But it subsequently disappeared from economics (except in the work of Marx, where this coexistence raised its own difficult questions).

This discovery requires answering two questions of economic theory. The first must explain enrichment and the second its connection with the accumulation of capital. Smith asked the first question at the University of Glasgow.[1] It can also be found in his "Introduction and Plan of the Work" of the *Wealth of Nations*. The point here for Smith was to explain an "observed" phenomenon, or rather one assumed to exist for a long time, namely that of "savage" or "primitive" societies which inhabited America and which were poor and egalitarian, because everyone worked. By contrast, the "refined" or "advanced" societies of Europe were rich and unequal because the richest Europeans did not work at all. Yet the poorest Englishman was richer than the most powerful of Indian princes. So how was it possible to explain that growing inequalities did not arise at the expense of the less fortunate?

Smith attempted to combine two answers that he gave to these two questions. The first was already present in his *Lectures on Jurisprudence*. Enrichment was thus explained by the progress of the division of labour which allows labour productivity to be increased. These advances in the division of labour are themselves the result of extending the scope of markets. The extent of markets refers to the flow of spending on markets by economic agents, an important notion which I shall return to. The second answer is the accumulation of capital, which appears at the heart of the *Wealth of Nations*. This results from saving, or what Smith calls the "incessant desire to improve one's lot", as we have seen.

Whatever the causes, which we will have to return to, enrichment therefore appears to be the result of these two phenomena, which are not easy to render compatible. To do this, Smith studied two states of societies—the "primitive" and the "advanced" state—since the question of enrichment was raised from a comparative perspective between these two states.

We will also see that Smith's exploration of capitalism took place in the context of the struggle against the mercantile system, which should be understood in this case as the intellectual construction asserting the importance of monetary policy. For Smith, as we saw in Chapter 4 of this book, the latter was quite useless and only asserted the exorbitant claim of merchants and manufacturers to embody the general interest under all circumstances. We will see how Smith countered Munand Locke (and probably Sir James Steuart too, though Smith did not cite him) with the concept of real wealth. For better or worse, Smith bequeathed this view of

[1] As is shown in Smith's *Lectures on Jurisprudence* (Smith A. [1762/1766–1978]).

wealth to economics as a discipline, which of course the *Wealth of Nations* helped found.

I will show in Chapter 6 that Smith, in the name of a "primitive state", actually described for us an economy that was not so primitive, since it comprised a division of labour and therefore also a decentralised exchange of goods. Smith's primitive state was also characterised by the fact that all agents worked, and traded the products of their labours in markets. These products were the "natural reward" for their labours, and so—by definition—were their *wages*. These workers were therefore *self-employed producers*, who paid their own wages (or, if one prefers, they were wage-earners by nature). The goods they produced constituted their wages, and thus constituted real wealth. Smith's primitive state of society therefore contained all the ingredients necessary to constitute a market economy, reduced to its essentials. Real enrichment was possible in this state (albeit slowly), and resulted in higher wages and population growth.

Chapter 6 also deals with how Smith's vision of the "primitive state" of societies was *both* a *historical stage* of development (that of hunting and gathering) and a *theoretical model*, of a market economy. Smith devoted only a small portion of the *Wealth of Nations* (its first five chapters) to this economy. But this was important. On the one hand, it helped him lay the foundations of his analysis since enrichment was indeed already conceivable in this primitive state. On the other hand, later economic theories converted into questions some of Smith's propositions of a market economy, which he himself took for granted.

In Chapter 7, I will study the capitalist economic model and the accumulation of capital. The central question raised here concerns the dynamics of capital accumulation: what are its effects on the distribution of income? What are the stages of accumulation? How does it start? By what processes does accumulation continue? What are its limits? The *Wealth of Nations* raised these questions—and they are still largely open today.

Finally, we will see in Chapter 8 of this book that the accumulation of capital challenges an important property of the market economy, namely that of the *anonymity* of market relations. The advanced state of societies (i.e. the capitalist economy) sees the appearance two new social relationships, in a way that Smith does not explain (and which are added to the division of labour): the wage dependency relationship and the relationship of indebtedness. I will show these are not (incomplete or degraded) derivative forms of market relations in the *Wealth of Nations*. Instead, they are different and *normally* liable to lead to conflicts and therefore instability. The latter does not exist in principle in a market economy, yet it permeates capitalism.

CHAPTER 6

Economic Progress Without Capital Accumulation

One of the intriguing questions raised by the *Wealth of Nations* is that Smith, from the very first pages of this book, contrasted what he called "early and rude state" and "advanced state" of societies. Smith seems to have been contrasting "American Indian" or Native American society on the one hand, and Western Europe, and on the other, especially Great Britain. The advanced state of societies is a way here of designating capitalism.

However, in this chapter, I will show that this identification is misleading. In Smith's early state, he actually describes an economy in which the division of labour exists, and hence the exchange of commodities. This economy is characterised by the fact that *all* the agents in this state work. They exchange the products of their work in markets, and these products make up their wages. These workers are therefore *self-employed*. We will see that this primitive state is not so much a historical phase, but the model of an economy which is not capitalist, yet which possesses all the essential characteristics of a market economy.

In this economy, labour appears as the *original* mode of appropriation. This is stated in the opening lines of the *Wealth of Nations* by the famous proposition that: "The annual labour of every nation is the fund which originally supplies it with all the necessaries and conveniences of life which it annually consumes, and which consist always either in the immediate

D. Diatkine, *Adam Smith and the Wealth of Nations*, Palgrave Studies in the History of Economic Thought, https://doi.org/10.1007/978-3-030-81600-1_6

produce of that labour, or in what is purchased with that produce from other nations" (*WON* Introduction (1). Smith's initial thesis, which was already included in his Glasgow *Lectures on Jurisprudence*, explains enrichment by the progress of the division of labour. This in turn depends on extent of the market (a concept similar to, but not identical to that of "demand"). Yet, before addressing this key issue, it is necessary to clarify two points. First of all, we will study the role of sympathy and the impartial spectator in market relations. I will show that, coming after many others, these central notions to Smith's *Theory of Moral Sentiments* (*TMS*) have no place in the *Wealth of Nations*, because market relationships take no account of sympathy, in principle. This is why they can be characterised by their anonymity. This anonymity of market relationships expresses the idea that exchange relationships (prices) cannot normally be dependent on the identity of agents (Section "The Anonymity of Market Relations: The Language of Goods").

I will next show why the early state of societies not only designates a historical stage, but above all a theoretical economy. The latter is characterised by the presence of a single class—that of the labourers—and consequently of a single type of income, namely wages (Section "The Early State of Societies and the Stage of Hunter-Gathering").

It is then possible to deal with the division of labour and the exchange of the products of labour, in markets that mean the "early state" is in fact a market economy. I will show in Section "The Division of Labour How Smith, with Great Audacity", assumed that a large number of theoretical problems had been solved, such as the process of specialisation or the endogenisation of endowments (talents).

Finally, we will look at the most important and delicate part of Smith's legacy: the concept of real wealth. In Section "Real Wealth and Value", I will address the difficult question of the presence or absence of a theory of value in the *Wealth of Nations*.

In this chapter, I will not deal with the question of market coordination, which examines how markets manage to render agents' interests compatible under the pressure of competition. In fact, this question could be fully addressed here. This curious absence will be partly explained in the next chapter, which deals with the famous analysis of price gravitation under the pressure of competition. And if this question is not addressed here, *it is probably because the Wealth of Nations assumed it to be solved*. As a result, the analysis of market price gravitation towards a natural price, put forward by Smith within the framework of the capitalist economy, should probably not be read as an awkward anticipation of the answers given to these important questions. The analysis was only raised much later, and I will return to it in the next chapter.

The Anonymity of Market Relations: The Language of Goods

As I have tried to show in Chapter 3, the theory of an impartial spectator attempts to answer to the question of the origin of the feeling of obligation, posited by Hume. This theory, as we have seen, is entirely constructed from the twofold relationship that associates the actor and the spectator: the actor learns to judge herself through the eyes of the spectators, then the impartial spectator. This relationship associates an individual (an actor) and a (the) audience. From this perspective, it could be called a social relationship (or political, using a very broad definition of this term).

By contrast, market relationships are distinguished from social relationships thus defined, by the fact that they are *anonymous.* Consequently, they are distinguished by not entailing sympathy. Given that market relationships are deprived of any theatricality, we will see later that they escape from the feeling of obligation and therefore the feeling of duty (as long as they remain anonymous). Only an agent's purchasing power counts in markets made up by commodities (i.e. products for sale) and prices. This anonymity is explained by the fact that in markets, in the final analysis, it is not two individuals but two commodities, or according to Smith two purchasing powers, which come together. We will see later the analytical consequences of this important position.

In a market, there is no showmanship, at least not between professionals—between businesspeople. With the end consumer—the final buyer—things are different. In this case, asymmetries of information about the qualities of products, the more or less well-founded trust of the consumer in *her* supplier (*her* grocer or *her* doctor or *her* lawyer) play a role. Here we are in the world of imperfect markets where information is incomplete and unequally distributed. This world is not of particular interest to Smith. The market economy for him was the economy of merchants, or of professionals in today's terms. Although Smith states in the *Wealth of Nations* that we are all in "in some measure" merchants because of the division of labour,[1] this obviously does not mean that we are always and everywhere merchants. We are mainly actors and spectators elsewhere.

Smith simply asserts that there is probably a propensity to exchange. He adds: "Whether this propensity be one of those original principles in human nature of which no further account can be given; or whether, as seems more probable, it be the necessary consequence of the faculties of reason and speech, it belongs not to our present subject to inquire" (WON 25).

In addition, Smith stated that exchange is a founding principle of an anthropology when he noted that: "Nobody ever saw a dog make a fair and deliberate exchange of one bone for another with another dog" (*ibid.*).

This anthropology of exchange has fuelled much debate about the relationship between morality and economics. I must therefore look at it too, because the anonymous nature of the commodity exchange seems to be belied by this famous passage: "But man has almost constant occasion for the help of his brethren, and it is in vain for him to expect it from their benevolence only. He will be more likely to prevail if he can interest their self-love in his favour, and show them that it is for their own advantage to do for him what he requires of them. Whoever offers to another a bargain of any kind, proposes to do this. Give me that which I want, and you shall have this which you want, is the meaning of every such offer; and it is in this manner that we obtain from one another the far greater part of those good offices which we stand in need of. It is not from the benevolence of the butcher, the brewer, or the baker that we expect our dinner, but from their regard to their own interest. We address ourselves, not to their humanity but to their self-love, and never talk to them of our own necessities but of their advantages" (WON 27).

Since sympathy is not benevolence, perhaps sympathy lies at the root of Smith's "use of reason" which he uses to establish an anthropology of exchange. Smith is very cautious on this point, but some commentators

[1] "When the division of labour has been once thoroughly established, it is but a very small part of a man's wants which the produce of his own labour can supply. He supplies the far greater part of them by exchanging that surplus part of the produce of his own labour, which is over and above his own consumption, for such parts of the produce of other men's labour as he has occasion for. Every man thus lives by exchanging, or becomes in some measure a merchant, and the society itself grows to be what is properly a commercial society" (WON, 37).

are less so. Jeffrey Young (1997) seems to me representative of this line of thinking, which tries to show that Smith's analyses in the TMS are also at work in the WON. In this way, Young strongly opposes the widely held thesis (illustrated, *inter alia*, by the work of Louis Dumont (1977), who developed Halévy's views (1926) on this point) that economics emerges as science and freed of morality in the *Wealth of Nations*. While I share his critical point of view, I nevertheless think that his enthusiasm takes him a little too far.

According to Young, the "natural price" (a very important notion to which we will return) is very close to the "fair price", if one supposes, as he does, that the natural price does not escape the judgement of an impartial spectator. Young's approach is as follows: he asks why people in a early state exchange, instead of stealing, which they could do if it is assumed that in this state the economy has no legal system (which Young assumes). Only the injunctions of the impartial spectator would be able to explain exchange. However, it seems to me that Young here transforms the early state into a Hobbesian state of nature.

This point needs to be clarified. In Smith's *Lectures on Jurisprudence*, the theory of property rights is a primary concern. Smith asserts that the impartial spectator can act as a judge when it comes to appropriation *by occupation*, that is to say appropriation of what was previously owned by no one.[2] This involves knowing, for example, if the rightful owner of game is the person who first saw an animal, or if it is the person who caught it. We have seen that Smith invokes the impartial spectator to settle this classic case, which Hume also addressed, by referring to rules of understanding in order to legitimise original property rights. When he deals with contracts, i.e. promises (*LJ (A)*, ii, 1–13), Smith resorts to the judgement of the impartial spectator to solve the very thorny problem of the obligation to keep one's promises, as we have seen (*LJ (A)*, ii, 43). By contrast, Smith does not at all mention the problem of fair prices, neither in the *Lectures on Jurisprudence* nor in the *Wealth of Nations*. If the impartial spectator is invoked to appreciate how much of a particular type of work is necessary to acquire good A, and how much of an equally particular work (but qualitatively different from the first) is necessary to acquire good B, it is also necessary to know the structure of wage rates (how many hours of type 1 work are equivalent to one hour of type 2

[2] See Chapter 3 above.

work) in order to determine the exchange ratio (we return to the wage structure later). That is why Smith stated that he was dealing with the heterogeneity of wage rates: "It is adjusted, however, not by any accurate measure, but by the higgling and bargaining of the market, according to that sort of rough equality which, though not exact, is sufficient for carrying on the business of common life" (WON 49).

Yet, this "rough equality" is not only hard for the impartial spectator to establish, but it is especially difficult to understand how it may result from the *higgling and bargaining* of the market. There is a risk of being faced with an aporia or puzzle: either the "impartial spectators" of economic agents all have the same information and the same criteria, and in this case there is no need to bargain; or, if this is not the case, then impartiality no longer has any role apart from invoking an *external* judge who imposes a fair price on economic agents.

Finally, the "pleasure of persuasion" expresses itself in a very particular way in the market. This can be seen in the very strange slip-of-the-pen made by one of the copyists of the *Lectures on Jurisprudence*. The text (*LJ (A)*) contains the following passage twice. First, the student taking the class notes was probably quite troubled. He wrote: "A bargain does this in the easiest manner. When you apply to a brewer or butcher [for] beer or for beef you do not explain to him how much you stand in need for these, but how much it would be in your [sic] interest to allow you them for a certain price. You do not address his humanity, but his self-love" (LJ(A), vi, 45 et 56).

I would love it if the copyist's troubles that made him *invert* the sense of the agents' interests were due to an amusing image suggested by Smith himself, in which Smith would have represented himself trying to persuade his butcher that it was in his advantage to barter a quarter of an hour of moral philosophy against 250 g of steak … Be that as it may, the next day, Smith (or the student) felt the need to be much more explicit: "If we should enquire into the principle in the human mind on which this disposition of trucking is founded, it is clearly the naturall (sic) inclination everyone has to persuade. The offering of a shilling, which to us appears to have so plain and simple meaning, is in reality offering an argument to persuade one to do so and so as it is for his interest" (LJ (A), vi, 56).

Here, things are simple, and even trivial: if the propensity to persuade is more easily deployed on the market than anywhere else, it is precisely because such persuasion needs neither language nor sympathy: a shilling is an argument that easily carries conviction.

The purchasing power of the currency is very visible, and I just need money to access all goods offered for sale. And if we assume, as Smith did in the Wealth of Nations, that this purchasing power is not "in reality" only confined to money, but exists for all commodities, then the supply of commodities is sufficient to persuade buyers to act in accordance with the interests of the suppliers. The silent "language" of commodities, with their purchasing power, replaces rhetoric and sympathy. From this point of view, the world of the market economy is a wordless world, in every sense of the expression: traders do not speak because traders do not promise anything. In the final chapter of this book, I show how Smith demonstrates that taking credit into account changes this.

In short, market relationships (between merchants) differ from all other social relationships by being anonymous.

Today, it is argued that conditions of perfect competition (which require an organised market and a clearing house) guarantee this anonymity. The anonymity of relationships and the lack of strategic behaviour on the part of agents are two closely related expressions.

Of course, this anonymity is not excessive, bearing in mind that merchants operate in the market. If they are not good professionals (if they do not master their techniques, rational and well-informed), then competition would quickly exclude them from the market. In other words, I think Smith's vision of economics in the early state was that of a market economy in which competition is deemed sufficient to resolve all conflicts of identity and interest, because market relationships are anonymous. This peculiarity of the market is by no means self-evident. But perhaps it provides an answer to Jean-Pierre Dupuy (1992, p. 50), who questions the fact that economic theory "seeks relentlessly—who knows why?—to base the social bonds on an absolute minimum of interpersonal communication". If one is willing to admit that market relationships are far from making up all "social bonds", then the anonymity of market relationships makes them exceptional. And it is precisely this "minimum of communication" that characterises them.

The general character of social and political relationships as theatrical[3] (and hence asymmetrical) relationships thus has a *very important exception*, when these relationships concern market transactions. In the market, agents are neither actors nor spectators. Merchants terminate the actor/spectator relationships which characterise the social and political relations set out in the *Theory of Moral Sentiments*. The relationship that binds them is characterised by symmetrical anonymity, which then rules out a theatrical relationship. Smith expresses this commonplace notion according to which relationships between things replace human relationships in the market. These regain all their importance outside the market; in particular, as we have seen, in the relationships between merchants and legislators.

The Early State of Societies and the Stage of Hunter-Gathering

We now need to deal with a new difficulty which concerns the relationship between the market economy and history. Indeed, Smith develops two theses that seem contradictory: on the one hand, "early states of societies" already include the essential relationships that characterise the market economy; on the other hand the advanced state (or the commercial society as Smith sometimes calls it) is the result of a long historical process that is studied by history which is "theoretical or conjectural", in the words of Dugald Stewart (*Account of the Life*..., *op. cit.*). This is the *theory of stages* as set out by Ronald Meek (1971).[4] This four-stage theory was characteristic of the influential Scottish Historical School, of which Smith was one of the initiators. This idea was a remarkable novelty in the eighteenth century, associating cultural, moral and political progress with economic development.

The first stage is that of hunting, gathering and fishing; the second stage is that of breeding; the third stage of agriculture; and the last stage involves trading. This theory of stages occupies a significant amount of space in the *Lectures on Jurisprudence* and in Book V of the *Wealth of Nations*.

[3] See above Chapter3.

[4] See also A. Brewer (1995); J. Jacquet (2007).

If we examine the temporality of the stages and the early state/advanced state opposition, then the immediate, simplest question which stands out asks whether the hunting stage is part of the "primitive" society (in terms used by anthropologists).

As Christian Marouby (2004) has shown, Native Americans were seen in the eighteenth century as the epitome of primitiveness, a state in which a "natural" society exists, which is "savage" and stripped of the "artifices" imposed by civilisation. I would add that while Native Americans were perceived as testifying to the "primitive" conditions of humans, Asian societies by contrast (especially "the Chinese empire") are perceived in the *Wealth of Nations* as representing the steady state towards which all societies converge, having "probably long ago acquired that full complement of riches which is consistent with the nature of its laws and institutions" (WON 111).

To describe the West Indies, Smith used the texts of early anthropologists such as Pierre Francois Xavier Charlevoix, Joseph Francois Lafitau, Jorge Juan and Antonio de Ulloa, which he quoted and which were in his library (Mizuta 1967). By associating primitiveness with savage Native American society, Smith was part of an approach which argued that the "savage" societies of the West Indies testified to the past of European societies. "Savagery" was thus associated with "primitiveness". This testimony justifies the studies in anthropology, one of the first examples being precisely one of the authors quoted by Smith, namely Lafitau. In 1724, Lafitau had published (*Mœurs des Sauvages américains comparées aux mœurs des premiers temps*) in which he systematically compares his survey of the Huron and Iroquois Native Americans with the information available concerning early European times (Homeric legends, historians of antiquity and the Bible). In the final analysis, these observations raise the question of *progress*: European societies had made progress, but "savage" societies had not. Why?

However, the description provided by the *Lectures on Jurisprudence* of the first stage (hunting and gathering) is very different from Smith's description of primitive societies, as Marouby has shown clearly.

This infidelity to the anthropologists' texts can be explained by bearing in mind the object of the stage theory. When Smith sets it out (in the *Lectures on Jurisprudence* and in Book V of the *Wealth of Nations*), he first develops a theory of the State in relationship to the theory of property rights. The stage of hunting is characterised by the fact that *minimum* conditions of appropriation appeared in this stage. What characterised the hunter-gatherer stage was the fact that game or fruits were *perishable* goods. Their appropriation was *limited in time*. The immediacy of exchange was therefore obvious. As a result, property did not need powerful institutions to be guaranteed. The presence of tribal elders may have sufficed to structure exchange, but this function did not require institutional specialisation.

Perennial forms of ownership appeared with the advent of stage of animal breeding. Livestock began being passed on from one generation to the next and required, according to Smith, forms of political organisation that were themselves more durable and *specialised*. Typically, these political organisations were what Smith called "Tartar monarchies". New forms for founding property rights emerged, related to the accession to ownership that raised the problem of the appropriation of offspring born to animal herds. Formidable legal problems arose, even if they were sometimes quite ironic. Smith stated, for example, that animal offspring belonged to the owners of the mother, except in the case of the swans which belonged to the owners of the father!

In any case, Smith assumed that the multiplication and, above all, the increasing durability of appropriated goods therefore required more developed legal systems and complex administrative structures. The transition from the agricultural to the commercial stage of society was hardly sketched out in the *Lectures on Jurisprudence (A)*, since the latter was characterised by international exchange. The *Wealth of Nations* hardly gives more information in the first chapter of Book V, where the theory of stages is used to describe the evolution of state military expenditures and to explain how the reduction in free time caused by the passage of one stage to another led to the gradual disappearance of conscription and militia, and the emergence of professional armies. The latter therefore appeared indispensable in societies where a large part of employment was no longer part time (as in the hunting stage), nor seasonal (as in the agricultural stage).[5]

To conclude this section rapidly: stage theory sketched out a theory of property rights and of the State. Marouby is therefore right in attributing

[5] Smith favoured professional armies, compared to A. Ferguson who supported militia forces. This debate was important in the wake of the 1745–1746 war between Scottish Jacobin militia and the English professional army, and on the eve of the American War of Independence. See Lisa Hill (2009, pp. 71–89).

this typical infidelity by Smith vis-à-vis his sources for the sake of developing *another* anthropology to that addressed by Lafitau. But, in my opinion, this was less an economic anthropology than a legal anthropology seeking to explain the emergence of institutions guaranteeing the right to property.

The historical arguments in the *Lectures on Jurisprudence* were numerous, yet were only intended, as anthropological references, to illustrate this theory of stages. While the early state of the societies referred only to the hunter-gatherer stage by way of illustration, it nevertheless referred theoretically to the market economy. This is what I am going to show now.

The Division of Labour

Smith explicitly justified the distinction between the "early state" and "advanced state" of society in the Introduction of the *Wealth of Nations*. Indeed, he claimed it was well known that the difference in wealth which separated the poorest from the richest English person was much greater than that which separated the poorest from the richest Native American. In addition, all Native Americans worked. On the other hand, in Britain, some persons did not work at all. And yet, the poorest British labourer was richer than the richest Native American.[6] This difference in situations between the "early state" (of Native Americans) and that of the "advanced state" (of the British) must of course be explained.

[6] "Among the savage nations of hunters and fishers, every individual who is able to work, is more or less employed in useful labour, and endeavours to provide, as well as he can, the necessaries and conveniences of life, for himself, or such of his family or tribe as are either too old, or too young, or too infirm to go a hunting and fishing. Such nations, however, are so miserably poor that, from mere want, they are frequently reduced, or, at least, think themselves reduced, to the necessity sometimes of directly destroying, and sometimes of abandoning their infants, their old people, and those afflicted with lingering diseases, to perish with hunger, or to be devoured by wild beasts. Among civilised and thriving nations, on the contrary, though a great number of people do not labour at all, many of whom consume the produce of ten times, frequently of a hundred times more labour than the greater part of those who work; yet the produce of the whole labour of the society is so great that all are often abundantly supplied, and a workman, even of the lowest and poorest order, if he is frugal and industrious, may enjoy a greater share of the necessaries and conveniences of life than it is possible for any savage to acquire" (WON, 10).

The first explanation of the enrichment given immediately by Smith follows from the progress in the division of labour. This has existed from the early state onwards, and even if exchange only concerned a relatively small number of goods, it necessarily implied property rights.

The effects of the progress of the division of labour analysed by Smith are famous and are regularly rediscovered by growth theorists. Smith admitted that growth can be explained by what we now call economies of scale.

To understand the effects of the division of labour on "the general business of society", Smith believed that these could be better understood by looking at some "trifling manufacture". For the division of labour is more easily observable in small factories (or manufactures); while in "those great manufactures, on the contrary, which are destined to supply the great wants of the great body of the people, every different branch of the work employs so great a number of workmen that it is impossible to collect them all into the same workhouse. We can seldom see more, at one time, than those employed in one single branch" (WON 14). One of the first difficulties of the *Wealth of Nation* is found here: what exactly does this opposition between "great" and "small manufacture" mean? In other words, what does the term the "general business of society" mean? Does it mean what Marx later called the social division of labour, that was first represented in Quesnay's *Economic Table* (which Smith knew about and commented on)? The answer to this question is of relevance to the rest of this chapter, and we will also find it in the following chapter.

For the moment, let us follow Smith who turned to the pin factory as an example. He hardly went far to find this example, as it was described in detail in the *Grande Encyclopédie* by Diderot and d'Alembert. Smith, however, stressed that he took care to verify this textbook example in a Scottish factory employing ten workers, where, although the division of labour was less extensive than in the example of the "Pins" article in the *Encyclopédie*, total production was still 48,000 pins per day, equivalent to 4,800 pins per worker, per day. This calculation of labour productivity is *absent* in the *Grande Encyclopédie*. It is *essential* in the *Wealth of Nations* and so emphasises the usefulness of Smith's visit to the factory. By contrast, according to Smith, a worker alone would produce little more than twenty pins a day. This considerable increase in the productivity of labour was caused above all by the breakdown of pin manufacture into 18 operations, each carried out by a specialised worker. Smith (following the *Encyclopédie*) described in detail the effects of specialisation on labour productivity, including: increased dexterity, the intensification of working time, the use of machines invented by workers or by "scientists or theorists".

In short, Smith described in simple terms what was later "rediscovered" in the twentieth century in the name of the "Taylor system" or "scientific management". Smith set out what are now called the economies of scale created by specialisation and thus provided us with what is still today the best explanation for the growth of labour productivity and hence enrichment.

Smith's modernity here has too often been emphasised for me to develop this point.[7] Equally impressive, however, is Smith's denunciation of the excesses of the division of labour. It appears in Book V, in which Smith justifies the community's consideration of the education of poor children (and the impossibility of setting up militias): "In the progress of the division of labour, the employment of the far greater part of those who live by labour, that is, of the great body of the people, comes to be confined to a few very simple operations, frequently to one or two. But the understandings of the greater part of men are necessarily formed by their ordinary employments".... "The torpor of his mind renders him not only incapable of relishing or bearing a part in any rational conversation, but of conceiving any generous, noble, or tender sentiment, and consequently of forming any just judgment concerning many even of the ordinary duties of private life". "Of the great and extensive interests of his country he is altogether incapable of judging", "It corrupts even the activity of his body, and renders him incapable of exerting his strength with vigour and perseverance in any other employment than that to which he has been bred. His dexterity at his own particular trade seems, in this manner, to be acquired at the expense of his intellectual, social, and martial virtues. But in every improved and civilised society this is the state into which the labouring poor, that is, the great body of the people, must necessarily fall, unless government takes some pains to prevent it" (WON 782).

[7] It should be noted that Smith's "modernity" has limits: he hardly described the beginnings of the Industrial Revolution, and the steam engine is mentioned only in a very incidental way, although Smith met Watt. See Charles P. Kindelberger (1976). I will come back to this point in the next chapter.

This famous passage foreshadows analyses of alienated labour that were developed in the nineteenth century, because we know Smith paid attention to the loss of political identity affecting workers, as a result of the extension of the division of labour. Similarly, and most importantly, as we shall see in the last chapter of this book, Smith addressed forms of wage subordination.

Returning to the first chapter of Book I of the *Wealth of Nations*, it concludes with the banal and yet crucial observation that the division of labour implies general interdependence, as much as it is affected by the latter. Such general interdependence is therefore the first answer to the question of enrichment, raised in the Introduction. Smith concludes the first chapter of this book as follows:

> Observe the accommodation of the most common artificer or day-labourer in a civilised and thriving country, and you will perceive that the number of people of whose industry a part, though but a small part, has been employed in procuring him this accommodation, exceeds all computation. The woollen coat, for example, which covers the day-labourer, as coarse and rough as it may appear, is the produce of the joint labour of a great multitude of workmen. The shepherd, the sorter of the wool, the wool-comber or carder, the dyer, the scribbler, the spinner, the weaver, the fuller, the dresser, with many others, must all join their different arts in order to complete even this homely production. How many merchants and carriers, besides, must have been employed in transporting the materials from some of those workmen to others who often live in a very distant part of the country! How much commerce and navigation in particular, how many ship-builders, sailors, sail-makers, rope-makers, must have been employed in order to bring together the different drugs made use of by the dyer, which often come from the remotest corners of the world! What a variety of labour, too, is necessary in order to produce the tools of the meanest of those workmen!"… "if we examine, I say, all these things, and consider what a variety of labour is employed about each of them, we shall be sensible that, without the assistance and co-operation of many thousands, the very meanest person in a civilised country could not be provided, even according to what we very falsely imagine the easy and simple manner in which he is commonly accommodated. Compared, indeed, with the more extravagant luxury of the great, his accommodation must no doubt appear extremely simple and easy; and yet it may be true, perhaps, that the accommodation of a European prince does not always so much exceed that of an industrious and frugal peasant as the accommodation of the

latter exceeds that of many an African king, the absolute master of the lives and liberties of ten thousand naked savages. (WON 23–24).

I will return to this important point soon. For the moment, it should also be noted that while Smith magnificently described general interdependence, he did not ask the question of how such decentralised co-ordination was possible. This question was raised much later in general equilibrium theory, while Smith assumed it to be resolved in the *Wealth of Nations*.

We thus find here an *initial* answer to the question of enrichment. Yet, this answer raises serious difficulties, some of which are still without solutions. Here, I will examine a few.

It is striking to note, for example, that Smith's description of the pin factory totally omits the presence of non-workers. This is why, in my opinion, it has its place more in the early state. The workers are alone, without masters or foremen, to organise and control the production process. As a result, the pin factory not only foreshadows the future Taylor system, but it also prefigures self-management, as only workers are associated with it! Master manufacturers—capitalists—or their representatives are *absent* in the model.

This is why Marx (may be surprised to see Smith using the technical division of labour in the workshop as a model of what he (Marx) called the social division of labour in a *given* economy.[8] For the factory, in which the technical division of labour reigned, seemed in fact to have been devised by Smith as a model of the social division of labour, with work being divided into trades, or into what we would call branches today. These were

[8] "But, in spite of the numerous analogies and links connecting them, division of labour in the interior of a society, and that in the interior of a workshop, differ not only in degree, but also in kind. The analogy appears most indisputable where there is an invisible bond uniting the various branches of trade. For instance the cattle-breeder produces hides, the tanner makes the hides into leather, and the shoemaker, the leather into boots. Here the thing produced by each of them is but a step towards the final form, which is the product of all their labours combined. There are, besides, all the various industries that supply the cattle-breeder, the tanner, and the shoemaker with the means of production. Now it is quite possible to imagine, with Adam Smith, that the difference between the above social division of labour, and the division in manufacture, is merely subjective, exists merely for the observer, who, in a manufacture, can see with one glance, all the numerous operations being performed on one spot, while in the instance given above, the spreading out of the work over great areas, and the great number of people employed in each branch of labour, obscure the connexion" (Marx 1867, vol I, 246) I.

connected with one another through trading relationships. The factory, in which work was planned by a central authority, was thus presented as the model of the whole of society, in which accomplished tasks were distributed in a decentralised way, under the influence of the competition and the market!

If Smith was the first theorist of the market and if Marx was right, then it must follow that the *Wealth of Nations* begins with a monumental blunder, by making a centralised economy (the pin factory) the model of a decentralised economy (the *general business of society*).

Nevertheless, a different reading of this chapter is possible. To be sure, it enables us to conclude, in a way that may seem paradoxical, that pin production, far from anticipating a hypothetical future based on self-management, actually fitted in well with the "early state of societies"; i.e. with a *hypothetical* market economy, in which only the self-employed exist as economic agents. But correcting this error by Smith came at a price that was perhaps prohibitive.

To understand how one can avoid Marx's point of view, one must follow how Smith concluded his analysis of the division of labour: "It is the great multiplication of the productions of all the different arts, in consequence of the division of labour, which occasions, in a well-governed society, that universal opulence which extends itself to the lowest ranks of the people. Every workman has a great quantity of his own work to dispose of beyond what he himself has occasion for; and every other workman being exactly in the same situation, he is enabled to exchange a great quantity of his own goods for a great quantity, or, what comes to the same thing, for the price of a great quantity of theirs" (WON 22).

These few lines deserve comment. Smith asserts, admittedly rather ambiguously, that each worker commands a surplus of *work* beyond what he himself can consume. The ambiguity, of course, lies in the use of the term *work* (and not labour) that should be translated as "output". In English and French, the term *work* means both to work and the output or product of work. And here we are indeed talking about this identification. If work and output can be viewed as the same, Smith's text implies that exchange work is the same thing as exchanging the output (or product) of work. This proposition is absurd according to Marx, given the contradictory relationship in capitalist production between work and the output of work, which is one of Marx's major theses. From Marx's *point of view*, to confuse them is therefore an error.

Yet, what can be understood by the expression "exchange work"? To use the image of the two boaters employed by Hume,[9] exchanging work does not necessarily mean "I row if you row", but rather to understand that if the two boaters want to cross the water, they will necessarily have to row together, in other words cooperate. Smith's text thus assumes that if workers are specialised to produce each the inputs necessary for the production of a good, then whether they cooperate or exchange amounts to the same thing. The productivity gains will be the same in both cases, compared to the situation in which they are not specialised. And this is what matters here for Smith.

At the end of the quoted text, Smith introduced a second equivalence. He stated, and this assertion is central in the *Wealth of Nations*, that the exchange products and "product prices" are the same thing. This statement is very important and we will return to it later. It means that the exchange of products is the same as buying and selling for money. This is what allowed Smith to assume that everything observed in the factory occurred "as if" each of the ten specialised workmen had exchanged the specific output of his labour for one-tenth of the total output.

We can accept both equivalences as Smith did. The first thus abolishes the distinction between the social division and the technical division of labour (in the Marx's sense), between exchange and cooperation, a distinction which fades to the point of disappearing. Moreover, the criticism that Marx levelled at Smith falls away too, since cooperating (within the self-managed pin factory) is the same as exchanging (as part of the *general business of the society*). But we can also reject these two equivalences, following Marx. For example, we may think that the exchange of two commodities is not the same thing as a monetary exchange, because this type of transaction (barter) is inconceivable as a general form of exchange..

In any event, this double equivalence is the foundation of the concept of *real wealth*, to which I shall return soon.

However, before coming to this point, I must emphasise one characteristic of the approach developed in the *Wealth of Nations*. Smith puts forward his thesis that the division of labour is limited by the extent of the market: "As it is the power of exchanging that gives occasion to the division of labour, so the extent of this division must always be limited

[9] See above, p. 21.

by the extent of that power, or, in other words, by the extent of the market"(WON 31).

This proposal is at the heart of the *Wealth of Nations*. The extent of the market is in fact the purchasing *power present* in the market. It has the quantity dimension multiplied by prices. This purchasing power is carried by the goods and is therefore not reserved for money. The extent of the market for American gold and silver was global, and according to Smith this was the only property that distinguished these precious metals from other commodities. Conversely, he wrote, a porter could not establish himself in a village in Scotland, because the extent of the market was too small, which was easily understandable. If the purchasing power present in the village for services of this type of work was such that, *given* the normal (or natural) wage rate, the income that a worker could derive from this activity was less than the wage normal, then no porter would specialise in this work in the village. Thus, each commodity (or service) faces a distinct market limit. The sequencing of phenomena is thus as follows: an extension of the market allows progress in the division of labour and together they generate high labour productivity, the ultimate indicator of enrichment. This proposal is therefore perhaps the most important to be found in the *Wealth of Nations*, from an economic point of view. It remains indeed the best explanation of enrichment, growth and development, we can still find today. From a political point of view, this thesis is the best argument for free trade.

However, this proposal nevertheless raises several problems. Let us look quickly at three of them.

1. One might be tempted to understand the extent of the market as designating demand, and so translate Smith's thesis as follows: the supply of goods is limited by the quantity demanded. Yet, we need to be careful here. The modern notion of demand always refers to the required *quantity* of a good or service (for a given price), and this quantity is associated with prices via a demand function.[10] But, as we have just seen, the extent of the market designates the purchasing power present on the market, that is to say the product

[10] Or indeed conversely, whereby the price of demand or supply is associated with a given quantity.

of a quantity multiplied by its price. The extent of the market is therefore a different concept from that of demand.

2. As will be shown in the following chapter, Smith went on to study how the accumulation of capital runs up against the extent of the market, which, under certain conditions, may be insufficient to absorb accumulated capital without causing a fall in the rate of profit
3. Another difficulty concerns the process of specialisation. This is at the heart of the enrichment process. But *how* is it carried out? Smith hardly raises this question, and yet it is crucial. He merely asserts that specialisation occurs easily: "In a tribe of hunters or shepherds a particular person makes bows and arrows, for example, with more readiness and dexterity than any other. He frequently exchanges them for cattle or for venison with his companions; and he finds at last that he can in this manner get more cattle and venison than if he himself went to the field to catch them. From a regard to his own interest, therefore, the making of bows and arrows grows to be his chief business, and he becomes a sort of armourer". "And thus the *certainty* of being able to exchange all that surplus part of the produce of his own labour, which is over and above his own consumption, for such parts of the produce of other men's labour as he may have occasion for, encourages every man to apply himself to a particular occupation, and to cultivate and bring to perfection whatever talent or genius he may possess for that particular species of business" (WON 28, author's italics).

So we see that Smith assumed that there were no problems in passing from a first state, characterised by the fact that bows and arrows were joint products of animal game; to a second state, in which specialisation was established and exchange between the means of production and the consumer good could take place. The reader cannot help asking firstly how the agent specialising in an activity has the "certainty" of being able to sell his bows and arrows. Smith suggested that a process of trial and error could take place. But, it is not easy to see how the productivity gains from specialisation could be known in advance. This central question is not solved by incidence whereby the producer "will exchange these objects more frequently", if there are more than two objects, because in this case interdependence clouds the simplicity of relations in a world with two goods.

What is sure is that this process of specialisation implies that each of the traders first has a *stock* of the goods he will have to acquire once specialisation takes place, as Smith states in the Introduction of Book II of the *Wealth of Nations*: "when the division of labour has once been thoroughly introduced, the produce of a man's own labour can supply but a very small part of his occasional wants. The far greater part of them are supplied by the produce of other men's labour, which he purchases with the produce, or, what is the same thing, with the price of the produce of his own. But this purchase cannot be made till such time as the produce of his own labour has not only been completed, but sold. A *stock* of goods of different kinds, therefore, must be stored up somewhere sufficient to maintain him, and to supply him with the materials and tools of his work till such time, at least, as both these events can be brought about" WON II, Introduction, 1, author's italics).

Such "commodity stores" are *stocks which are not capital*. This point will surprise economists, who are accustomed to equating any stock with capital. We can note that Smith himself did not make such an assimilation, which seems obvious to us. I will come back to this in the next chapter.

On the other hand, Smith then states with some audacity that the differentiation of talents, which he has just made the *cause* of the division of labour, is in fact, the *effect*:

> The difference of natural talents in different men is, in reality, much less than we are aware of; and the very different genius which appears to distinguish men of different professions, when grown up to maturity, is not upon many occasions so much the cause as the effect of the division of labour. The difference between the most dissimilar characters, between a philosopher and a common street porter, for example, seems to arise not so much from nature as from habit, custom, and education. When they came into the world, and for the first six or eight years of their existence, they were perhaps very much alike, and neither their parents nor playfellows could perceive any remarkable difference. (WON 28)

This juxtaposition between cause (talents are exogenous) and effect (talents are endogenous) is surprising for several reasons. On the one hand, these two propositions contain an element of common sense and are therefore both perfectly acceptable. On the other hand, the juxtaposition simply expresses that the list of talents (and therefore the list of available resources) *is not* given. More generally, it seems that Smith refused (as we will see later) to consider as *given* the list (however long it is) of the goods and services traded in *a given economy*.[11] Instead, he sought to understand its genesis. This allows us to begin to understand what Smith means by *the general business*.

If the list of "talents" is not a given prior to the division of labour, but results from it, then it becomes difficult to assume as a given list all the goods and works exchanged as the general business, no matter how great the list. In this context, general business cannot be represented, because the system of interdependence is not given, but instead is the result of a process that must be studied.

In fact, we can only consider a subset of the division of labour, capable of observation, as the pin factory was.

Finally, we must add a point on which Smith insists and whose importance will be seen in the following chapter. The division of labour is always more difficult to implement in agriculture than in manufacturing, because of the constraints involved in the exploitation of the land. It therefore took longer to develop in the countryside than in the cities.

Real Wealth and Value

The concept of *real* phenomena in economics is the result of an abstraction since nobody ever *perceives real* measures. Nobody "earns" or "receives" a real salary.[12] Nevertheless, no one confuses the variations of their real income with those of their monetary income, even if they often find it difficult to measure the relative shares of these variations.

This process of abstraction is familiar to all, and is set out most clearly in Chapter 5 of Book I of the *Wealth of Nations*. This chapter is entitled "Of the Real and Nominal Price of Commodities, or their Price in Labour, and their Price in Money". The construction of the real price consists of changing the unit of account, which everyone can do when, for example, they evaluate a good in terms of the time spent to acquire the property. In this case, a person divides the price of the good by their income per unit of time. Chapter 5 of Book I starts by putting forward a banal definition of wealth. It states that wealth is the power to buy "the necessaries, conveniences, and amusements of human

[11] This given situation was called the "nomenclature hypothesis" by C. Benetti and J. Cartelier (1980).

[12] Of course, a part of the wages can be paid in-kind. Cases of wages being paid totally in-kind only arise in extreme forms of domesticity or slavery.

life". This purchasing power of "things" transforms them into economic magnitudes, measured by their price.

Smith then encountered the difficulty of choosing the unit for measuring wealth. As wealth is a purchasing power, it is impossible to identify within its movements those attributable to variations in the purchasing power of wealth and those attributable to variations in the purchasing power of the unit of wealth: i.e. the price standard, whatever it may be. Of course, prices appear to everyone as being measured in money. But the value of money varies over time. Consequently, given the variation of the monetary price of a good, it is impossible to know if it is the power to purchase the good which has changed or if it is that of the money. To solve this problem, Smith proposed expressing the prices of goods in terms of the amount of work needed to acquire them. To calculate this quantity, it sufficed to divide the monetary price of commodities by a reference wage rate, for example the wage of a worker deemed representative. Smith in no way claimed that this change in the price unit would make it possible to determine (to calculate) these prices.

The solution proposed by Smith was still adopted by economists and statisticians, and is easy to understand. Let us assume firstly and for the sake of simplicity, that workers do not need any other goods than wheat. In addition, let us assume as constant (and known), over time, the quantity of wheat per unit of working time that workers need. In doing so, we assume the wage rate as given. It follows that if one expresses the price of good i not in money, but in wheat whose purchasing power of work is assumed to be constant, then we can check that when the wheat price of good i varies, it is in fact its purchasing power of the labour of good i that has changed, and not the value of the money. To check this, very simple case, all that needs to be done is to divide the monetary price of good i by the price of wheat.

Smith's argument depends on the assumption of the physical homogeneity of the wage in wheat, and the constancy of its rate (the amount of wheat per unit of labour time). The assumption of physical homogeneity could be removed by replacing wheat with a basket of goods whose composition will remain constant (or which we can try to evaluate and correct for variations). This is what is done today in calculating the indices of consumer prices. The difficulties of this approach are often considered to be important, but technically manageable. The assumption of the constancy of the reference wage rate, on the other hand, raises a theoretical problem. Some commentators[13] have in fact admitted, as Smith seems to have done, that even if the wage per unit of working time varies (in composition and quantity), the effort and trouble the worker faces to obtain the goods which are the objective the worker must attain in order to live *normally* (norms which vary with time and place) does not change over time. In short, it is the trouble and effort expended to support the worker's "cost of living", which for the worker is seen as constant, even if "living standards" improve. In other words, it was certainly impossible to compare directly the "baskets of goods" consumed per unit of time by a British worker and a Native American. Nevertheless, Smith seems to have assumed that these different baskets of goods were a *standard* that workers would strive to achieve and that they would sacrifice the same pain and effort to acquire these different baskets, be they Native American or British. Ricardo criticised Smith on this point in the very first pages of the *Principles of Political Economy and Taxation*. For him, Smith's assumption that the cost of the wage goods-basket remained constant from the *point of view of the worker* was irrelevant because the cost of labour, *seen instead from the point of view of the employer* varied, as did the prices of the goods in the basket, the equivalent of which the employer had to give to the worker. This change in points of view testified to a break in the classical school that should not be underestimated.

It seems, however, that the issues raised in Chapter 5 were not just about the question of price indices. Smith solemnly asserted that wealth is indeed a form of *power* (following Hobbes, whom Smith probably quoted wrongly here). Yet, it was not a political or military *power*, but the *purchasing power* over the "labour or over all the produce of labour which is then in the market" (WON 48). It is important to understand that the power to purchase labour conferred by wealth is first and foremost defined as the power to command labour through the exchange of products. However, I will show in Chapter 8 that the *Wealth of Nations* is very attentive to the different forms of subordination of workers to employers, that is to say to wage dependency. But commanded labour is a different concept to dependent work.

The first price paid for acquiring property is therefore not money, nor even another good, but labour. Work is a deed of property, the original

[13] See F. Duboeuf (2004) and J. Mathiot (1990).

deed of any property which, for Smith (as we have seen)[14] results from the judgement of the impartial spectator who thus allocates what previously did not belong to anyone.

If wealth is the power to command labour, as Smith argued, then we have to take a difficult step, which Smith (like many economists) may not have taken. It requires showing under what conditions the product of labour becomes a component of wealth (a commodity), i.e. acquiring a positive price. This difficult question is most often asked in a partial and roundabout form found in the theory of price determination, in which a product with a positive price is obviously a commodity. So can we find a theory (or the beginnings of a theory) of price determination in the *Wealth of Nations*?

To answer this question, one of the most controversial issues of the *Wealth of Nations* needs to be addressed, so let us see what the text says.

Smith concluded Chapter 4 of Book I by announcing that he proposed to examine "What are the rules which men naturally observe in exchanging them either for money or for one another, I shall now proceed to examine. These rules *determine* what may be called the relative or exchangeable value of goods" (WON 44, author's italics).[15]

We must be careful here as Smith may have used the verb "to determine" in quite a different sense to how it is used today. Nowadays, price determination requires a distinction to be made between, on the one hand, the parameters on which prices depend (for example, the endowments available to economic agents, their objectives or preferences, and the techniques they are likely to use), and secondly the unknowns (i.e. the (finite) list of prices to be determined as a *solution* to a system of equations parameterised accordingly). Economists seek to know under which conditions this solution exists; under what conditions it is (preferably) unique; and under what conditions it is revealed (possibly) by the market, characterised by competition. The question then is whether this objective (which is the aim of theories of value) is actually the one pursued

[14] See above, p. 45.

[15] Smith then reminds his reader of the Aristotelian distinction between use value and exchange value, as well as the paradox of water and diamonds that was known to Greek philosophy (Plato, *Euthydemus*, 304, b). Plato quoted Pindar: "What is rare, Euthydemus, is paid for dearly indeed, while water is cheap, though it is, as Pindar has said, that which is best".

in Chapters 6 and 7 of the *Wealth of Nations*. This is in fact not clear, as further reading shows. Indeed, after this proposal, Smith added:

"In order to investigate the principles which regulate the exchangeable value of commodities, I shall endeavour to show:

> First, what is the real measure of this exchangeable value; or, wherein consists the real price of all commodities.
>
> Secondly, what are the different parts of which this real price is composed or made up.
>
> And, lastly, what are the different circumstances which sometimes raise some or all of these different parts of price above, and sometimes sink them below their natural or ordinary rate; or, what are the causes which sometimes hinder the market price, that is, the actual price of commodities, from coinciding exactly with what may be called their natural price.

After reading this three-point programme, which outlines the contents of Chapters v, vi and vii in Book I of the Wealth of Nations, price determination (in the modern sense of the term) was not Smith's objective.[16] Instead, he was seeking more to show how prices are regulated, that is to say, to understand what forces influence the evolution of prices. The first point aimed to show that the measurement of prices by the quantities of labour which goods allow their possessors to purchase is a more adequate measure than their measurement by the quantity of money against which they can be exchanged. We have seen this assumes that prices are *already* known. Similarly, we will see in the next chapter that the purpose of the second point was to distinguish the three types of income which, in advanced state societies, are the components of most prices. Finally, the last point has a clear objective. The natural price is *defined* (though not *determined* in the present sense of the term) by the fact that it informs sellers what to pay in wages, rents and profits at their *natural rates* as assumed by Smith, which are given elsewhere. This was to show that if current prices (market prices) deviate from natural prices for some reason, then the forces of competition would "regulate" them, and compel them to return to the natural level, sooner or later. We will see that the objective

[16] Smith adds: "For which I must very earnestly entreat both the patience and attention of the reader: his patience in order to examine a detail which may perhaps in some places appear unnecessarily tedious; and his attention in order to understand what may, perhaps, after the fullest explication which I am capable of giving of it, appear still in some degree obscure".

pursued here was simple, namely to show that the privileges (monopolies) granted to certain merchants, by obstructing such price gravitation, had the effect of blocking the market price above the natural price, which at the same time prevents the rate of profit from falling to the level of its natural rate. I showed in the precedent chapter how politically important is this point. The colonial monopoly gives to British merchants the deception that the rate natural rate of profit is higher than it actually is.

The issue is therefore about studying what controls or regulates price movement (gravitation, which, under the impact of competition, leads market prices to converge on natural prices). But in this outline, Smith made no mention of looking for the principles which determine—in the modern sense of the term—the relative prices of goods. In the final analysis, his aim more simply was to highlight the effects of monopolies.

That said, a very famous example seems to belie this last assertion. It should therefore be examined. At the very beginning of Chapter 6—i.e. after the announcement of its outline—we find the following proposition: "In that early and rude state of society which precedes both the accumulation of stock and the appropriation of land, the proportion between the quantities of labour necessary for acquiring different objects seems to be the only circumstance which can afford any rule for exchanging them for one another. If among a nation of hunters, for example, it usually costs twice the labour to kill a beaver which it does to kill a deer, one beaver should naturally exchange for or be worth two deer. It is natural that what is usually the produce of two days' or two hours' labour, should be worth double of what is usually the produce of one day's or one hour's labour" (WON 65).

It *seems* obvious that this is the formulation of the labour theory of value as Ricardo went on to formulate it. Indeed, it *seems to determine*, in the current sense of the term, relative prices (in this case only one relative price, that of beaver in terms of deer) by the quantities of labour required to acquire (or produce) each of the goods. However, even "in that early and rude state of society", the story is not so simple because Smith knew well that these amounts of work were heterogeneous.[17] And, logically, he pointed out that wage rates allowed the outputs of work to be compared

[17] "If the one species of labour should be more severe than the other, some allowance will naturally be made for this superior hardship; and the produce of one hour's labour in the one way may frequently exchange for that of two hours' labour in the other" (WON, 65).

against each other.[18] However, if the "baskets" of goods that make up wages are not homothetic (which is generally the case), then these baskets cannot be compared independently of the prices of the goods making up the "baskets". Yet, if we were dealing with a Ricardian statement of the embedded labour value theory, as suggested by a first reading, then it is nevertheless very incomplete, because we need to know other parameters involved in price determination than those stated here by Smith. It is easy *today* to specify these parameters.[19] In any case, the necessary conclusion is simple: Smith tells us that the amount of work that a commodity can command in the early state of the societies is equal to the amount of labour required for its production (or acquisition), because the price only pays the wages of the workers. In fact, Smith did not determine which prices govern trade in more advanced states. It is even doubtful that he was trying to do so. Indeed, we will see that Smith assumed the natural rates of wages and profits as given, within a given "locality". It is enough to assimilate such a "locality" with a given economy to share the intuition according to which the rates of profit and salary cannot be assumed to be given *independently* of each other, as the net income of this economy is distributed between profits and wages (rent may be omitted in a Ricardian context).

By contrast, Ricardo used the title "Value" for the first chapter of his *Principles of the Economy and Taxation*. In it, he attempted to generalise the idea that exchange ratios are determined by the amounts of labour needed to produce goods.

[18] Wages are defined by Smith as the "natural recompense of labour" (WON, 82). I have already noted that game was the wage of hunters, paid by themselves (or by nature).

[19] In the first place, it must be assumed that this exchange takes place during a unit time period. Secondly, it is necessary to assume that deer and beaver are the only goods produced, traded and consumed in the economy. Thirdly, the quantities of beaver (and deer) produced are equal to the quantities consumed. These conditions must be met to determine the relative price of deer in terms of beaver! These conditions amount to assuming a very simple economy. It was studied by P. Sraffa in the first chapter of *Production* of Commodities by Means of Commodities (1960, Cambridge, Cambridge University Press) which demonstrates the social division of labour reduced here to two branches producing simultaneously two goods.

Conclusions

1. Exchanges substitute relationships between goods/commodities for person-to-person relationships. This is why exchange relationships are generally anonymous, as we have seen. We will see in the last chapter of this book that this last peculiarity is *threatened* in the advanced state of society, i.e., in the capitalist economy.
2. Smith's twofold equivalence still plays a major role, which is to provide the foundation of a particular conception of commodities (defined here as goods and services produced for sale in the market). We have seen how Smith expressed this in a brutal way, when he looked for the principle on which the mercantile system—his foremost enemy—was based. According to Smith, this principle is grounded in a commonplace error, by which "it is easier to buy than to sell", and that it was by virtue of this principle that the mercantile system required the power of public authorities to ensure foreign trade surpluses, i.e. the import of gold. However, Smith claimed that this proposal did not stand up to the objections that what was bought with money was also bought with the products, and what was bought with products was in the final analysis bought with labour. In order to be able to maintain that what is bought by money was also bought by products and works/output, Smith had to confer on the products of labour a property that was considered to be the peculiarity of money, namely that of possessing purchasing power.[20]

So it was not so much the historical temporality that linked early states with advanced states, but rather the framework of a theoretical hypothesis which made wages the only component of prices in the early states of societies. The economy described in these conditions was a market economy, and its "early" dimensions should not be misleading. It was not the ancestor of the advanced states, but it was something else other than being a capitalist economy.

[20] To be sure, since Aristotle we have known that a good can be viewed by its possessor in two ways: as far as it may be useful to her, and insofar as it may be exchanged and thus *sold*. If this is the case, the good has an exchange value, but that does not mean that it has purchasing power. The generally accepted assumption up to the *Wealth of Nations* was that *regular* exchange could only be monetary, because only money had purchasing power.

In this economy, labourers are independent. They produce and exchange goods. They had all the qualities required for traders and merchants. Admittedly, they were wage workers, but they paid their own wages. It is through the exchange that they commissioned the work of others. The fact that these workers used tools and raw materials that were not capital would later worry Ricardo. But according to Smith, hunters no more accumulated bows and arrows to no end than they would accumulate beavers to no end. And it was precisely because bows were not accumulated for profit, that they did not constitute capital from Smith's perspective (as we shall see), even though they were certainly a means of production. Their appropriation remained limited by direct needs. As hunters desired, like everyone else, to improve their condition, they worked, and the productivity of their labour increased (slowly) as the market for their products extended and the division of labour developed (slowly). The first pages of Chapter 8 ("Of the Wages of Labour"), bear witness to this in an astonishing way: "In that original state of things, which precedes both the appropriation of land and the accumulation of stock, the whole produce of labour belongs to the labourer. He has neither landlord nor master to share with him".

> Had this state continued, the wages of labour would have augmented with all those improvements in its productive powers to which the division of labour gives occasion. All things would gradually have become cheaper. They would have been produced by a smaller quantity of labour; and as the commodities produced by equal quantities of labour would naturally in this state of things be exchanged for one another, they would have been purchased likewise with the produce of a smaller quantity. (WON 82)

We thus see clearly that "the early state" did not refer so much to a historical period, as to a very simple economy, without "owners and masters".

The study of this market economy model only took up a minor, although inaugural, place in the *Wealth of Nations*. The main question that Smith was seeking to answer was to understand why we (in Western Europe, in the eighteenth century) were so rich. Smith gave the following answer: because the enrichment which the division of labour had already permitted in the early state was accelerated in the advanced state by the accumulation of capital. This is what we will examine in the following chapters.

References

Benetti, C., & Cartelier, J. (1980). *Marchands, salariat et capitalistes.* PUG Maspero.

Brewer A. (1995). The concept of growth on eighteenth century economics. *History of Political Economy, 27.*

Duboeuf F. (2004), Prix réels, prix naturels dans la Richesse des Nations : de la réflexion éthique à l'analyse économique. *Oeconomia, Economie et Sociétés, 38*(8–9).

Dumont, L. (1977). *Homo aequalis.* Gallimard.

Dupuy, J. P. (1992). *Libéralisme et justice sociale—le sacrifice et l'envie.* Hachette.

Halévy, E. (1926). *The growth of philosophic radicalism.* The Macmillan Company.

Hill, L. (2009). Adam Smith on war (and peace). In Ian Hall & Lisa Hill (Eds.), *British international thinkers from Hobbes to Namier.* Palgrave-Macmillan.

Jacquet, J. (2007). *L'Économie politique smithienne et l'histoire: les rapports entre la Richesse des nations et l'école historique écossaise*, PhD, Université d'Évry-Val d'Essonne.

Kindelberger, C. P. (1976). The historical background. Adam Smith and the Industrial Revolution. In par T. Wilson et A.S. Skinner (Eds.), *The market and the state: Essays in honour of Adam Smith.* Oxford University Press.

Marouby, C. (2004). *l'économie de la nature essai sur Adam Smith et l'anthropologie de la croissance.* Le Seuil.

Marx, K. (1867). *The capital.* Progress Publishers.

Mathiot, J. (1990). *Adam Smith Philosophie et Economie, PUF, coll.* Philosophie.

Meek, R. (1971). Smith, Turgot and the four stages theory. *History of Political Economy, 3*, 1.

Mizuta, H. (1967). *Adam Smith library.* Cambridge University Press.

Smith, A. (1762/1766–1978). *Lectures on Jurisprudence.* In R. L. Meek, D. D. Raphael & P. G. Stein (Éds.), *The glasgow editions of the works and correspondence of Adam Smith.* Oxford University Press.

Young, J. T. (1997). *Economics as a moral science.* Cheltenham, Edward Elgar.

CHAPTER 7

The Accumulation of Capital

Under what conditions is the enrichment of all possible, when not everyone works and non-workers get rich the most? The whole difference between the early state and the advanced state of societies is contained in this question, which Smith raised immediately in the Introduction of the *Wealth of Nations*. He had already asked it in *almost* identical terms in the *Early Draft* text, probably written in 1763[1]:

> It cannot be very difficult to explain how it comes about that the rich and the powerful, should, in a civilized society, be better provided with the conveniencies and necessaries of life than it is possible for any person to provide himself in a savage and solitary state. It is very easy to conceive that the person who can at all time direct the labours of thousands to his own purposes, should be better provided with whatever he has occasion for than he who depends upon his own industry only. But how it comes about that the labourer and the peasant should likewise be better is not perhaps so easily understood. In a civilized society the poor provide both for themselves and for the enormous luxury of their superiors. The rent which goes to support the vanity of the slothful landlord is all earned by the industry of the peasant. The monied man indulges himself in every sort of ignoble and sordid sensuality, at the expense of the merchant and

[1] See R. L. Meek, D. D. Raphael and P. J. Stein (LJA 561).

D. Diatkine, *Adam Smith and the Wealth of Nations*, Palgrave Studies in the History of Economic Thought, https://doi.org/10.1007/978-3-030-81600-1_7

> tradesman whom he lends out his stock at interest. All the indolent and frivolous retainers upon a court are, in the same manner, fed, clothed, and lodged by the labour of those who pay the taxes which support them. Among savages, on the contrary, every individual enjoys the whole produce of his own industry. There are among them no landlords, no usurers, no taxgatherers. (Smith, LJA 563)

This text is extremely violent. Donald Winch (1978, p. 89) was surprised not to find it in the *Wealth of Nations*, while many other passages of the *Early Draft* are repeated word for word. It seems to me that this absence in the *Wealth of Nations* may be linked with Smith's novel consideration of the accumulation of capital, which depends on savings out of profits. This consideration necessarily then modified his point of view about "superiors" (as we shall see), in particular concerning interest-bearing loans, which were subjected in the *Early Draft* to very typical criticisms, that disappears completely in the *Wealth of Nations*.

To recall, Book I of the *Wealth of Nations* had two aims. The first was to explain enrichment by progress in the division of labour, such progress being self-sustaining as the extent of the market increased. This in turn was the cause and consequence of progress in the division of labour. The second aim was to understand the "natural" evolution of revenues, and more especially of the rates of wages, profits and rents. Smith wanted to show that wage and rent rates were positively correlated to the rate of growth of wealth, whereas profit rates were negatively correlated to the growth rate. The conclusion of Book I states this very clearly—although it is very rarely read. This is probably because it comes at the end of a fastidious chapter (even in Smith's opinion) on rent, and it is appropriate to quote this conclusion extensively here.

"The whole annual produce of the land and labour of every country, or what comes to the same thing, the whole price of that annual produce, naturally divides itself, it has already been observed, into three parts; the rent of land, the wages of labour and the profits of stock; and constitutes a revenue to three different orders of people; to those who live by rent, to those who live by wages and to those who live by profit. These are the three great, original and constituent orders of every civilised society, from whose revenue that of every other order is ultimately derived.

"The interest of the first of those three great orders, it appears from what has been just now said, is strictly and inseparably connected with the general interest of the society. Whatever either promotes or obstructs the one, necessarily promotes or obstructs the other. When the public deliberates concerning any regulation of commerce or police, the proprietors of land [the landlords] never can mislead it, with a view to promote the interest of their own particular order; at least, if they have any tolerable knowledge of that interest. They are, indeed, too often defective in this tolerable knowledge. They are the only one of the three orders whose revenue costs them neither labour nor care, but comes to them, as it were, of its own accord, and independent of any plan or project of their own. That indolence, which is the natural effect of the ease and security of their situation, renders them too often, not only ignorant, but incapable of that application of mind which is necessary in order to foresee and understand the consequences of any public regulation.

"The interest of the second order, that of those who live by wages, is as strictly connected with the interest of the society as that of the first. The wages of the labourer, it has already been shown, are never so high as when the demand for labour is continually rising, or when the quantity employed is every year increasing considerably. When this real wealth of the society becomes stationary, his wages are soon reduced to what is barely enough to enable him to bring up a family, or to continue the race of labourers. When the society declines, they fall even below this. The order of proprietors may, perhaps, gain more by the prosperity of the society than that of labourers: but there is no order that suffers so cruelly from its decline. But though the interest of the labourer is strictly connected with that of the society, he is incapable either of comprehending that interest or of understanding its connection with his own. His condition leaves him no time to receive the necessary information, and his education and habits are commonly such as to render him unfit to judge even though he was fully informed. In the public deliberations, therefore, his voice is little heard and less regarded, except upon some particular occasions, when his clamour is animated, set on and supported by his employers, not for his, but their own particular purposes.

> His employers constitute the third order, that of those who live by profit. It is the stock that is employed for the sake of profit which puts into motion the greater part of the useful labour of every society. The plans and projects of the employers of stock regulate and direct all the most important operations of labour, and profit is the end proposed by all those plans and projects. But the rate of profit does not, like rent and wages, rise with the prosperity and fall with the declension of the society. On the

> contrary, it is naturally low in rich and high in poor countries, and it is always highest in the countries which are going fastest to ruin. The interest of this third order, therefore, has not the same connection with the general interest of the society as that of the other two. Merchants and master manufacturers are, in this order, the two classes of people who commonly employ the largest capitals, and who by their wealth draw to themselves the greatest share of the public consideration. As during their whole lives they are engaged in plans and projects, they have frequently more acuteness of understanding than the greater part of country gentlemen. As their thoughts, however, are commonly exercised rather about the interest of their own particular branch of business, than about that of the society, their judgment, even when given with the greatest candour (which it has not been upon every occasion) is much more to be depended upon with regard to the former of those two objects than with regard to the latter. Their superiority over the country gentleman is not so much in their knowledge of the public interest, as in their having a better knowledge of their own interest than he has of his. It is by this superior knowledge of their own interest that they have frequently imposed upon his generosity, and persuaded him to give up both his own interest and that of the public, from a very simple but honest conviction that their interest, and not his, was the interest of the public. The interest of the dealers, however, in any particular branch of trade or manufactures, is always in some respects different from, and even opposite to, that of the public. To widen the market and to narrow the competition, is always the interest of the dealers. To widen the market may frequently be agreeable enough to the interest of the public; but to narrow the competition must always be against it, and can serve only to enable the dealers, by raising their profits above what they naturally would be, to levy, for their own benefit, an absurd tax upon the rest of their fellow-citizens. The proposal of any new law or regulation of commerce which comes from this order ought always to be listened to with great precaution, and ought never to be adopted till after having been long and carefully examined, not only with the most scrupulous, but with the most suspicious attention. It comes from an order of men whose interest is never exactly the same with that of the public, who have generally an interest to deceive and even to oppress the public, and who accordingly have, upon many occasions, both deceived and oppressed it. (WON 265–267)

This passage is as violent as it is illuminating. The three essential classes (or orders) have three revenues. Landlords were generally numbed by their own consumption of luxury, while wage labourers had neither the time, the training nor the political means to take part in public debate.

Only merchants and master manufacturers had the taste and means to share (in all candour) their political aims in line with their interests, with the country gentlemen governing the country.

The hegemony thus exercised by this class of merchants and master manufacturers was the simplest definition of the mercantile system: in other words, capitalism as a political moment. As we have seen, it was a product of European history, which had inverted "the natural progress of opulence", which Smith thought he had observed unfolding in the English colonies of North America.

He then therefore had to explain the sequence of investment which characterised the *natural* course of capital accumulation. This study was very ambitious because it had to start by explaining why capital accumulation began and then what its dynamics were: what sectors were first affected? What were the stages of this process? Smith did not answer this first question. By contrast, it is crucial that Smith demonstrated his thesis that a "natural" sequence of accumulation is conceivable, because its *inversion*[2] created the mercantile system, whereas the "natural" sequence would lead to a system of natural liberty, which Smith believed was sketched out in the English colonies of North America. The capitalist economy is studied as of Chapter 6, in Book I of the *Wealth of Nations*, entitled "Of the component Parts of the Price of Commodities". This economy is defined by the existence of two classes of non-workers: landowners who enjoyed the monopoly of landownership, which allowed them to have rents; and capitalists (whom Smith called "merchants and master manufacturers") who advanced funds necessary to pay workers, in view of obtaining profits. These new classes were thus identified by their incomes: rents and profits. Moreover, workers were mainly dependent workers (a point which struck Marx and which will be discussed in the following chapter).

I will first show (section "Capital and the Advanced State of Societies") how Smith defined capital more precisely than we often think, by distinguishing between capital and stocks. I will show that Smith defines what we call today investment through the employment of *productive* workers. This is an important, difficult and forgotten concept.

Section "The Dynamics Of Capital Accumulation" of this chapter studies the dynamics of the accumulation of capital that Smith draws out

[2] I will study this inversion p. 183 and sqq.

from his critique of the mercantile system. We shall see how Smith tried to show: (i) that the continued accumulation of capital leads to a downward trend in the rate of profit; the privileges (monopolies) obtained by the merchants and the manufacturers being obstacles to offset; (ii) that the continuation of capital accumulation results in an increase of rent and wage rates; and (iii) that *foreign trade* is necessary to avoid a fall in the rate of profit.

The first proposal is generally accepted by most economists who will defend it with very different arguments. The second is highly debatable, while the third was criticised by Ricardians to the extent that John Stuart Mill saw it as an absurd leftover of the mercantile system, even though Smith was the system's "*destroyer*" (Mill [1888] Chap. 17).

The demonstration of the first two propositions is the central aim of Chapters 6–11 of Book I of the *Wealth of Nations*, which conclude (as we have seen) with the solemn statement that the interest of the capitalist *class*, unlike the interests of the other two *classes*, is *always* opposed to the general interest of society.

The demonstration of the third proposition is the subject of Chapter 1, Book III, "Of the Natural Progress of Opulence", which I believe is central to the *Wealth of Nations*.

Subsequently, I will be able to turn to Smith's support of international free trade.

This approach to the dynamics of accumulation is very ambitious. The *answers* provided by Smith are not usually acceptable. But it is worth dwelling on them, to highlight these *issues* which are sometimes forgotten, being set aside as too difficult.

Two very important aspects of capitalist society are reserved for Chapter 8 of this book: the relationship of wage dependency and the relationship of financial dependency.

Capital and the Advanced State of Societies

The plurality of social classes is therefore an essential characteristic of the advanced state societies. Smith discovered simultaneously the accumulation of capital and the mercantile system. As I have already shown here in Chapter 4, it was probably among the Physiocrats that Smith found the name of his enemy—the mercantile system. But at the same time, and in contrast to Quesnay (along with Turgot),[3] Smith discovered that the net product contains not just a net agricultural product, but also profit.

The first difficulty concerns the very definition of the concept of capital, which not only refers to a stock of goods (i.e. a quantity that does not change during a period of time chosen arbitrarily).

Capital and Stock

We need to wait until Book II of the *Wealth of Nations* to study the effects of capital accumulation on enrichment. In the "Introduction" to this Book, Smith considers a situation of autarky, right from the outset.[4] Yet he immediately adds:

> But when the division of labour has once been thoroughly introduced, the produce of a man's own labour can supply but a very small part of his occasional wants. The far greater part of them are supplied by the produce of other men's labour, which he purchases with the produce, or, what is the same thing, with the price of the produce of his own. But this purchase cannot be made till such time as the produce of his own labour has not only been completed, but sold. A stock of goods of different kinds, therefore, must be stored up somewhere sufficient to maintain him, and to supply him with the materials and tools of his work till such time, at least, as both these events can be brought about. A weaver cannot apply

[3] Smith knew Turgot and flattered himself by the esteem and the friendship in which Turgot held him in his letter to Duc de la Rochefoucauld, dated 1 November 1785 (Smith, *Correspondence,* p. 286). The proximity of the two authors was great, (see: P. D. Groenewegen (1968) the same author, "Adam Smith, the Physiocrats and Turgot", *Elgar Companion to Adam Smith,* J. Young T. [ed.], Edward Elgar, Cheltenham, 2009). In Turgot's *Réflexions sur la formation et la distribution des richesses* emphasis is placed on the importance of capital advances in the circulation of the whole of the economy: the search for profit being viewed as an extension of the search for rent, just as capital itself is analysed as a generalisation of land, landed capital stock being the original form of capital: "Tout capital en argent, ou toute somme de valeur quelconque, est l'équivalent d'une terre produisant un revenu égal à une portion déterminée de cette somme" (Turgot 1766–1970, p. 154). This is the title of the Chapter LVIII, in which Turgot defines capital. All capital, whatever its form (money, land or goods), generates an income (interest, rent or profit). It follows that the profit is not analytically different from land rent. Once admitted, the principle whereby the owners of the land extract a share of output (which was not obvious), Turgot generalised profits to all owners. Assimilating profit with a quasi-rent was an idea which went on to experience a singular fortune, but which seems deeply contradicted by the *Wealth of Nations.*

[4] To my knowledge, this occurrence of autarky is unique to the *Wealth of Nations.*

> himself entirely to his peculiar business, unless there is beforehand stored up somewhere, *either in his own possession or in that of some other person*, a stock sufficient to maintain him, and to supply him with the materials and tools of his work, till he has not only completed, but sold his web. This accumulation must, evidently, be previous to his applying his industry for so long a time to such a peculiar business. (WON 276 author's italics)

If stock and capital are assimilated, as it is very tempting to do, then the distinction between market economy (early state) and capitalist economy (advanced state) obviously disappears. As soon as there is the division of labour (and therefore the market exchange), capital is necessarily mobilised.

Thus the first difficulty that I am going to address seems to lie in an incoherence of the *Wealth of Nations*: the beginning of Book II contradicts the "Introduction and Plan of the Work" by removing any relevance of the opposition between the early and advanced states of society. However, it is not necessary to assume such an inconsistency in Smith's book, as he also provides us the means to distinguish capital and stock.

As the reader has no doubt noticed, Smith takes care in suggesting that the funds necessary for a weaver may belong to him, or may be *advanced* by another. In the latter case, it is clear to Smith that this *advance* would not be granted if a profit were not expected by the person advancing these funds, proportional to the amount of the advance. By contrast, the consumer fund owned by the weaver is not used for a profit, but for future consumption. Moreover, it was noted above (see p. 146) that the first pages of Smith's chapter on wages are devoted to recalling the possibility (at least theoretically) that, in the early state of society, the surplus may be distributed proportionally to the quantities of wage labour. Consequently, and according to Smith, growth is conceivable without capital.

We will see that it is precisely this proportionality to advances—i.e. to capital—that distinguishes profits from wages in *Wealth of Nations*. So, as we shall soon see, Smith defines capital as a stock used by its owner in view of earning a profit in relation to its *value*.[5]

[5] Of course, it was still possible for the weaver to use his stock as capital. The separation of workers and the means of production (which was so crucial for Marx) are not logically necessary in the *Wealth of Nations*, even if it plays an important political role. We have seen that it was only transitory in the English colonies of North America.

Last but not least, Smith was very careful to distinguish two types of stocks right from Chapter 1 of Book II. He notes that the stock of resources of an individual or a society always breaks down into two parts. The first is the consumption funds (which includes non-rental housing); the second is the capital, i.e. the funds intended to produce a profit. Once again, the *intention* of its holder is a necessary condition (but of course not sufficient) which means that a stock is capital. The search of profit for profit's sake, the use of savings for accumulation and *not for future consumption* are what distinguish stock and capital in the final analysis, just as Smith distinguished the early state from the advanced state of societies.

From the beginning of Chapters 6 of Book I, Smith notes:

> As soon as stock has accumulated in the hands of particular persons, some of them will naturally employ it in setting to work industrious people, whom they will supply with materials and subsistence, in order to make a profit by the sale of their work, or by what their labour adds to the value of the materials. (WON 64–65)

This proposition (to which we need to return to in the next chapter) shows that a stock does not yield a profit, like a tree producing fruit naturally. And, the stock itself does not constitute capital, any more than the tree. Of course, this definition is problematic, as Smith knew well. It is not enough to look for profit to obtain it. It is only once the process of production has been completed and sales realised that the capitalist (or the investor) will know—perhaps—if the funds he has advanced were capital and if the accumulated stocks have not led to losses. For this to be so, the stocks must all generate the natural rate of profit, and therefore it must be assumed that competition between capitals will lead to the equalisation of profit rates. This ensures the social validation required for stock to be transformed into capital. Smith seemed to assume, as Ricardo explicitly did, that the economy will thus reach an *equilibrium*, in the sense that this situation designates a state of the economy in which nothing encourages agents to change their positions. But how was this situation to be reached? How could a merchant manufacturer know that the rate of profit was higher elsewhere? Smith knew perfectly well how difficult it is to answer this question, given that capitalists have trouble even knowing their own rate of profit. Smith begins Chapter 9 on the profits with a proposition that is difficult to contest: "Profit is so very fluctuating that the person who carries on a particular trade cannot always tell you himself what is the average of his annual profit" (WON 103).

However, he adds on the next page that one can get a rough idea of the average profit rate from the "interest of money". Intuitively, we understand then that it was (is) the community of capitalists—as expressed by the banking system and by financial markets that fix the interest of money—which organised(s) this social sanction. Yet this process was, and still is today, as easy to see, as it is hard to theorise. Everyone knows that if the rate of profit is lower than the expected rate, then either new capital needs to be reallocated, or the capitalist will face bankruptcy; i.e. will disappear. Smith's approach ought therefore to have given a prime place to financial and monetary relations (which largely covered the monetary policy implemented by the banking system) in the *Wealth of Nations*. However, as I will show in the last chapter here, Smith marginalised them, as the *Wealth of Nations* was practically built on the *denial* of monetary policy.

Wages, Profit and the Advanced State of Societies

Despite these difficulties, we can see that a capitalist economy manifests itself in its most basic form by the coexistence of at least two components of price, namely wages and profits. They are necessary and sufficient to define the advanced state:

> The value which the workmen add to the materials, therefore, resolves itself in this ease into two parts, of which the one pays their wages, the other the profits of their employer upon the whole stock of materials and wages which he advanced. He could have no interest to employ them, unless he expected from the sale of their work something more than what was sufficient to replace his stock to him; and he could have no interest to employ a great stock rather than a small one, unless his profits were to bear some proportion to the extent of his stock. (WON 66)

The wage rate and the profit rate are therefore now the two key variables in the distribution of income, since they make it possible to identify these components. And, to drive home the point, Smith added:

> The profits of stock, it may perhaps be thought are only a different name for the wages of a particular sort of labour, the labour of inspection and direction. They are, however, altogether different, are regulated by quite

> different principles, and bear no proportion to the quantity, the hardship, or the ingenuity of this *supposed* labour of inspection and direction. They are regulated altogether by the value of the stock employed, and are greater or smaller in proportion to the extent of this stock. (WON 66, author's italics)

It should therefore be noted that the inspection and direction activities carried out by the capitalist are supposedly types of work. These are certainly very important activities, but their remuneration is neither a salary nor a profit. A part of profits is undoubtedly devoted to them, but the *Wealth of Nations* is silent on this.

Capital is therefore neither a physical quantity (a factor of production as economists most often see it today) nor even a particular commodity (i.e. a physical quantity multiplied by its price). This is so, even if all goods (with rare exceptions)[6] are part of, or have been part of the manufacturer or merchant's capital, at some point in their existence. Capital is a *general* commodity, so to speak, because it exists only in relation to profit and therefore in relation to the rate of profit: a number per unit of time which has to be increased as much as possible. As a *general* commodity, capital has only one rival: money.[7] This generality expresses the fact that given equal rates of profit, capitalists *should* be indifferent to investing in one branch or another (although the *Wealth of Nations* considers one important exception to this norm, as we shall see). It is in this sense that capital can be considered as a "general" commodity. This search of profit for profit's sake characterises capitalism, both in the *Wealth of Nations* as well as in Ricardo's *Principles,* and in the work of Marx.

Productive and Unproductive Labour

It is therefore the existence of the capitalist class which in the final analysis distinguishes the advanced state of societies from the early state. This insatiable quest for capital is then detached from any direct or indirect private utility of its owner.

[6] "In some parts of Scotland a few poor people make a trade of gathering, along the sea-shore, those little variegated stones commonly known by the name of Scotch Pebbles. The price which is paid to them by the stone-cutter is altogether the wages of their labour; neither rent nor profit make any part of it" (WON 69).

[7] I will return to this relationship between money and capital in the last chapter of this book.

How is the accumulation of capital beneficial by its acceleration of growth, i.e. by enriching everyone? It is curious to note, as we saw in the previous chapter, that this acceleration does not manifest itself where one would have expected it in the first place. To be sure, the use of machinery is stressed in the first chapter of the *Wealth of Nations* as improving the productive power of labour. But, the accumulation of capital is characterised mainly by the allocation of profits to investment, conceived as the employment of *productive workers*.

Chapter 3 of Book II is devoted to the distinction between productive and unproductive work and has been much discussed.[8] I will simplify this here by noting that the distinction is ultimately based on a wage being paid to an unproductive worker which does not "return" to the employer in one form or another. By contrast, the wage *advanced* to a productive worker is only granted on the condition that it returns to the employer, with a profit after the sale of the product of labour. In other words, it is not the nature of the activity nor of the product which are decisive (although Smith insists on this point), but that of the motive for the payment of wages by the employer. Finally, productive work *does not cost* the employer *anything*. On the other hand, the wages paid to the unproductive workers (servants, military personnel or teachers) are "destroyed": they do not return to the employer, who in this case does not act as a capitalist. He spends his income and does not invest it. Logically, productive work is only productive when the employer knows that the funds he has advanced are "recognised" as capital. Thus, capital which may yield a positive profit *ex ante* may become ruinous capital *ex post,* while productive employment *ex ante* may turn out to be unproductive *ex post*. It is for this reason, I believe, that Smith was led to adding "objective" determinants (such as product durability) to differentiate between productive and unproductive work. This complicates the discussion unnecessarily.

Be that as it may, it is this allocation of profits to investment (in the employment of profit-producing workers) rather than consumption of luxury goods (the employment of unproductive workers) which ultimately explains the positive effect of capital accumulation on total income growth. Growth is thus the consequence of "parsimony".[9] Capitalists thus

[8] See M. Blaug (1968, p. 56).

[9] I must point out here a considerable novelty that separates the *Wealth of Nations* from *The Theory of Moral Sentiments*. We have seen here (Chapter 3) that in the latter, Smith strongly asserted the interdependence between the "rich" and the "poor": spending (on

are the parsimonious class *par excellence* and this is a class which employs productive workers. Once net income is defined, the *Wealth of Nations* states that the growth rate of the economy will depend on the proportion of net income which is subsequently allocated to productive employment. This is the positive effect of capital accumulation.

The Dynamics of Capital Accumulation

The Gravitation, Natural and Market Prices

The *Wealth of Nations* seeks to explain two very different phenomena: the first concerns the gravitation of market prices towards natural prices, and the second is the decline in the natural rate of profit. Smith suggests that both follow from competition. This is undeniable with regard to gravitation, but it is probably inaccurate with regard to falling profit rates.

Let us start with gravitation. Prices fluctuate in markets all the time, but Smith wants to show that these fluctuations are not arbitrary. Market prices gravitate around natural prices and therefore tend to conform to them, under pressure from competition. The distinction between market and natural quantities is often considered as the essential contribution of *Wealth of Nations*. This gravitation is studied in Chapter 7 of Book I, containing one of the most famous passages of the *Wealth of Nations.* Along with the metaphor of the "invisible hand", it lies at the origin of Smith's current renown. For Lionel Robbins, for example, it placed Smith

luxury goods) by the former creates employment for the latter. This relationship between the "rich" and the "poor" was modified considerably by Smith in the *Wealth of Nations.* On the one hand, extravagant spending is mainly undertaken by landowners. On the other hand and above all, in the *Wealth of Nations*, Smith widely highlighted a new type of behaviour, namely the "incessant" desire to "improve one's lot". This desire leads to parsimony, i.e. to *savings*. Workers' savings are necessarily scarce and are naturally intended to support future consumption and this is (by definition) the only kind of saving that exists in early state of societies. In contrast, savings by capitalists are abundant, and are intended to be used to employ "productive workers", with a view to future profits.

on the same level as Walras and Pareto.[10] The "central result", according to Robbins was of course this gravitation.

Even more recently, Arrow and Hahn began their *General Competitive Analysis* (*op. cit.*) with a thorough tribute to Smith, who, in their view, highlighted the property of markets they were studying.

I will show here that this interpretation may be exaggerated. Indeed, it is hardly clear that this chapter of the *Wealth of Nations* had the ambition which the modern theory of general equilibrium gave itself in the 1960s. As we shall see, Smith sought above all to understand how monopolies prevented the "natural progress of opulence". This "natural progress" was the one followed by the accumulation of capital that was first invested in agriculture (the countryside), then in the factories (the city), and whose "surplus" finally "disgorges" into foreign trade. This dynamic is central, because in the final analysis it justifies Smith's advocacy of free trade. And yet it has seemed unintelligible to Smith's most attentive readers. Hollander (1973) or Aspromourgos (2009) tend to consider these arguments, too, as dross which it is better to minimise or even sometimes to omit. On the other hand, Albert Jeck (1974) and Heinz Kurz (1992) have explored an alternative way to understand under what conditions it is possible to comprehend, if not share, these analyses of the *Wealth of Nations*. I will try to extend their approach.

Since Ricardo, the traditional, accepted reading has been to distinguish between the process by which magnitudes gravitate around natural levels on the one hand, and the accumulation of capital on the other hand. However, we will see that the *Wealth of Nations* combines these. This is one of the reasons for which I have placed gravity behaviour in this chapter. Yet two important notions need to be specified beforehand. The first concerns the notion of the "extent of the market", which I have already mentioned. The second is that of "effectual demand" that we will look at here.

[10] "Although Adam Smith's great work professed to deal with the causes of the wealth of nations"—"yet, from the point of view of the history of Theoretical Economics, the central achievement of his book was his demonstration of the mode in which the division of labour tended to be kept in equilibrium by the mechanism of relative prices—a demonstration"—"is in harmony with the most refined apparatus of the modern School of Lausanne" (Robbins [1935], pp. 68–69).

The extent of the market is the purchasing power present in the market, during a given period of time.[11] As we have seen, the extent of the market is therefore the product of quantity (per unit of time) multiplied by price. The extent of a *given* market may thus associates an infinity of price/quantity relationships. If the extent of the market is sufficient, then a price/quantity combination exists that will allow *at least* for the payment of wages at their natural rate and of profits needed to bring the quantity of a good thus determined to the market. Smith called this price/quantity combination "effectual demand", which therefore associates a natural quantity with a natural price that pays wages and profits at their natural rates, natural rates that once more are assumed given and hence known. This effectual demand will not exist if the extent of the market is insufficient. In this case, the good in question will simply not be produced.[12] That is why Smith took care to distinguish effectual and absolute demand (WON 73). A poor man could certainly wish to own a "coach and six", but such absolute demand has no effect because it lacks purchasing power.[13]

This approach to prices seems to have been common in the eighteenth century. Traditionally prices (in general) were defined as the relationship between the extent of the market (i.e. the purchasing power present in the market) and the quantity of goods present in the market.[14]

Smith assumed that the rates of natural wages were given: i.e. he assumed that they were common knowledge to all workers. Similarly, Smith assumed that all capitalists had knowledge of the rate of ordinary

[11] For example, if €10,000 of wheat is sold in a day, then this may be considered as the extent of the market.

[12] As we saw in the previous chapter, Smith explained for example that a porter would not be able to set up in a village.

[13] The difference with the contemporary view of demand (following Walras) is to be noted. In contrast to the market commissioner who calls out prices "by chance", absolute demand is taken into account "by chance".

[14] The extent of a market E (where there is purchasing power in the market) is defined by a product Qp. It follows that $p \equiv E/Q$, where p is the unit price and Q is the quantity brought to the market. This is an old definition, and can be found as such in Locke, for example: "He that will justly estimate the value of any thing must consider its quantity in proportion to its vent, for this alone regulates the price" (Locke, 1632, p. 66). *Vent* here refers to the extent of the market.

profits, in "each society, each locality": "There is in every society or neighbourhood an ordinary or average rate both of wages and profit in every different employment of labour and stock" (WON72).

The natural rates of wages and profits therefore defined natural prices:

> When the price of any commodity is neither more nor less than what is sufficient to pay the rent of the land, the wages of the labour, and the profits of the stock employed in raising, preparing, and bringing it to market, according to their natural rates, the commodity is then sold for what may be called its natural price.
>
> The commodity is then sold precisely for what it is worth, or for what it really costs the person who brings it to market. (WON 72)

It is the merchant who "brings the commodity to market" and who anticipates that his earnings will allow him to recover his advances and will provide him with the highest possible rate of profit. The natural price is therefore the price that provides rates of remuneration judged to be "natural" by agents in the "society" or the "locality" in question. To be sure, the quantity of good actually present in the market is not necessarily equal to the natural quantity that satisfies effectual demand.

"The market price of every particular commodity is regulated by the proportion between the quantity which is actually brought to market, and the demand of those who are willing to pay the natural price of the commodity, or the whole value of the rent, labour, and profit, which must be paid in order to bring it thither. Such people may be called the effectual demanders, and their demand the effectual demand" (WON 73). When the market price does not equal the natural price, agents see that profit and/or wage rates (Smith saw rents as being reserved)[15] are different to their natural rates and adjust their capital (or their labour) accordingly, so that the quantities brought to market are modified. Smith assumed that the market price would thus gravitate around the natural price until converging on it: "The natural price, therefore, is, as it were, the central price, to which the prices of all commodities are continually gravitating" (Ibid., p. 127)

[15] "The accidental and momentary fluctuations that occur in the market price of a crop fall mainly on the shares of the price going to wages and profits. The share going to rent is less affected" (WON 76). Indeed, rents are fixed by leases that cannot be adjusted to these fluctuations.

So what is at stake in this analysis? It is surely not the fact of market coordination via competition, which the "invisible hand" is meant to represent; a metaphor that Smith only used some 400 pages later (as William Grampp (2000) has remarked). The issue is simpler: it is a case of showing that if this regulation through competition is hampered one way or another, then the rates or remuneration will remain different to their natural level.

In fact, the rest of the chapter is entirely dedicated to emphasising this point. Having set aside "trade secrets" and "production secrets", which Smith said would not go unnoticed for long, as well as natural conditions (that affect for example "the rents of some vineyards in France"), he turns to "police regulations" such as corporations or apprenticeship regulations which he then attacks.

Smith's gravity analysis does not therefore study how interests are naturally identified, to draw on E. Halévy's expression (1901–1904–1995).[16] Instead, it aims to express economically the political collusion of economic agents and legislators, a collusion which Smith called the mercantile system. The political importance of this analysis should therefore not be underestimated.

Moreover, it should be stressed that the conventional character of natural wage and profit rates is different in the *Wealth of Nations* to Ricardo's analysis, which is largely organised around demonstrating the existence of a necessary relationship between the natural rates of wages and profits. That is why Smith's text must be taken at face value and each "locality" needs to be viewed as being defined by the community of capitalists constituting it, grounded on the convention, (the local rate of interest) relating to the natural rate of profit (as well as on the convention for wage rates). Each capitalist, as we have seen, is ignorant of profit rate achieved by others, and hardly knows his own. Wage rates also follow from convention, but as we shall see in the next chapter, they are to a large extent *public* information, even if numerous obstacles prevent its dissemination. However, there is little information which is as private as the profit rate actually achieved, and which summarises all the secrets of a private firm. These profits rates are hardly private knowledge and are certainly not public, as we have seen.

[16] Halévy is very careful on this point. Some of his readers are less so.

The Natural Evolution of Profit, Wage and Rent Rates

I turn now to some of the most difficult issues in the *Wealth of Nations*. The first concerns the fall of the natural rate of profit; the second, the evolution of natural wage rates and rent rates; while the third is about what Smith means by the "natural progress of opulence".

According to Smith, natural profit rates tend to fall. He attributes this to competition, but such attribution is not necessary. This led to misinterpretations, which is why Smith's attribution was criticised by Ricardo in the *Principles of Political Economy* and then by Marx in Volume 3 of *Capital*. They both sought to explain the decline in the natural rate of profits by other "circumstances".

Smith's position may be understood as follows. Each capitalist seeks accumulation for accumulation's sake, in a process that never ends. It follows that *if* the extent of the market is *given*, and therefore for a *given* state of the division of labour and so a *given* level of employment and technology, then manufacturers of commodities will naturally choose first the most profitable employment of their capital, and then progressively less profitable ones (again, we know *today* that while these assumptions are acceptable concerning the partial equilibrium (*local* functioning of a market), they are not acceptable in analysing capital accumulation in a given economy). Smith describes this process:

> As capitals increase in any country, the profits which can be made by employing them necessarily diminish. It becomes gradually more and more difficult to find within the country a profitable method of employing any new capital. There arises in consequence a competition between different capitals, the owner of one endeavouring to get possession of that employment which is occupied by another. (WON 352)[17]

This proposition must be examined. *Natural* profit rates fall when capital accumulation continues, *all other things being equal;* i.e. if techniques remain unchanged because *the extent of the market is assumed to remain*

[17] It should be noted that the fall in the profit rate is the natural consequence of the assumption about the constancy of the extent of the market, and not of competition. This is because the rate also falls if there is only one capitalist. Competition will be exacerbated as accumulation continues under these conditions. But it is difficult to assume that competition that is the *cause* of the falling natural rate of profit. I owe this comment to C. Benetti.

constant so that the division of labour is unchanged, despite the accumulation of capital. This is why natural prices (and therefore the *natural* rate of profit) must fall.

However, this is only an interpretation that extends Smith's central thesis that the division of labour is limited by the size of the market to capital accumulation as well, though the extent of the market will not be affected by the accumulation of capital. Again, the *all things being equal* clause is difficult to accept here. Nevertheless, it is possible to understand the thesis of falling profit rates as a prototype of the "trend laws" which appeared later in the writings of other economists, who were faced with the very difficult question of general interdependence. Smith, for his part, was content in Chapter 9 ("Of the Profits of Stock") to rely on the common *accepted* thesis that the rate of interest evolved in the opposite direction to enrichment. This idea served as a cornerstone for many "mercantilist" propositions which sought to demonstrate that a trade surplus was the expression (or the cause) of the enrichment of society by causing a fall in the interest rate. This proposition was also based on the empirical finding that interest rates were generally higher in poor countries and cities than in rich countries and cities.

The *Wealth of Nations* willingly adopted this thesis, while changing its significance. Hume, in his essay *Of Interest*, had already refused to associate the rate of interest with the quantity of money. Smith here stated that the interest rate could not be significantly different to the rate of profit. Smith also mentioned the idea that as the interest rate was the price of borrowed capital, it would be even higher when profit rates were high. Thus, the interest rate was "controlled" (*regulated*) by the rate of profit, and its decline should unambiguously indicate the decline of the latter.

According to Smith, the accumulation of capital tends (other things being equal) to lower the rate of profit. On the other hand, he also thought that it tends to raise the rates of wages and rent. Yet although the natural rate of profit tends to fall with continued capital accumulation, natural wage rates are never as high, Smith argued, as when the rate of growth of overall income is high. His argument was very simple: "The demand for those who live by wages, therefore, necessarily increases with the increase of the revenue and stock of every country, and cannot possibly increase without it. The increase of revenue and stock is the increase of national wealth. The demand for those who live by wages, therefore, naturally increases with the increase of national wealth, and cannot possibly increase without it".

> It is not the actual greatness of national wealth, but its continual increase, which occasions a rise in the wages of labour. It is not, accordingly, in the richest countries, but in the most thriving, or in those which are growing rich the fastest, that the wages of labour are highest. England is certainly, in the present times, a much richer country than any part of North America. The wages of labour, however, are much higher in North America than in any part of England. (WON 87)

It is not easy to determine the origin of these propositions on wages in the English colonies of North America, and I will not risk trying here. But we can see that Smith found this colonial situation to be exemplary.

If wage rates are proportional to the rate of growth of the economy, what about rent? Smith was clear: "As soon as the land of any country has all become private property, the landlords, like all other men, love to reap where they never sowed, and demand a rent even for its natural produce" (WON 67).

A first question is therefore to understand how the landlords may "reap where they never sowed", as everybody wants to reap where they have never sowed (Matthew: 26). But I will not answer this question.

However, from a theoretical point of view, rent raises delicate questions. There is an asymmetry between rent and the two other components of price, which Smith expressed by saying that the natural rates of wages and profit are the *causes* of high or low natural prices of commodities, while rent is *the effect* of these prices. This asymmetry is explained by the fact that the rent is paid independently of the advances that may have improved the soil. As a result, rent is therefore unrelated to both the capital advanced by the farmer and the wage labour the farmer employs. In order for the natural quantity of a commodity to be brought to the market, its price must be enough to repay advances, as well as to pay profit and wages at their natural rates: i.e. the price has to cover what Smith calls the *prime cost*. But sometimes the natural price is such that it can pay a "supplement" added either to the natural wage (if, exceptionally, the worker brings the commodity to the market), or to the profit (if, as usually happens, it is the merchant who brings the goods to the market). This proposition by Smith is curious: Why would the natural price be higher than the prime cost?

To answer this question, we may note that Smith sets out here a conflict between landlords and capitalist farmers, which is won by the former:

> Rent, considered as the price paid for the use of land, is naturally the highest which the tenant can afford to pay in the actual circumstances of the land. In adjusting the terms of the lease, the landlord endeavours to leave him no greater share of the produce than what is sufficient to keep up the stock from which he furnishes the seed, pays the labour, and purchases and maintains the cattle and other instruments of husbandry, together with the ordinary profits of farming stock in the neighbourhood. This is evidently the smallest share with which the tenant can content himself without being a loser, and the landlord seldom means to leave him any more. (WON 160)

Smith here described the landlord—in person—who *imposes* the ordinary rate of profits in the vicinity on the capitalist farmers. Such landowners were clearly visible (there was no spontaneous competition of capital here), and were in a position to impose the competitive game on the farmers and thus prevent them from appropriating rent. Because they had the monopoly of land ownership they could do so:

> The rent of the land, therefore, considered as the price paid for the use of the land, is naturally a monopoly price. It is not at all proportioned to what the landlord may have laid out upon the improvement of the land, or to what he can afford to take; but to what the farmer can afford to give. (WON 161)

This proposition may seem surprising. If the rent, which results from monopoly, is a component of the price, then how can the latter be qualified as "natural"? The answer to this question may require looking at the origin of the monopoly. Landownership is the heritage of a given social class. This monopoly of landownership is thus different in nature from the monopoly resulting from an artificial monopoly imposed by the manufacturers because of privileges they have obtained from the sovereign, or from a natural monopoly like that of certain wine-growing regions. Land rent then would not be the result of an impediment to competition, but that of a monopoly which may not be "natural", but is at least "historic", so to speak.

In any case, rent here clearly *follows* prices, as it results from the difference between the natural price and the prime cost; i.e. the sum of profits and wages paid at their natural rates.

Of course, the price of land still needed to be explained. Historicity was not enough. Who would own land that does not earn rent? Rent and landownership should be determined simultaneously. The *Wealth of Nations* did not ask this question.

By contrast, in the *Wealth of Nations* Smith strove to show that rents increase with income. This demonstration occupies the last chapter of Book I. Here I only set out the argument summarily. Smith's analysis of rent was based on two principles. First, a piece of land always produces a surplus of wheat; i.e. more wheat than is necessary directly or indirectly (in the form of seeds, tools, wages) to reproduce it. Second, and above all, this wheat will always find effectual demand; i.e. someone ready to work to acquire it. I propose interpreting this latter assumption as simply as possible. An economy is *always* in a state of underemployed, as is the case in economies where agriculture still occupies an important place.[18] On this basis, Smith classified, quite impressively, all goods to which natural resources are dedicated progressively, as societies enrich themselves. Accordingly, the only land that farming requires to remain fallow is assigned to grazing. Livestock is then a joint product of wheat whose price is zero, as the cost of fallow is zero. The effectual demand for meat then has to be sufficiently high for its price to become positive, so the land is reserved for breeding (and only then). Land that is still dedicated to wheat can then generate rent for its owners, just like land devoted to livestock. The same reasoning applies to all goods which were first joint products of self-consumption, and which gradually saw effectual demand appear. Specialisation may then take place, which leads to progress in productivity. Smith continued his analysis step-by-step (via wood and coal) through to mining products and mining rents, and finally on to the price of precious metals. This gave meaning to his complicated analysis. At each stage, rent increases and Smith concluded this long chapter as follows:

> I shall conclude this very long chapter with observing that every improvement in the circumstances of the society tends either directly or indirectly

[18] It should be noted that this was of course the case in the eighteenth century in Britain, as is indeed still the case today in our global economy.

> to raise the real rent of land, to increase the real wealth of the landlord, his power of purchasing the labour, or the produce of the labour of other people.
>
> The extension of improvement and cultivation tends to raise it directly. The landlord's share of the produce necessarily increases with the increase of the produce. (WON 264)

It was therefore necessary to show that general enrichment was always accompanied by the enrichment of landowners. We have seen the political importance of this proposition above.[19] Its theoretical foundation (the theory of rent) was quickly criticised, and Ricardo's theory of rent replaced Smith's. But Ricardo's arguments led to the same conclusions: landowners get rich with the accumulation of capital.

The Natural Progress of Opulence and the Invisible Hand

- The primacy of agriculture

In the fifth and last chapter of Book II ("Of the Different Employment of Capitals"), Smith tries to show that we can classify the sectors of activity (agriculture, manufacturing and "distant trade") according to two criteria. The first is that of *income* per unit of capital invested; the second is that of *employment* per unit of capital invested. Investments in agriculture would create more income and employment per unit of capital invested than for capital invested in manufacturing. In turn, investments in the latter sector would create more income and employment per unit of capital than capital invested in distant trade. Clearly, the argument used here is not always convincing and it is probably for this reason that this chapter is often omitted by commentators, or that Smith is criticised for having been influenced by the Physiocrats. Nevertheless, being less interested in Smith's results than in his questions, I accept without further discussion the theses that conclude Book II of the *Wealth of Nations* and which are devoted to the accumulation of capital.

So let us accept the idea that there is indeed a sectoral order of investments which maximises income *and* employment per unit of capital invested. In the next chapter (the first of Book III), Smith wanted to show that this order of investment would in fact be spontaneously preferred by

[19] See above pp. 162–163.

investors had it not been "reversed" by the mediaeval barbarism that had led to the mercantile system. This spontaneous order is referred to by Smith as the "natural progress of opulence".

Smith tried to explain how the accumulation of capital generates what could be called the *sectoral division of the economy,* to distinguish these three sectors from the division of labour studied at the beginning of Book I.

This sectoral division was hierarchical, and it needed first to be shown that the accumulation of capital necessarily *began* in the agricultural sector, as progress in the division of labour allowed the manufacturing sector to emerge, with capital *from* agriculture being invested in manufacturing. Finally, capital was *then* invested in distant trade. The important point in this development model did not concern its *results,* which are very questionable, as already noted. As I suggested, these results were predetermined by Smith's hypothesis that capital accumulation in Europe presented an *inverted* image of the natural course of opulence. The model was built on the basis of this inversion and Smith made every effort to establish this inversion. But the important *point* was the *question* asked, which was very daring. Indeed, Smith set out to understand the dynamics of capitalism, how it began in one sector of activity and then spread to other sectors which capitalism engendered in this very way. This is the question of economic development, which still remains today difficult to answer theoretically.

The first sector of activity concerned the production of goods that allowed individuals to survive (*necessaries*). Indeed, initially, the accumulation of capital could only concern goods essential for survival, first of all food, say, "wheat". Housing and clothing (other *necessaries)* were products linked to "wheat" but *self-consumed,* because they too were not exchanged, and therefore devoid of purchasing power. As mentioned above, Smith supposes that wheat was the *only* commodity which has *immediate* purchasing power over labour as the surplus of wheat always found mouths to feed. The exchange (if this term can be used here) of the surplus wheat for labour was therefore the only exchange of commodities to exist in this first stage; assuming that labour was available or resulted from population growth, and given the importance of labour in the creation of real wealth.[20] Agriculture therefore constituted the first sector of investment.

A second sector based on crafts and manufacturing, then follows. This sectorisation was combined with a division of labour, by a process analogous to that set out in Chapter 2 of Book I. But in this case, the hunters and armourers are replaced by farmers and craftsman, who are all capitalists:

> Without the assistance of some artificers, indeed, the cultivation of land cannot be carried on but with great inconveniency and continual interruption. Smiths, carpenters, wheelwrights, and ploughwrights, masons, and bricklayers, tanners, shoemakers, and tailors are people whose service the farmer has frequent occasion for. Such artificers, too, stand occasionally in need of the assistance of one another; and as their residence is not, like that of the farmer, necessarily tied down to a precise spot, they naturally settle in the neighbourhood of one another, and thus form a small town or village. (WON 378)

There follows a first proposition:

> Neither their employment nor subsistence, therefore, can augment but in proportion to the augmentation of the demand from the country for finished work; and this demand can augment only in proportion to the extension of improvement and cultivation. Had human institutions, therefore, never disturbed the natural course of things, the progressive wealth and increase of the towns would, in every political society, be consequential, and in proportion to the improvement and cultivation of the territory or country. (Ibid.)

As we can see, the relations between towns and the countryside are shown here to be *asymmetrical* due to the existence of an upstream and a downstream production. Towns allowed the countryside to achieve

[20] "As subsistence is, in the nature of things, prior to conveniency and luxury, so the industry which procures the former must necessarily be prior to that which ministers to the latter. The cultivation and improvement of the country, therefore, which affords subsistence, must, necessarily, be prior to the increase of the town, which furnishes only the means of conveniency and luxury. It is the surplus produce of the country only, or what is over and above the maintenance of the cultivators, that constitutes the subsistence of the town, which can therefore increase only with the increase of this surplus produce" (WON 377).

productivity gains because they provided markets with "the surplus" output of the countryside, though the converse was true only after a certain delay. This asymmetry was both characteristic (though it later disappeared completely from the economic analysis) and intriguing.[21] It was at the origin of the criticism of *agricultural bias* that was levelled at the *Wealth of Nations*.[22] However, sequence of "countryside (agriculture and mining) – towns (manufacturing)" was extended to "foreign trade":

> When the capital stock of any country is increased to such a degree that it cannot be all employed in supplying the consumption and supporting the productive labour of that particular country, the surplus part of it naturally disgorges itself into the carrying trade, and is employed in performing the same offices to other countries. (WON 372)

Towns provided outlets for surpluses produced in the countryside, but this was followed by "carrying" or "foreign trade", which provided outlets for surpluses produced by towns. These propositions would seem to negate Jean-Baptiste Say's later law of demand, and were strongly criticised by Ricardo and Stuart Mill. Yet it is possible to highlight the conditions that make them intelligible. This follows as agriculture occupied a key role in the analysis, being the point of departure. Albert Jeck (1974) has given a convincing explanation based on the asymmetry between towns and the countryside which characterised the *Wealth of Nations*, and he draws on three propositions in it.

Proposition 1: it argues that the fundamental form of exchange takes place between towns and the countryside:

[21] This was formulated by Turgot (1766–1970, pp. 160) "Il faut cependant observer que le laboureur, fournissant à tous l'objet le plus important et le plus considérable de leur consommation (je veux dire leurs aliments, et de plus la matière de presque tous les ouvrages), a l'avantage d'une plus grande indépendance. Son travail, dans l'ordre des travaux partagés entre les différents membres de la société, conserve la même primauté, la même prééminence qu'avait, entre les différents travaux qu'il était obligé dans l'état solitaire de consacrer à ses besoins de toute espèce, le travail qui subvenait à sa nourriture. Ce n'est pas ici une primauté d'honneur ou de dignité; elle est de *nécessité physique*. Le laboureur peut, absolument parlant, se passer du travail des autres ouvriers; mais aucun ouvrier ne peut travailler si le laboureur ne le fait vivre". This asymmetry necessarily disappeared when Smith is interpreted using modern price theories (see T. Aspromourgos (2009) or A. Witztum (7.2010).

[22] See for example, S. Hollander (1973, p. 286).

> The great commerce of every civilised society is that carried on between the inhabitants of the town and those of the country. It consists in the exchange of rude for manufactured produce. (WON 376)

Foreign trade then occurred beyond trade between towns and the countryside. Taken literally, foreign trade refers to all trade taking place with all areas outside the zone made up by a town and its surrounding countryside. This includes trade between towns and between places (for example, Genoa, Venice or Glasgow, Amsterdam and London). I will return to this at the end of the chapter.

Proposition 2: it is set out as of Chapter I of the *Wealth of Nations*, namely that the division of labour is less advanced in agriculture than in manufacturing, because agricultural production faces time constraints (seasonal, for instance), which do not exist in manufacturing.[23]

Proposition 3: there was a second difference between agriculture and the other two sectors. In the so-called primary sector, a significant share of the raw materials (the soil and its natural fertility, minerals, etc.) is *free*,[24] whereas manufacturing had to pay for all inputs. Thus, as has already been seen, the *Wealth of Nations* established a principle of sectoral interdependence which could be described as "diachronic". This principle guides the interdependence between an upstream and a downstream, in which agriculture and mines (the countryside) were upstream, while *foreign trade* was downstream. Factories (the city) came in between, transforming the raw materials produced in the primary sector into goods (commodities) sold through trade (locally between towns and countryside, and *foreign trade*). The natural price at which goods were finally sold had to be such that it paid for all the inputs added successively to "free" inputs supplied by nature. Smith could therefore assert that all of these activities were necessary to each other, and that the primary sector remained the priority.

[23] "The spinner is almost always a distinct person from the weaver; but the ploughman, the harrower, the sower of the seed, and the reaper of the corn, are often the same. The occasions for those different sorts of labour returning with the different seasons of the year, it is impossible that one man should be constantly employed in any one of them. This impossibility of making so complete and entire a separation of all the different branches of labour employed in agriculture is perhaps the reason why the improvement of the productive powers of labour in this art does not always keep pace with their improvement in manufactures" (WON 16).

[24] This signifies that opportunity cost does not apply here. This not was not absent in the *Wealth of Nations*, as it can be found in Smith's analysis of specialisation.

- Intersectoral dynamics

However, all this can explain the sectoral hierarchy set out in the *Wealth of Nations*, but not the dynamics which needs to explain the successive implementation of the three sectors.

The first chapter of Book III, which follows on from the one just commented on, describes a dynamic process according to which the "natural progress of opulence" implies that the (secular) order of investments chosen " naturally" by the capitalists would one in which agriculture leads to *foreign trade*, via manufactures. In addition, Smith deduced from this that such a "natural" course would be optimal, as we would say today. This is because it yields the highest possible rate of growth in value added and employment. The analysis of the process mobilised two propositions, on top of the previous three:

Proposition 4: Natural profit rates tend to fall.

Proposition 5: At *equal* net profit rates, an investor will prefer to invest near home than far away.

An interpretation of Proposition 4 has already been given above, so it is not useful to return to it. On the other hand, Proposition 5 is curious. In fact, the arguments used here typically combine economic considerations (the risk associated with the investment) and *aesthetic considerations*: as the *Wealth of Nations* notes, having one's capital "under [one's] view" presents very particular *charms*:

"Upon equal, or nearly equal profits, most men will choose to employ their capitals rather in the improvement and cultivation of land than either in manufactures or in foreign trade. The man who employs his capital in land has it more under his view and command, and his fortune is much less liable to accidents than that of the trader"... "The capital of the landlord, on the contrary, which is fixed in the improvement of his land, seems to be as well secured as the nature of human affairs can admit of. The beauty of the country besides, the pleasures of a country life, the tranquillity of mind which it promises, and wherever the injustice of human laws does not disturb it, the independency which it really affords, have charms that more or less attract everybody; and as to cultivate the ground was the original destination of man, so in every stage of his existence he seems to retain a predilection for this primitive employment" (WON 378).

This preference for nearby investment seems therefore to have been justified by risk. This however contradicts—to say the least—the analysis of risk developed in Chapter 10 of Book I, in which Smith rightly seems to consider that natural rates of profit are net of risk.[25] If this were the case, then there only remained the *aesthetic* dimensions which made it possible to order the preferences of investors in what seemed to be the three sectors of activity: at equal profit rates (net risk), investment in agriculture was preferred, because it was "more beautiful" than investment in manufacturing, while the latter was preferred for the same reasons to investment in trade. The reader will probably find such aesthetic considerations included in a theory of investment choice extravagant. But they may appear less so if one bears in mind the parable of the "poor man's son" (see Chapter 2). I will return to this in conclusion, because we find these considerations at the heart of Smith's "invisible hand".

But let us return to the dynamics of capital accumulation. In defending the idea that foreign trade, including re-exportation, is necessary for general prosperity, Smith argued that:

> When the produce of any particular branch of industry exceeds what the demand of the country requires, the surplus must be sent abroad and exchanged for something for which there is a demand at home. Without such exportation a part of the productive labour of the country must cease, and the value of its annual produce diminish. The land and labour of Great Britain produce generally more corn, woollens, and hardware than the demand of the home market requires. The surplus part of them, therefore, must be sent abroad, and exchanged for something for which there is a demand at home. It is only by means of such exportation that this surplus can acquire a value sufficient to compensate the labour and expense of producing it. (WON 372)

[25] "In all the different employments of stock, the ordinary rate of profit varies more or less with the certainty or uncertainty of the returns. These are in general less uncertain in the inland than in the foreign trade, and in some branches of foreign trade than in others; in the trade to North America, for example, than in that to Jamaica. The ordinary rate of profit always rises more or less with the risk" (WON 128). Commentators, such as Edwin West (1990) consider sometimes that Smith had forgotten in the last chapter of Book II what he had written in Chapter 10 of Book I.

This proposition, like others already cited, is not self-evident, and it is natural to feel the same mistrust that they later aroused in Ricardo. Indeed, he worried how any quantity of capital could *not be* used. Ricardo then quoted Say who showed that demand was determined by the conditions of production. Any supply of goods generates income which is spent and such spending is equal to the value of these goods.

In other words, all production generates an income which is always divided between consumption and savings. And the share that is saved is necessarily invested, except when there is a "lack of common sense", as Smith himself explained (see Chapter 8). This proposition was true not just at the individual level, but also at the level of a *given* economy. The idea that capital might be superfluous thus seemed completely absurd, at least as long as the profit rate was positive. Ricardo's concern was not therefore necessarily justified. Let us see why.

As I said, we are initially in the framework of a purely agricultural, capitalist economy, with the assumption that there are two goods: wheat and iron. During this first stage, the net product is made up of wheat, produced in the agricultural sector, while iron is produced jointly with wheat for self-consumption. The surplus of wheat is "exchanged" for the surplus of population. Let us assume this describes the "agricultural stage" of societies, and the rate of profit is then equal to r_a.

A first bifurcation then takes place, which introduces the sectoral division. The conditions of this bifurcation are only sketched out, as indeed are those of the division of labour between hunters and bowmakers in Chapter 2 of Book I. It must be assumed that the conditions of iron production evolve in a way such that certain capitalists (who produce both wheat to exchange for surplus labour and iron which they use themselves to produce wheat) anticipate *the appearance of an iron market*. The extent of this market is sufficient so that investments in the production of iron yield a rate of profit r_m, with $r_m = r_a + \pi_a$, where r_a is the rate of profit in agriculture and π_a is the "aesthetic premium" necessary to quit the "delights" of producing wheat (Proposition 5).

What holds for iron, also holds for all manufactured commodities, and so capitalist craftsmen and therefore towns develop: as craftsmen were not attached to a fixed place, they could group together in agglomerations and hence benefit from economies of scale that were not negligible (as we have seen).

These dynamics do not end there, because the relationship between towns and the countryside is not symmetrical. As the progress of the division of labour is faster in manufacturing (in towns) than in agriculture (in the countryside) (Proposition 2), the rate of growth of income and employment of the two sectors is not identical. Moreover, given that the change in profit rates decreases when the growth rate of real wealth is positive, it follows that the profit rate tends to fall more quickly in towns than in the countryside.

Is this development dramatic? No so, according to Smith: "[h]ad human institutions, therefore, never disturbed the natural course of things, the progressive wealth and increase of the towns would, in every political society, be consequential, and in proportion to the improvement and cultivation of the territory or country" (WON 378).

Indeed, a manufacturer, anticipating a decline in profit rates if he continues to invest in his factory or workshop (Smith chose the example of a blacksmith) would prefer to invest in agriculture, as the premium π_a would tend to disappear under the effect of falling profit rates in manufacturing. This switch in investment would however require available land. If this is the case, then a stable cyclical growth regime would be established. This was in fact what Smith boldly assumed to have happened in the English colonies of North America:

> In our North American colonies, where uncultivated land is still to be had upon easy terms, no manufactures for distant sale have ever yet been established in any of their towns. When an artificer has acquired a little more stock than is necessary for carrying on his own business in supplying the neighbouring country, he does not, in North America, attempt to establish with it a manufacture for more distant sale, but employs it in the purchase and improvement of uncultivated land. From artificer he becomes planter, and neither the large wages nor the easy subsistence which that country affords to artificers can bribe him rather to work for other people than for himself. (Ibid.)[26]

By contrast, in Europe, land was not available as it was held in large estates inherited from the Middle Ages and protected by the archaic laws of primogeniture.

[26] In the next chapter, I return to the importance of the analysis of wage dependency in the *Wealth of Nations*.

> In countries, on the contrary, where there is either no uncultivated land, or none that can be had upon easy terms, every artificer who has acquired more stock than he can employ in the occasional jobs of the neighbourhood endeavours to prepare work for more distant sale. The smith erects some sort of iron, the weaver some sort of linen or woollen manufactory. Those different manufactures come, in process of time, to be gradually subdivided, and thereby improved and refined in a great variety of ways, which may easily be conceived, and which it is therefore unnecessary to explain any further. (Ibid.)

This important proposal must be understood as "the artificer" suffering a decline in the profit rate, if he continues to invest. And it is to avoid this fall in returns that he switches to being a manufacturer. It is certainly a pity that Smith did not seek to "explain any further" how this transformation from "blacksmith" to "manufacturer" took place, even if he assumed that this craftsman was already a capitalist.

This second bifurcation therefore supposes that our craftsman anticipates an increase in the extent of the market by engaging in foreign trade, in order to avoid the fall in his rate of profit following his pursuit of accumulation. The blacksmith seeking to open up new markets thus provides us with the basic state of the core formulation that later shocked Ricardo. Indeed, Ricardo could certainly have asked why an artisan would raise "more funds than he could use". But all it takes to become clearer is to modify this last proposition, as I have just done, by adding the words "without incurring a drop in his rate of profit".

In Europe, a blacksmith who could not become a *gentleman farmer*, yet who nevertheless still wanted to continue accumulating capital, had to anticipate an extension of his market by *foreign trade,* in order to increase his profit rate further, or at least to avoid it falling.

Cosmopolitanism and the "invisible Hand" of the Wealth of Nations

It is now necessary to understand what Smith means by *foreign trade*. Does he mean international trade? Actually, it is not so simple. Smith wrote *The Wealth of Nations* and not *The Wealth of* the *Nation*. His use of the plural was certainly not due to chance, for several reasons. The first is obvious enough, as the United Kingdom (of England and Scotland) was (and is) itself a plurinational state. In addition, it had colonies, the most important being Ireland, making it an Empire. Finally, we have seen how the awareness of this colonial Empire, which was becoming immense and costly, was an important element in the political context in which Smith wrote the *Wealth of Nations*. Last but not least, the *Wealth of Nations* does not look at "one" economy, but the world economy as a whole, which is obviously not a "single" economy. Smith's idea of an economy was therefore different to how economists generally picture it.

In fact, Smith described an economy using the notion of neighbourhood. To support and clarify this, I will use three propositions that are in the *incipits* of three important chapters.

> 1. There is in every society or neighbourhood an ordinary or average rate both of wages and profit in every different employment of labour and stock. (WON 72)

And:

> 2. The whole of the advantages and disadvantages of the different employments of labour and stock must, in the same neighbourhood, be either perfectly equal or continually tending to equality. (WON 116)

This "neighbourhood" is therefore the area in which competition operates, and so equalises profit and wage rates, in the absence of any obstacle (natural or artificial).[27] Since Ricardo, it has been common to define economically the *nation* as the space in which capital is in competition. Profit rates would thus be equalised between London and Birmingham, but not between London and Lisbon. The identification of an economy with the national political space is thus a remarkable simplification. So, it may be asked whether Smith's "neighbourhood" was Ricardo's "nation". This may be doubted if we add a third proposition, which we have already encountered, to the first two.

> 3. The great commerce of every civilised society is that carried on between the inhabitants of the town and those of the country. (WON 376)

[27] The monopoly of landownership was historical, as we have seen.

This association of the city and its surrounding countryside constitutes a *civitas* or city-state, in the classic sense of the term. At the time, this was one of the frames of reference for political and social life, and would have been normal for Smith's readers. As Charles Tilly (1989) has shown, three political forms coexisted and were connected in mediaeval and modern Europe, namely: empires, kingdoms and cities.[28] The three preceding quotations testify to the importance of the city-state as the elementary unit of economic space within the complex political space of the British Empire. This *non*-coincidence of political and economic spaces seems to be typical of the *Wealth of Nations*. It therefore seems justifiable to take quotations 1, 2 and 3 literally, and to assume that the area in which the force of competition was exerted was that of the city-state, made up of one urban agglomeration (or perhaps several), surrounded by its adjacent countryside. Each city-state was therefore characterised by a set of natural rates of remuneration specific to it. However, these city-states were not independent islands from each other, since they were integrated into commercial networks through foreign trade. Capital therefore did circulate, but the rates of profit did not equalise. These networks were global and constituted the *general business of society* that was cosmopolitan in nature.

This is why the *Wealth of Nations* is about not the wealth of *the* nation. Again, a comparison with Quesnay is enlightening. His *Economic Table* was built on an initial *given* state of a "rich agricultural kingdom" which had reached the height of opulence and in which some classes advanced *given* resources *annually* (the productive class and class sterile) while the landowners spent a given income inherited from the previous year. The kingdom (the nation) coincided exactly with the economy. That was why the *general business* of the society was *clearly* described by the *Table*. The circulation of advances and net proceeds ensured the *annual* reproduction of the economy within a given political framework. Foreign trade was incidental, in the very simple sense that its loss (due to the war, for example) would not jeopardise the reproduction of the economy. The economy that Quesnay's *Table* shows was therefore entirely enclosed within the limits of the "agricultural kingdom". Smith knew this perfectly, as he described it clearly in the last chapter of Book IV of the *Wealth of Nations*. We must admit that what was obvious for Quesnay (and indeed

[28] *Cities and the Rise of States in Europe, A.D. 1000 to 1800,* Tilly and Blockmans (eds.).

for us) was not at all so for Smith. If this is so, it seems to me, it is because in seeking to understand the mercantile system as a historical phenomenon, Smith immediately thinks of it as being the result of the process of capital accumulation in Europe. Smith therefore characterised the mercantile system, and indeed the commercial society which resulted from it, by a sequence of sectoral investments: first in *foreign trade*, then in manufacturing and only finally agriculture. For Smith, this investment dynamics explained the mercantile system as being, as we have seen, the result of the inversion of the "natural course of the progress of opulence". For Quesnay (and for most later economic theories), the sectors of activity were *given*. But this was not so for Smith, who tried instead to *explain* how they came about.

Thereafter, economists (quite rightly) simplified their analytical framework. They assumed that the limits of nations (borders) coincided with financial and monetary spaces. There is no more dramatic example of this reversal than the destiny of Smith's metaphor of the "invisible hand".[29] In Chapter 2 of Book V, the invisible hand appears for the third time in Smith's writings. He mentions it in the "History of Astronomy", published after his death with the title *The Principles Which Lead and Direct Philosophical Enquiries Illustrated by the History of Astronomy*:

> Heavy bodies descend, and lighter substances fly upwards, by the necessity of their own nature; nor was the invisible hand of Jupiter ever apprehended to be employed in those matters. But thunder and lightning, storms and sunshine, those more irregular events, were ascribed to his favour, or to his anger. (Smith [1980, pp. 49–50])

The invisible hand of Jupiter obviously had ironic connotations which it partly lost in the *Theory of Moral Sentiments* (see Chapter 3 above) and in the *Wealth of Nations*, in which the invisible hand refers to certain unintended effects of human action. In the first book published by Smith, it refers to the spending of riches which provide employment for the poor, as we have seen. In the *Wealth of Nations*, the meaning of the invisible hand is more complex, but it is not difficult to disentangle, provided it is put into context.

As we have seen, Book IV of the *Wealth of Nations* is dedicated to a critique of policies inspired by the mercantile system, a system which

[29] See E. Rothschild (2002).

assumed the interests of merchants to be the same as the general interest. Having looked at the "principle" on which the mercantile system was based in the first chapter of this book, Smith examined in luxurious detail the laws implemented to ensure surpluses on foreign trade, the first law relating to protectionist measures. These measures were demanded by merchants and manufacturers, and Smith argued that they were all contrary to the general interest. It was precisely at this point that he used his famous metaphor:

"But the annual revenue of every society is always precisely equal to the exchangeable value of the whole annual produce of its industry, or rather is precisely the same thing with that exchangeable value. As every individual, therefore, endeavours as much as he can both to employ his capital in the support of domestic industry, and so to direct that industry that its produce may be of the greatest value; every individual necessarily labours to render the annual revenue of the society as great as he can. He generally, indeed, neither intends to promote the public interest, nor knows how much he is promoting it. By *preferring the support of domestic to that of foreign industry*, he intends only his own security; and by directing that industry in such a manner as its produce may be of the greatest value, he intends only his own gain, and he is in this, as in many other cases, led by an invisible hand to promote an end which was no part of his intention. Nor is it always the worse for the society that it was no part of it. By pursuing his own interest, he frequently promotes that of the society more effectually than when he really intends to promote it. I have never known much good done by those who affected to trade for the public good. It is an affectation, indeed, not very common among merchants, and very few words need be employed in dissuading them from it" (WON 456, italics are mine). Thus, each investor faces two contradictory forces. The first is the search for the highest possible rate of profit. This search tends to push the investor to look abroad if profit rates are higher there. Such behaviour was commonly accepted by all in the eighteenth century. Capital is mobile and subject to a centrifugal force, which is why Quesnay was weary of it. However, Smith added that there was also a centripetal force, namely the preference of investing at home (justified here by risk, although I have shown the weakness of this justification). It was the equilibrium between these centrifugal and centripetal forces which was evoked by the metaphor of the invisible hand. This is very different to market coordination.

Smith went on to add the following proposition which was seen as a direct attack on planning, 150 years later:

> What is the species of domestic industry which his capital can employ, and of which the produce is likely to be of the greatest value, every individual, it is evident, can, in his local situation, judge much better than any statesman or lawgiver can do for him. The statesman who should attempt to direct private people in what manner they ought to employ their capitals would not only load himself with a most unnecessary attention, but assume an authority which could safely be trusted, not only to no single person, but to no council or senate whatever, and which would nowhere be so dangerous as in the hands of a man who had folly and presumption enough to fancy himself fit to exercise it. (Ibid.)

It is possible that Smith's prodigious lucidity did indeed allow him to anticipate planning; but there is reason to doubt this. By contrast, it has enough just to read what is written to understand that a statesman had no reason to know anything about trade in tea, spices or cotton, or be concerned about them in any way. Reading the *Wealth of Nations* will not help at all, and even today a good management manual cannot substitute for the practical business experience which politicians lacks. If the statesman in all his "folly and presumption" believed he should get involved in commerce, he would necessarily fall into the hands of merchants, the most powerful of whom were the shareholders of the privileged companies.

On the other hand, merchants knew better than anyone where their interests lay. They had no knowledge of the common good for which they hardly cared. We know this, and Smith concluded Book 1 of the *Wealth of Nations* on this point. More novel was his insistence on the curious preference which led capitalists to invest "near their home" rather than faraway, at equal rates of profit. I have already commented on this strange proposition (see p. 192 and sqq.), which finds its full meaning here.

Indeed, Smith's position was not easy. He had to do two things. On the one hand, he showed that the mercantile system was "partial and oppressive" and resulted from the confusion of merchants' interests with the general interest. On the other hand, he showed that the search for profit for its own sake was the key to everyone's enrichment. Yet this latter assertion was menaced by "foreign trade". Why, after all, should capitals not all be invested "elsewhere", if profit rates are higher there? While the search for monopolies required contacts with local legislators, the search for profit was global. Moreover, Smith knew there was nothing more volatile than capital. As he wrote in the last paragraph of Book III:

> The capital, however, that is acquired to any country by commerce and manufactures is all a very precarious and uncertain possession till some part of it has been secured and realised in the cultivation and improvement of its lands. A merchant, it has been said very properly, is not necessarily the citizen of any particular country. It is in a great measure indifferent to him from what place he carries on his trade; and a very trifling disgust will make him remove his capital, and together with it all the industry which it supports, from one country to another. (WON III. 426)

Merchants were not therefore necessarily very loyal subjects, at least when they were not investing in agriculture: far from it. And they were not mistaken by menacing legislators to migrate to more comfortable habitats if necessary. However, why did Smith use the qualification "in a great measure"? He introduced this restriction because he believed there existed an obstacle to shifting movable wealth at equal profit rates, because investors preferred to invest close to home rather than further away. The centrifugal force of the insatiable search for profit was fortunately balanced by a centripetal force which kept capitalists at home. The invisible hand supposed—no more or less—this balance of forces.

Capitalists, by maximising profits, and *in as far as they preferred to invest at home rather than faraway*, in fact behaved unknowingly in accordance with the public interest. They were therefore led to pursuing a goal they knew nothing about. By contrast, when seducing legislators by proposing especially elegant systems which only they—the capitalists—could imagine, would allow them to obtain the monopoly profits they coveted. Here, as I have already pointed out, Smith warned legislators most strongly against capture by merchants: they know what is good for them but ignore the common good. They should therefore stick to their affairs and not feign concern for public affairs. This situation hardly corresponds to the miracles of market coordination. I want to emphasise again that the class of merchants and manufacturers were the target of Smith's critique. Smith thus stood apart from the denunciation, which became ritualised, of *specific* demands of *individual* industrialists or traders seeking State protection or subsidies.

Understanding what the general interest meant was not the business of merchants, or shopkeepers as Smith sometimes called them. It was the business of legislators.

References

Aspromourgos, T. (2009). *The science of wealth: Adam Smith and the framing of political economy*. Routledge.

Blaug, M. (1968). *Economic theory in retrospect*. Cambridge University Press.

Grampp W. (2000). What did Smith mean by the invisible hand?. *Journal of Political Economy, 108*(3).

Groenewegen, P. D. (1968). Turgot and Adam Smith. *Scottish Journal of Political Economy, 15*(3), 271–287.

Groenewegen, P. D. (2009). Adam Smith, the physiocrats and Turgot. In J. T. Young (Ed.), *Elgar companion to Adam Smith*. Edward Elgar.

Halévy, E. (1926). *The growth of philosophic radicalism*. The Macmillan Company.

Hollander, S. (1973). *The economics of Adam Smith*. The University of Toronto Press.

Jeck, A. (1974). The macrostructure of Adam Smith's theoretical system: A reconstruction. *The European Journal of the History of Economic Thought, 1*(3), 551–576.

Kurz, H. (1992). Adam Smith on foreign trade: A note on the 'vent for surplus' argument. *Economica, 59*(236), 475–481.

Locke J. (1632–1704). *Some considerations of the consequences of the lowering of interest*…. https://la.utexas.edu/users/hcleaver/368/368LockeSomeConsiderationsAlltable.pdf

Meek R. L., Raphael D. D. and Stein P. J. ed. (1978). Adam Smith, *Lectures on Jurisprudence, The Glasgow edition of the works and correspondence of Adam Smith*. Oxford University Press (Clarendon Press).

Mill, J. S. (1888). *Principles of political economy* (6th ed.). Longmans.

Robbins, L. (1935). *An essay on the nature and significance of economic science*. Macmillan.

Rothschild, E. (2002). *Economic sentiments. Adam Smith, condorcet and the enlightment*. Harvard University Press.

Smith, A. (1980). *Essays on philosophical subjects, with Dugald Stewart's 'Account of Adam Smith'*. In W. P. D. Wightman, J. C. Bryce and I. S. Ross (Eds.)

Tilly, C. (1989). Cities and states in Europe 1000–1800. *Theory and Society, 18*(5), 563–584.

Turgot. (1766–1970). *Réflexions sur la formation et la distribution des richesses*, 1766, *in* Turgot, *Écrits économiques*. Paris, Calmann-Lévy.

Turgot, A. R. J. (1970). *Ecrits economiques*. Calmann-Lévy.

West, E. (1990). *Adam Smith and modern economics*. Edward Elgar.

Winch, D. (1978). *Adam Smith's politics*. Cambridge University Press.

Witztum A. (2010). Interdependence, the invisible hand, and equilibrium in Adam Smith. *History of Political Economy, 42*(1).

CHAPTER 8

Employment, Money and Interest in the *Wealth of Nations*

Smith associates the accumulation of capital and hence the advanced state of societies, with wage dependency. But he does not explain this relationship. In a little less enigmatic way, he associates bank money and financial relationships with the accumulation of capital.

Employing a worker, borrowing or lending are the all activities that share the fact of removing, at least partially, the *anonymity* that characterises market exchange relations, as the relationship of wage dependency implies the subordination of the worker to *his (or her)* sole employer, while the borrower is bound to *his (or her)* creditor by a *promise* made to the latter.

Smith never states that these new dependency relationships (in wage earning and finance) are *necessary* in defining the advanced state. However, he stresses that they are frequent, that they are sources of common conflicts and that government measures are required to mitigate their effects. Yet these dependency relationships are not the main cause of Smith's deep concern.[1]

[1] We saw in Chapter 5 that Smith most feared the political dangers which the mercantile system placed on Britain.

D. Diatkine, *Adam Smith and the Wealth of Nations*, Palgrave Studies in the History of Economic Thought, https://doi.org/10.1007/978-3-030-81600-1_8

Nevertheless, this chapter does testify to Smith's limited confidence in the spontaneous order of the market in such important areas as employment, interest and money.[2]

I will start by looking at how Smith addressed wage dependency, which manifests itself by the emergence of various forms of violence in economic relationships (section "Wage Dependency"). I will then study financial dependency, which also causes turmoil during banking and financial crises. This will provide us with the opportunity to highlight the role of a curious character, namely the "projector" who has a troubling resemblance with the "son of the poor man" studied in Chapter 3. Moreover controlling projectors requires a rule: the state must set a maximum limit on the interest rate (section "The Two Theories of Money in the Wealth of Nations and the Disqualification of Gold").

Wage Dependency

Two phenomena are brought together by Smith to describe the wage relationship in advanced states.

The first phenomenon stems from the presence of non-workers (landowners and capitalists), and of course from their incomes (rent and profit). Both of which we have just studied it.

The second phenomenon is that of subordination or dependency of workers to their employer.

Smith points out that in advanced states, workers are most often dependent on their masters. According to him, the ratio throughout Europe of the number of self-employed workers to those working under the authority of a master was 1–20 (WON, 83). Smith was sensitive to such dependency, as he described it as a form of oppression, as we shall see, because this wage relationship is special and very different from an exchange relationship. Smith was very clear on this point.

Wage dependency is therefore not expressed in the *Wealth of Nations* by the mere addition of a new market—a market for labour or for labour power—alongside other markets. Instead, it expresses a ***new type*** of economic relationship.

[2] Some macroeconomic issues of the *Wealth of Nations*, though very different to those we tackle in this chapter, did not escape the attention of J. R. Hicks (1990). In his posthumous text Hicks notes: "I shall show that he [Keynes] had mighty predecessors, the most important being no other than Adam Smith".

The presentation of the advanced state of societies is, as we have seen, done in the following famous terms:

> As soon as stock has accumulated in the hands of particular persons, some of them will naturally employ it in setting to work industrious people, whom they will supply with materials and subsistence, in order to make a profit by the sale of their work, or by what their labour adds to the value of the materials. (WON, 66–65)

We know how much this sentence sparked Marx's indignation:

> Stop, before we follow the passage further. In the first place, whence come the 'industrious people' who possess neither means of subsistence nor materials of labour – people who are hanging in mid-air? If we strip Smith's statement of its naïve phrasing, it means nothing more than: capitalist production begins from the moment when the conditions of labour belong to one class, and another class has at its disposal only labour-power. This separation of labour from the conditions of labour is the precondition of capitalist production. (Marx, 1863, p. 246)

The indignation of Marx here summarises his attitude towards Smith: for Marx, Smith's formulation is "naïve", and it is precisely this "naivety" that allows him (Marx) to see and therefore to say what others cannot, and so understand what became Marx's theory of exploitation and surplus value.

For Smith went on almost immediately to add:

> The value which the workmen add to the materials, therefore, resolves itself in this case into two parts, of which the one pays their wages, the other the profits of their employer upon the whole stock of materials and wages which he advanced. He could have no interest to employ them, unless he expected from the sale of their work something more than what was sufficient to replace his stock to him; and he could have no interest to employ a great stock rather than a small one, unless his profits were to bear some proportion to the extent of his stock. (WON, ibid.)

Marx then emphasised how close Smith was to his own theory of surplus value. According to Marx,[3] Smith finally abandoned the view which Marx found in Steuart (*Theories of surplus value*, I, Steuart) that profit could

[3] Ibid.

only exist as a result of exchanges out of equilibrium ("profit upon alienation"). Yet in the *Wealth of Nations*, profit exists even when a commodity is sold for what it is worth. There are only two steps left to reach Marx's theory. First, we must distinguish between labour itself which cannot be a commodity and labour power which, according to Marx, is a commodity. Second, a common explanatory principle needs to be found for rent, interest and profit (i.e. surplus value), in order to render the Smith's theory coherent, from the point of view of Marx.

Nevertheless, what sparked Marx's indignation, as we have seen, was the fact that Smith ignored the historical process that the presence of "industrious people" implied. Primitive accumulation is completely absent in the *Wealth of Nations*, even though the very terminology used by Smith calls for it. How did societies go from the early state to the advanced state? How and why did "industrious people"—still called proletarians today—emerge? The very close proximity of these two authors and the very great distance that separates them at the same time can be expressed from Marx's *point of view*.

But is it also expressed from Smith's *point of view*? Was Smith the innocent herald of Marx's theories? It is probably difficult to answer these questions directly. But, as I showed previously, we may propose an alternative interpretation to Marx's.

It is true that the formulation "As soon as there is …" *evokes* a historical development and that is how Marx interpreted it. In fact, if one assimilates the early state with the hunter-gather society, and the advanced state with commercial society, then it becomes necessary to account for the passage of one stage to another (via the other stages envisaged by the Scottish School of History), within *general theory of history*. However, the need to understand the transition between the two models of *economic theory* disappears, if we adopt the view (as I have already noted) that the early state is distinguished from the advanced state not because the latter was generated (indirectly) by the former, but because they are actually two different economic models.

This interpretation draws a line between economic theory and the science of history. It distances Smith from Marx, and it allows us to recall the very important difference in approach between these two authors regarding labour.

It should be recalled here that Smith put forward two concepts of labour. The first makes labour "the first price" that initially paid for all things (we have seen that labour in this case confers a title of ownership).

The second concept of labour sees labour as productive work. The use of the productive labour of the worker "the labour of a manufacturer adds, generally, to the value of the materials which he works upon, that of his own maintenance, and of his master's profit. The labour of a menial servant, on the contrary, adds to the value of nothing" (WON, 330). This is not the place to study the considerable impact on the history of ideas of how these two concepts came together.[4] I will therefore limit my analysis to the effects of how these two concepts are brought together in the *Wealth of Nations*.

In Chapter 4 of this book, I showed that Smith remained faithful to the old conception of labour which makes it the original title of property. Whoever gives up their labour thus gives up their title to the product of their activity, which then becomes the "product of labour" belonging to the master. This view turned the employer into a worker *par excellence* (helped by *his* "collaborators", i.e. members of *his* household, including *his* wife, children, employees, possibly slaves and beasts of burden). It was a view that was no more shocking in the eighteenth century than it is today.

However, Smith was studying the boundary between self-employment and dependent work. This is why Smith studied various forms of work dependency, from slavery to modern wage labour, in both the *Lectures on Jurisprudence* and in the *Wealth of Nations.*

Slavery is, of course, the extreme case of dependency. According to Smith, slavery is not only immoral but also inefficient,[5] because the more dependent labour is, the lower its productivity is, as Smith shows, for example, in Chapter 2 of Book III of the *Wealth of Nations*. Serfdom, for its part, was characterised by the workers' dependence on the land and resulted from an evolution of agricultural slavery that extended via serfdom through to sharecropping. Outside of agriculture, serfdom was extended by the menial domestic work of servants. From this point of

[4] The interconnection between the concepts of labour generating property rights and labour generating profit lies at the origin of the thesis according to which the worker is the sole, legitimate owner of the product of his labour and the corollary that labour appropriated by non-workers is therefore the result of theft. We know that this popular thesis was strongly criticised by Marx, from the *Poverty of Philosophy* through to the *Critique of the Gotha Program*.

[5] On this see A. Lapidus (2002). Smith's thesis of the inefficiency of slavery will be reused by opponents of slavery. It is now largely abandoned since the work of Fogel and Engerman (1974).

view, in the *Lectures on Jurisprudence* Smith refers to a very characteristic indication during the first discussion of the gravitation mechanism. Smith argues that wage rates should adjust to the price of wheat, since the price of wheat's capacity to command labour is constant. While discussing this idea, whose role in the *Wealth of Nations* we have already seen, Smith remarked (in contradiction to his thesis) that there is, in fact, an inverse relationship between variations in the price of wheat and those of monetary wages. This latter observation contradicts Smith's own argument that, in the event of *falls* in the price of wheat, market wages do not adjust to the falls but in fact *increase*. This is because servants prefer to establish themselves as self-employed workers in this case. Indeed, in the *Lectures on Jurisprudence* Smith states that: "Every one abhors naturally the subjected and mean condition of a meniall (sic) servant, liable to the caprice and extravagance of a master; he [the labourer] will work for days wages much more willingly than become your servant" (LJ(A), vi.79). Working for daily wages, of course, means being a daily labourer, leasing one's "hands" for a limited time (by the day, for example, or by job) and always to different employers. Domestic subjugation is thus a sufficiently disgusting situation that labourers prefer, as soon as possible, to work daily or do piecework, leasing out their hands to accomplish *particular* tasks and so escape subordination to a single master. Moreover, and above all, this refusal of servitude concerned not only servants, as labourers in workshops would also endeavour to become self-employed where possible. Indeed, Smith added immediately that in case of real wage increases (consecutive to a drop in the price of wage goods): "The maid servant who had been employed at spinning sets up for herself, though before she could not have lived by her own labour" (LJ(A), 79).

This "maid servant" is representative in the *Wealth of Nations* of the modern wage condition, as this analysis is found again in Chapter 8 of Book I. Why is the condition of servants or dependent labourers not only ineffective, but also despicable?

The servant is subject to the capriciousness of his (her) master as he (or she) is part of his household. Smith saw clearly, as everyone knew at the end of the eighteenth century,[6] that domestic service was practically a servile condition, because anonymity was virtually non-existent while dependency was almost total. Servants were largely paid in-kind and their preferences were imposed on them by their master. This condition existed not only for servants. It was very often shared by apprentices and journeymen working for master craftsmen. They could only marry and start a family if they managed to *establish* themselves, that is to say to set up on their own account. From this point of view, the worker (or hired labourer), who went every morning to sell his labour on the Place de Grève in Paris, for example, was able to come to the market to rent out his services to different employers. And, if he had a conflict with one employer, he could still look for other work, by going *en grève* and returning to the *Place de Grève* to find another employer.[7] There was therefore, according to Smith, a continuity between the servile condition and that of the dependent worker. It was accompanied by increasing productivity which further increased when workers became self-employed and hence independent.

Strictly speaking, and even if Smith's vocabulary (like Locke's) suggested that the wage rate was the "price of labour", the worker did not sell anything to his (or her) employer, but entered into the service (in his/her "house") giving up to the master his/her title to the product of labour. That is why, ultimately, dependent workers *are not merchants*.

If a spinner works for a master, then it was (according to Smith), because the prices of the goods and the means of production were such that she could not live "alone" from her work, and could not use it for herself. She was *forced* (she had no choice) to become dependent on a master. We find an echo of this idea in Marx when he showed that workers had to be "free" to sell their labour power, and that this "freedom" was

[6] This theme was one of the classics of the era. An illustrative example highlights this well. In 1773, the French polymath and playwright Pierre-August de Beaumarchais managed to get his play *The Barber of Seville* staged at the Comédie-Française, and in 1778 he wrote the *Mariage of Figaro*. As we know, in the first of these plays Figaro was an independent barber who helped Count Almaviva kidnap Rosine, while in the second play he has become a servant of the Count. Figaro's almost servile condition is then expressed in his conflict with his master when the latter wants to exercise his *primae noctis* right to bed Suzanne first when she marries Figaro.

[7] In the nineteenth century, the meaning of this expression changed totally, as *en grève* came to mean going on strike.

"conferred" on them by the primitive accumulation of capital which separated them from the means of production. It was under this condition that workers were (are) sellers of the enigmatic commodity which was (is) their labour power.[8] Admittedly, Marx looks at why the wage rate does not appear for what he thought it to be, namely as the price of labour power, because in real life, the price presents itself as the "price of labour". This "conceals the free labour of the employee for the capitalist". For his part, Smith frequently spoke about the natural price and the current price of labour, but he suggested that what was presented as a price was in fact not one.

We can clearly see a misunderstanding here. For Marx, the wage rate was indeed a price, although it was not clear what the price was for, namely labour power. For Smith, the wage rate resembled a price, but it was not really one, because the wage dependency relationship is not an exchange relationship.

The description of this dependence in the *Wealth of Nations* is that of an impressive source of violence, which was only later found in Marx. This is shown in a text in Chapter 8 of Book I, "Of the Wages of Labour", which should be quoted in full. Having shown how, in the early state of society, the increase of the wage rate and hence the enrichment of independent workers were possible (see *above,* pp. 141 and sqq.), Smith added: "But this original state of things, in which the labourer enjoyed the whole produce of his own labour, could not last beyond the first introduction of the appropriation of land and the accumulation of stock. It was at an end, therefore, long before the most considerable improvements were made in the productive powers of labour, and it would be to no purpose to trace further what might have been its effects upon the recompense or wages of labour" (WON, I, 82).

In the advanced state, the worker therefore no longer enjoys "all the product of his labour", because, as we have seen, the master must advance wages and the means of production, and will not do so if he (the master) does not expect a profit.

Let us now see how Smith describes the fixing of the wage rate in an advanced state, i.e. in a capitalist economy: "What are the common wages of labour depends everywhere upon the contract usually made

[8] It may be noted that Marx (in Section II of Book I of *Capital*) was perhaps the first to equate the wage rate with a price (that of labour power), which supposed to obey the general laws governing prices.

between those two parties, whose interests are by no means the same. The workmen desire to get as much, the masters to give as little as possible. The former are disposed to combine in order to raise, the latter in order to lower the wages of labour" (WON, 83).

Apparently, we are dealing here with a description of "bargaining" which is identical to the bargaining that is supposed to take place between two traders. But, as I have shown, market bargaining or negotiation is, in a way, *silent*, as goods and their prices "speak" in the place of individuals (when there is no asymmetric information about the quality of products, which is considered to be normal). But here, we are not dealing with silence, but with *war*. In the course of the wage "bargaining", the silence is broken, and we can also draw attention to another asymmetry which concerns the speakers. Workers *shout* in the *street,* whereas employers, in the first instance, act in the *secrecy* of *their workshops*. Indeed, Smith immediately pointed out that in this *siege warfare*, employers can hold out longer:

> "It is not, however, difficult to foresee which of the two parties must, upon all ordinary occasions, have the advantage in the dispute, and force the other into a compliance with their terms. The masters, being fewer in number, can combine much more easily; and the law, besides, authorises, or at least does not prohibit their combinations, while it prohibits those of the workmen. We have no acts of parliament against combining to lower the price of work; but many against combining to raise it. In all such disputes the masters can hold out much longer"... "We rarely hear, it has been said, of the combinations of masters, though frequently of those of workmen. But whoever imagines, upon this account, that masters rarely combine, is as ignorant of the world as of the subject. Masters are always and everywhere in a sort of tacit, but constant and uniform combination, not to raise the wages of labour above their actual rate. To violate this combination is everywhere a most unpopular action, and a sort of reproach to a master among his neighbours and equals. We seldom, indeed, hear of this combination, because it is the usual, and one may say, the natural state of things, which nobody ever hears of. Masters, too, sometimes enter into particular combinations to sink the wages of labour even below this rate. These are always conducted with the utmost silence and secrecy, till the moment of execution, and when the workmen yield, as they sometimes do, without resistance, though severely felt by them, they are never heard of by other people. Such combinations, however, are frequently resisted by a contrary defensive combination of the workmen; who sometimes too, without any provocation of this kind, combine of their own accord to raise the price

of their labour. Their usual pretences are, sometimes the high price of provisions; sometimes the great profit which their masters make by their work. But whether their combinations be offensive or defensive, they are always abundantly heard of. In order to bring the point to a speedy decision, they have always recourse to the loudest clamour, and sometimes to the most shocking violence and outrage. They are desperate, and act with the folly and extravagance of desperate men, who must either starve, or frighten their masters into an immediate compliance with their demands. The masters upon these occasions are just as clamorous upon the other side, and never cease to call aloud for the assistance of the civil magistrate, and the rigorous execution of those laws which have been enacted with so much severity against the combinations of servants, labourers, and journeymen. The workmen, accordingly, very seldom derive any advantage from the violence of those tumultuous combinations, which, partly from the interposition of the civil magistrate, partly from the necessity superior steadiness of the masters, partly from the necessity which the greater part of the workmen are under of submitting for the sake of present subsistence, generally end in nothing, but the punishment or ruin of the ringleaders". (WON, 84)

It was obvious to Smith that the masters constitute a "brotherhood", in which information is exchanged. The ultimate appeal to civil magistrates testifies that it would really be necessary to be "ignorant of the world as of the subject" to imagine that the relationship of wage dependency can really be thought of as a particular case of exchange of goods and services. In Chapter 6 of this book, I mentioned the fact that for many commentators the propensity to exchange could provide the foundation of an anthropology of economics. If this were the case, we would immediately see that the wage dependency relationship is certainly not an exchange relationship.

Moreover, this denunciation of the balance of power between the masters and the workers must be measured in respect to Smith's head-on condemnation of guilds which appeared to him as remnants of feudalism (WON, 135 and *sq.*). In the final analysis, they were destined to allow masters to get their underpaid apprentices to work much longer than was necessary for their employees.

In the British world of the eighteenth century, as is still largely the case today, membership of a social class was a decisive element of *identity*, and class conflict was a *normal* assertion of such identity. But it is precisely because class conflict is also a conflict of identities that it cannot be easily reduced to being a mere conflict of interest.[9] This is because while conflicts of interest can often be resolved by competition in the market, the same is not true of identity conflicts. This is why it is not competition, *on its own,* that renders the decisions of employees and employers about hiring or firing compatible.

This *norm* of class membership was clear to Smith and there is no indication that an eighteenth- century reader was surprised by this in any way. It is therefore possible to ask whether wage dependency, which Smith emphasised strongly was a source of oppression as well as being generalised, is in fact also compatible with the system of natural liberty that Smith defended with great caution.

It is difficult to answer this counterfactual question. Nevertheless, admitting (following Smith) that the situation of the English colonies of North America was close to that which would prevail under the system of natural liberty, then it must be admitted that in this latter state, the wage condition may be *transitory*, as we have seen above. According to Smith, the wage rate was particularly high in these colonies, and it was possible to exploit available land, while being free of the servitudes imposed in Europe by large landed property ownership. This mediaeval heritage had therefore to disappear at the same time as the mercantile system.[10] And so it may be asked what revolutions Europe therefore needed to bring it closer to the American situation.

The Two Theories of Money in the *Wealth of Nations* and the Disqualification of Gold

This book aims therefore to show how the concept of real wealth was a weapon against the partisans of the mercantile system: Mun and Locke, but also probably Sir James Steuart, whose "fake principles" Smith was

[9] For a different point of view, see the classic work by Albert O. Hirschmann (1977).

[10] It should be noted that Smith did not mention indentured servants. The transportation costs of immigrants were "advanced" at the time by carriers and emigrants were then "sold" to employers. At the end of the contract period (several years), the workers were freed, provided with a nest egg and left to set up as farmers on land "acquired" from Native Americans by large American or British landowners. It is estimated that this status covered 48% of free immigrants in the eighteenth century moving to the North American colonies. See H. Zinn (1980).

pleased to "destroy [...] without ever even quoting him".[11] Smith's concept of wealth is thus closely related to the concept of commodity money developed in Chapter iv of Book I of the *Wealth of Nations*. It is time to come back to this point (section "The Exchange of Commodities by Means of Commodities").

Smith went on to consolidate his position. Not only was gold relegated to being a mere commodity, but as a monetary standard it lost all its relevance in favour of bank money. Indeed, a *second* theory of money, the theory of money as a symbol, as a "voucher" (Benetti, 1991) is set out in Chapter ii of Book II (section "Gold, Money and Banks"). The article concludes by recalling that Smith anticipated certain macroeconomic questions about banks' monetary practices.

The Exchange of Commodities by Means of Commodities

Chapter iv of Book I appears to be one of the most conventional in the *Wealth of Nations*. Smith starts by assuming that as soon as the division of labour is established, then "Every man thus lives by exchanging, or becomes in some measure merchant, and the society itself grows to be what is properly a commercial society" (WON, 37). The problem is that the "double coincidence of wants" arises sooner or later. To resolve this problem, it is therefore prudent to have "at all times, besides the peculiar produce of his own industry, a certain quantity of some one commodity or other, such as he imagined few people would be likely to refuse in exchange for the produce of their industry" (ibid.).

However, and quite curiously, the history of this agreement on a generally accepted commodity that can be used to mediate exchange—in other words the history of the transformation of the barter economy into a monetary economy—*is specifically not* the story Smith chose to tell us. Indeed, Smith's first example uses cattle, drawing on Homer's *Iliad*, in which it is said that Diomede's armour was worth nine oxen, whereas Glaucos's was worth 100. It is generally recognised that the choice of a unit of account, firstly to record credits and debts, is as old as writing itself. But that this choice involved cattle (*pecus*) as an intermediary of exchange is much more doubtful, and this is obviously not what Smith proposes. Instead, he sought to demonstrate that an initial agreement on a

[11] Cf. supra Chapter. 4, p. 74.

unit of common measure (a *numéraire*) leads to a second agreement on a fungible commodity, which may be used as a means of exchange precisely because its value is linked to the unit of account. This approach is found in the anterior texts to the *Wealth of Nations*. Money is viewed first as a "measure of value", and subsequently as "the instrument of commerce, or medium of exchanges and permutation".

It is in fact interesting to compare the *Wealth of Nations* with Smith's previous writings, his *Lectures on Jurisprudence* (LJ) as well as the *Early Draft* (ED). The structures of these three texts are the same. This is normal, as they were written within a short space of time (the two last years during which Smith was teaching at the University of Glasgow).

In the two versions of the *Lectures on Jurisprudence*, in the *Of Police* chapter (Smith's translation of the Greek *politeia*, the "regulation of a government in general"), he states that it has three components: (1) the maintenance and cleanliness of roads; (2) security; (3) cheapness or plenty which is its source.

After stating that enrichment follows the division of labour, and that the latter is a function of the extent of the market, Smith aims to study: (i) the laws of exchange, which regulate the price of commodities; (ii) money as the measure of value and hence as an instrument of commerce; (iii) the causes of the slow progress to opulence; (iv) taxes; and (v) the positive and negative effects of commerce (LJ, 352–394; LJ B, 494–554). The *Early Draft* has the same structure. It is only having presented the convergence of market prices on natural prices that Smith tackles the question of money.

The *Early Draft* was probably written in 1762. In it, Smith starts by noting that as far as money as a measure of value is concerned "I have little to say that is very new or particular" (ED, 33), thus anticipating Book I, Chapter iv of the *Wealth of Nations*. This is not the case when Smith examines money as an "instrument of commerce" immediately afterwards. Smith sketches out certain ideas which are developed in Book II, Chapter ii, of the *Wealth of Nations*. Gold is seen as a "dead stock", which is better replaced by bank money via the circulation of commodities. "Banks and bank notes [...] enable us, as, it were, to plough up our high roads, by affording us a sort of communication through the air by which we do our business equally well". And he adds: "That, therefore, to confine them by monopolies or any other restraints, except such as are necessary to prevent frauds and abuses, must obstruct the progress of opulence" (LJ, 576). Banks' function is thus very clear: they replace gold which is useless and costly, by a currency with no cost. Thirdly and lastly, Smith launches his attack against gold and bullion, as well as mercantilist policies, which are studied in Book IV of the *Wealth of Nations*.[12]

The comparison with the *Wealth of Nations* is revealing. The latter examines money before studying price convergence, but also before examining the new distinction which Smith makes between the real price and the nominal price (Chapter v), as well as before the study of the components of natural price (Chapter vi). However, both in the *Wealth of Nations* and in the previous texts, Smith stresses money's function as a measure of exchange (in Chapter iv, Book I). The difficulty of barter lies not so much in the double coincidence of wants, but rather that barter provides no common price measure. This is understandable in as far as an agreement that a commodity may act as a "medium of permutation" implies agreement on a common measure. This explains why Smith insisted on the fungible nature of gold, which explains in the final analysis the unanimous adoption of precious metals as a measure of value, and therefore as a "medium of permutation". The first novelty of the *Wealth of Nations* is to assert that gold—a commodity among others—is an erroneous measure of the value of commodities and to put forward labour instead. The latter is not a commodity, but a title of ownership over a commodity. The second novelty of the *Wealth of Nations* lies in seeking to demonstrate not only that gold is a poor measure for exchange, but also that it is best not used.

Gold, Money and Banks

Smith returned to the question of money in Book II of the *Wealth of Nations*, in which he studied bank money: i.e. money based on credit. This was the second use of money, when money is lent out for interest. The main problem Smith encountered centred on taking the two usages of money into consideration (the two chrematistics) which Aristotle had already described in his *Politics*, First part, Chapter 9. Money can be used as a means of exchange and Aristotle formulated one of the first versions of the barter fable. But money can also be used to make loans earning interest. Neither of these two functions, however, really found their place in Smith. The role of money as a means of exchange was taken

[12] See before Chapter 4.

by commodities and the second function of money was taken by capital, a point which I will now examine. In the *Wealth of Nations*, the relationship between money and capital is addressed in Chapters i, ii and iv of Book II, and so we may ask what the links are between bank money and the accumulation of capital and what role banks play.

If bank money did not exist, then money would be made up of metal specie, yet the stock of gold and silver required for money would only constitute a fraction of capital. Would this stock not have to be imported, if only to compensate for wear and tear? And would not such indispensable imports merely express foreign trade surpluses? If this were the case, then the arguments of the proponents of the mercantile system would be singularly strengthened. Smith's main arguments were put forward on two levels: on the one hand, he asserted that labour and the products of labour, which amount to the same thing, is wealth; and on the other hand, gold may be substituted by bank money.

However, underlying the former approach, Smith saw that there was a new difficulty, which had nothing to do with the standard for money (gold), namely the fact that bank money appeared to cause a form of instability which metallic money seems did not.

We may therefore look at three questions. The first concerns knowing how bank money could be substituted for monetary gold (section "Gold and Capital"). The second arises from the fact that banks may be "imprudent". How can this occur without being trivial? Banks' imprudence requires prudential measures to be *imposed* on them (section "The Confusion Between Money and Capital: Banks and Their Clients"). The third question extends this approach to financial instability. In this case, savers themselves may be "imprudent". This raises the same question. Imprudence by agents explains market instability and requires the State to fix a legal minimum rate of interest, set at as low a rate as possible (section "The Confusion Between Money and Capital: Relations Between Lenders and Borrowers").

Gold and Capital

In times when payments were made in gold or silver (not as often as we may think), the place of bullion in an economy was rather cumbersome. In fact, Smith defined net revenue as gross revenue less than what was required to maintain fixed capital. Circulating capital, minus a share required to maintain fixed capital, thus would constitute disposable income (used for consumption or saving), if it was not necessary to deduct money:

> As the machines and instruments of a trade, etc., which compose the fixed capital either of an individual or of a society, make no part either of the gross or of the net revenue of either; so money, by means of which the whole revenue of the society is regularly distributed among all its different members, makes itself no part of that revenue. The great wheel of circulation is altogether different from the goods which are circulated by means of it. The revenue of the society consists altogether in those goods, and not in the wheel which circulates them. (WON, 289)

Species thus constituted the only share of circulating capital which was neither part of income nor part of the gross income of the society. In other words, in today's language, money had no direct *private* utility (as consumer goods which constitute consumption have), nor indirect private utility (as with the means of production to which fixed capital belongs). This property of money was for long hidden by the existence of species, because metal had a private utility and a cost of production. These masked a specific problem of money while not resolving it, namely the determination of the value of money in a way that is distinct from the value of the bullion. In the terms of the *Wealth of Nations*, this problem expresses itself by the fact that the value of monetary gold does not contribute to the net income of a society, even though it may actually use up some of its gross revenues to extract or import metal. The income used for importing gold to mint money is therefore a cost which does not generate any revenue.

However, this difficulty seems easy to remove as bank money is a convenient substitute for monetary gold. This substitution looks to be fortunate from a theoretical point of view, but for two *bad* reasons. The first gives the impression that because the cost of paper is negligible the problem of metal seems to be resolved. But we shall see that this impression is false. The second reason lies in the idea that as the question of the value of commodity money is no longer raised, then only the *quantity* of bank money issued could regulate the purchasing power of money (value). However, the *Wealth of Nations* does not adopt this position, and I will try to explain what appears to be strange in the text.

For Smith, the quantity of money "necessary to circulation" is given at the same time as the total value of goods to be circulated (for any given velocity of circulation of money). *If* certain conditions are met,[13] Smith claimed that only a quantity of paper money would be issued that was sufficient to replace gold and silver, in order to ensure the circulation of commodities. Paper would replace bullion, which, having lost its monetary use and hence no longer having any local utility, would be exported as a commodity and exchanged against other commodities. The share of these revenues not consumed would be saved and accumulated. Thus dead capital, which generates no profit (gold) would be replaced by capital capable of implementing productive work.[14] Smith used the impressive comparison here of the "wagon-way through the air".

> The judicious operations of banking, by substituting paper in the room of a great part of this gold and silver, enables the country to convert a great part of this dead stock into active and productive stock; into stock which produces something to the country. The gold and silver money which circulates in any country may very properly be compared to a highway, which, while it circulates and carries to market all the grass and corn of the country, produces itself not a single pile of either. The judicious operations of banking, by providing, if I may be allowed so violent a metaphor, a sort of wagon-way through the air, enable the country to convert, as it were, a great part of its highways into good pastures and corn-fields, and thereby to increase very considerably the annual produce of its land and labour. (WON, 320)

The "wisdom" attributed to banks here should be noted, and I will return to it later. In the meantime, it must be asked how all this fortunate substitution between bank money and metallic money takes place. There is nothing obvious about this. Indeed, it would be expected that any issue of bank money would actually add to the money in circulation, rather than substitute for it. The result would be a fall in the value of money. This led Hume in his essays "Of Money" and "Of Interest" to argue that an expansion in the quantity of money has, finally, no real impact. And it is precisely this argument which Smith used (in Chapter iv of Book II) to argue that the secular decline in the rate of interest was not due to

[13] The "real effects doctrine" was attributed to Smith, and is based on abolishing this "if".

[14] I draw here on the analysis by S. Diatkine and M. Rosier (1999).

the inflow of money from the Americas, an inflow which according to Smith (and Hume) would have led to a rise in all prices, leaving interest rates unchanged. The fact that Smith did not use any "quantitativist" arguments in Chapter ii has seemed strange to many commentators since at least Jacob Viner (1928, p. 87). Today, it is usual to interpret Smith's position as an anticipation of what is called the "monetary approach to the balance of payments". In its initial form, this analysis aims to show that an expansion of the quantity of money issued by the monetary authorities would not lead to rising prices (at equilibrium), if an economy is sufficiently "small": i.e. if prices are determined elsewhere, by world prices. According to this hypothesis, prices cannot react to growth in the demand for goods following a rise in the quantity of money, which instead leads to a rise in imports and hence an outflow of money for equilibrium to be re-established. The quantity of money then returns to its new equilibrium.

Thomas M. Humphrey (1981) was keen to show that this approach had been anticipated by Smith. David Laidler (1981) remarked that monetary policy, and its determinant the Central Bank, were not at the heart of Chapter ii of Book II of the *Wealth of Nations*. I would add that the denial of monetary policy follows the criticism of the mercantile system which is at the heart of Smith's work. Another path needs therefore to be taken.

The analysis starts with circulation being based only on bullion. Gold was a fraction of the circulating capital in an economy, a fraction which was expensive to acquire and maintain. Subsequently, bank credit allowed gold to be replaced in circulation. It is then necessary to understand how this "replacement" occurred and what happened to the bullion in the process. Smith's metaphor of a "wagon-way through the air" means that agents who held bank notes used their gold, which it no longer made sense to hold, to import goods (all the more so because bank notes, in contrast to bullion, had no purchasing power abroad). The price of gold would not rise, because it was fixed, Smith stated, in the same way as all other prices. Indeed, gold is a commodity with a *world* market. Its price on the market depends on the relationship between the existing quantity of gold in the world and the extent of its market.[15] The gold price Smith argued was therefore not affected by the creation of local bank

[15] By contrast, the discovery of mines in America changed the quantity of gold brought to the global market (over the long term), and hence the price of gold. Hence Smith's acceptance of Hume's (very fragile) argument that a fall in the long-term interest rate

money. This point is suggestive of the hypothesis concerning a "small economy". This is expressed clearly in the quotation which practically concludes Chapter ii of Book II.[16] Smith stated that the quantity of paper money cannot influence the price of bullion, because the gold price of commodities, as their price in terms of any commodity, depends on the final analysis on *real* market conditions: in other words the extent of the market and the existing quantities of both bullion and other commodities. The quantity of local paper money issued would have no impact on the real conditions prevailing in the global gold market. This was a reiteration of the view according to which gold was a commodity which was only distinguishable from others by the fact that it had a global market, and this was the basis of the proposition that the issue of paper money had no effect on the price of gold.

Gold could then be exported to import commodities, and the only remaining gold in the economy would be that need by goldsmiths and as bank reserves.

Henceforth, any quantity of extra (and hence surplus) bank notes coming to the market (and we will shortly see why for Smith this was normally the case) would have no purchasing power if banks did not guarantee to convert bank notes into the gold they hold in reserves.[17] Smith's position may be expressed as follows:

> The goods to be bought and sold being precisely the same as before, the same quantity of money will be sufficient for buying and selling them. The channel of circulation, if I may be allowed such an expression, will remain precisely the same as before. (WON, 293)

cannot be explained by variations in the value of money: higher gold prices having the same impact on the numerator and the denominator of interest rates.

[16] "A paper currency which falls below the value of gold and silver coin does not thereby sink the value of those metals, or occasion equal quantities of them to exchange for a smaller quantity of goods of any other kind. The proportion between the value of gold and silver and that of goods of any other kind depends in all cases not upon the nature or quantity of any particular paper money, which may be current in any particular country, but upon the richness or poverty of the mines, which happen at any particular time to supply the great market of the commercial world with those metals. It depends upon the proportion between the quantity of labour which is necessary in order to bring a certain quantity of gold and silver to market, and that which is necessary in order to bring thither a certain quantity of any other sort of goods" (WON, 328–329).

[17] That is why Smith was against the "option clause" that allowed banks possibly to pull out of this obligation which encourages them to maintain reserve ratios.

The amount of paper money likely to enter circulation was therefore fixed. It may be concluded that no extra money could enter through this "channel", whose *dimensions were fixed by the purchasing power of commodities to be circulated*. Holders of paper money in excess just had to exchange their cash for gold coins at the emitting bank. What could be concluded from this? Simply that gold was a commodity with a utility and a cost, whereas *neither specie nor bank money were commodities*. The cost of bank money is zero, as is its private utility. It thus becomes clear that the substitution of bank money for specie did not provide any solution to the problem of the value of money.[18]

This result is not surprising, given that Smith's definition of wealth is the purchasing power of all commodities, as I have recall above. All commodities are a form of money, so that commodities themselves are the source of their own circulation. They drive themselves, so to speak. The purchasing power of commodities and the ability to command labour constitute the "channel of circulation", and also define its dimensions. Commodities do not need money. The *Wealth of Nations* thus provides us with the first expression of the problem faced by economic analysis until today, in constructing a theory of money which is compatible with *real wealth*, which Smith tries to formulate with such care, in contrast to "illusionary" wealth, followed by "mercantilist" wealth.

The Confusion Between Money and Capital: Banks and Their Clients

Let us leave aside the delicate issue of the value of money. Monetary stability is only acquired under certain conditions. If these are not met, there is a real risk of the destruction of capital. Smith notes this, immediately having referred to the "wagon-way through the air":

> The commerce and industry of the country, however, it must be acknowledged, though they may be somewhat augmented, cannot be altogether so secure when they are thus, as it were, suspended upon the Daedalian wings of paper money as when they travel about upon the solid ground of gold and silver. Over and above the accidents to which they are exposed from the unskillfulness of the conductors of this paper money, they are liable to

[18] Carlo Benetti (1991) emphasises the fact that if—as Smith argues—no income is associated with money, then the exchange value of money is zero. That is why it is possible to agree with him that the coherence in the *Wealth of Nations* would require withdrawing money from all commodities and converting it into "vouchers".

> several others, from which no prudence or skill of those conductors can guard them. (WON, II, 321)

Let us then see how Smith describes this instability. The creation of bank money starts initially with the discounting of bills of exchange. This is followed by the opening of credits in current accounts. If banks were *only* to create money to ensure the cash flow of their customers, then they would not face any risks as there would be no over-issuance:

> What a bank can with propriety advance to a merchant or undertaker of any kind, is not either the whole capital with which he trades, or even any considerable part of that capital; but that part of it only which he would otherwise be obliged to keep by him unemployed, and in ready money for answering occasional demands. If the paper money which the bank advances never exceeds this value, it can never exceed the value of the gold and silver which would necessarily circulate in the country if there was no paper money; it can never exceed the quantity which the circulation of the country can easily absorb and employ.
>
> When a bank discounts to a merchant a real bill of exchange drawn by a real creditor upon a real debtor, and which, as soon as it becomes due, is really paid by that debtor, it only advances to him a part of the value which he would otherwise be obliged to keep by him unemployed and in ready money for answering occasional demands. The payment of the bill, when it becomes due, replaces to the bank the value of what it had advanced, together with the interest. The coffers of the bank, so far as its dealings are confined to such customers, resemble a water pond, from which, though a stream is continually running out, yet another is continually running in, fully equal to that which runs out; so that, without any further care or attention, the pond keeps always equally, or very near equally full. Little or no expense can ever be necessary for replenishing the coffers of such a bank. (WON, 304)

Here, the bank clearly only *needs* to lend money necessary for the transaction to be cashed in by the borrower. To the extent that the bank is *obliged* to do so, this is not due to market forces. For the borrower, such an advance avoids holding sterile capital. But does the bank know it is acting within prudent limits? These limits are broached when the borrower provides a fake bill of exchange, which has not been issued, for example, as a means for settling a transaction that has *already* taken place, but as a means for settling a future transaction on commodities that need to be produced, specifically with the help of borrowed money. In short, in this case which is not exclusive, the fake bill of exchange is used for investment and not for cash flow. How is the bank distinguish between loans of money and loans of capital? The *Wealth of Nations* answers this by stating that the bank must pay attention to its "pond". Markets therefore cannot inform banks. If they lend "too much", by discounting fake bills of exchange, they will only know about it *afterwards*, by observing that their "pond" is emptying out continuously.[19] Indeed, clients will then ask the bank to convert bank money into bullion. Bank reserves will fall, and will be increasingly costly to rebuild. Banks are therefore strongly encouraged to stop issuing money.

Smith thus tells us that banks (and lenders more generally, as we shall see below) have to deal with two types of borrowers who use money differently.[20] One type borrows money, which mediates exchange, to meet deadlines. The other type borrows money which acts as capital, to produce goods the borrowers hope to sell in the future. Therefore, if banks only discount real bills of exchange, bank money will replace specie and the benefits of bank money will take place without hindrance. But banks also discount "circulating" (fake) bills of exchange, and are unable to distinguish between the two a priori. In this case, bank money supplements savings, leading to a disequilibrium in financial markets. Merchants thus always have the possibility of transforming money into capital.[21] The demarcation between money and capital is not "objective", but results from economic decisions which must be sanctioned socially by the banking system: this is never accomplished and never definitive. I will therefore show that prudence by banks requires them to be able to distinguish between lending for money and lending for capital, between "ordinary" merchants who borrow money and projectors who borrow capital. And we shall see that the usual distinction between the short term and long term is not of great help.

Indeed, here "projectors" who are typical characters in the *Wealth of Nations* come into play.

[19] This principle has been called the "Reflux Law" by partisans of the *Banking Principle*.

[20] These two uses of money are less well known, as I have recalled, because they were described in Aristotle's *Politics*.

[21] In terms used by Marx (or Aristotle), merchants were free to move from a *commodity-money-commodity* transaction sequence (in which money facilitates exchange), towards a *money-commodity-money + extra money* transaction sequence (in which money functions as capital).

Who are they? They are merchants and manufacturers or capitalists. It may be asked whether all capitalists are projectors.

The first characteristic of a projector is to be an innovator. However all manufacturing merchants are not projectors. The *Wealth of Nations* leaves room for routine capitalists. They can be found as lenders or shareholders.

A second important characteristic hinges on whether projectors are necessarily imprudent. Innovation is not synonymous with imprudence. After all, we know that routine is sometimes (and perhaps often) imprudent.

The definition of prudence in Smith's *Theory of Moral Sentiments* is the subject of the first section of the sixth part of this book, dedicated to the "Character of Virtue", which was inserted into the last edition during Smith's lifetime. Prudence is the first virtue, ahead of benevolence and self-control, which together are the three components of virtuous behaviour described here by Smith. The economic dimension of prudence is described as:

> The man who lives within his income, is naturally contented with his situation, which, by continual, though small accumulations, is growing better and better every day. He is enabled gradually to relax, both in the rigour of his parsimony and in the severity of his application; and he feels with double satisfaction this gradual increase of ease and enjoyment, from having felt before the hardship which attended the want of them. He has no anxiety to change so comfortable a situation and does not go in quest of new enterprises and adventures, which might endanger, but could not well increase the secure tranquillity, which he actually enjoys. If he enters into any new projects or enterprises, they are likely to be well concerted and well prepared. He can never be hurried or driven into them by any necessity, but has always time and leisure to deliberate soberly and coolly concerning what are likely to be their consequences. (TMS, VI, I, 12)

Accordingly, when the projector invests his saved profits and remains within the limits of his savings, he innovates prudently. But this is not necessarily the case, since the projector may invest more than his available savings by borrowing. The money issued by the bank may then be destined, for example, to acquire goods that will be sold at a profit in the future. This money then functions as a form of capital and may lead to the bankruptcy of both the borrower and lender. However this sanction is not immediate, and banks only realise belatedly that they have created "fictitious" savings. Smith sets out in detail practices that he judged (correctly) as being widespread and which allowed for the "raising money by circulation". These consisted of borrowing from some persons to reimburse others. Circulating bills of exchange were thus created and could fool banks, which believed that their "ponds" could fill up, thanks to such bills, even though initial loans had not been reimbursed. Such excessive monetary creation was sanctioned more or less rapidly, when the bills emitted by banks came back to their cash desks to be converted into specie. Realising that their gold reserves were running down, banks would then reduce their discounting and so trigger the clamour and fury of the *projectors*:

> The difficulties, accordingly, which the Bank of England, which the principal bankers in London, and which even the more prudent Scotch banks began, after a certain time, and when all of them had already gone too far, to make about discounting, not only alarmed, but enraged in the highest degree those projectors. Their own distress, of which this prudent and necessary reserve of the banks was, no doubt, the immediate occasion, they called the distress of the country; and this distress of the country, they said, was altogether owing to the ignorance, pusillanimity, and bad conduct of the banks, which did not give a sufficiently liberal aid to the spirited undertakings of those who exerted themselves in order to beautify, improve, and enrich the country. It was the duty of the banks, they seemed to think, to lend for as long a time, and to as great an extent as they might wish to borrow. The banks, however, by refusing in this manner to give more credit to those to whom they had already given a great deal too much, took the only method by which it was now possible to save either their own credit or the public credit of the country. (WON, 312)

Smith then describes the overtrading following over-emission and its effects on the relationships between banks and their customers. We will soon find this again in relations between lenders and borrowers. The cries of projectors are often cried by capitalists taken collectively: by confusing an exceptional rate of profit with the natural rate of profit, they actually all identify themselves with projectors.

It is thus clear why banks become so "adventurous" so easily. According to Smith, it is because they cannot know in advance whether their loans will be used to mediate exchange (as money) or as capital. Why should they refuse to finance a "beautiful" project, when a loan is supported by "good" collateral providing full guarantees? If the project succeeds, the entrepreneur will reimburse loans by shares in the company, which the banker will accept willingly, either to keep them, or to sell them at a profit to customers. The transformation of money into capital is the history of successful capitalism, as well as being its oldest story. Indeed, historians know well that this is the very successful story of capitalism. *Yet it is exactly this history which Smith wants to hear nothing about*. According to him, it is real savings and only such savings which can and should be transformed into real investment, while any deviation from this norm is a source of danger.

Bank money was certainly convertible for specie at banks' cash desks, but this conversion is the only potential. Normally it never takes place. The collapse of John Law's system in Paris, or the crisis in 1772 in London and Scotland showed that when conversion is effective, it was usually too late to go ahead: the promise of converting bank money into species, when it must be honoured, never in fact is honoured, or at least not entirely, as it leads to a bank run which may cause a collapse of the bank concerned, because reserves are never sufficient to meet the demands for converting all bank money.

That is why it is important to emphasise to what extent Smith, who founded financial orthodoxy (essentially on the hypothesis that capital accumulation is the fruit of real savings), was at the same time aware of the fragility of such accumulation. This fragility follows from the fact that information available to agents is *necessarily* limited and misleading, as this information concerns the future value of endowments of other agents. Such information which is in fact so intimate that the agents in question do not know it about themselves.[22]

This explains why, for example, a first series of prudential rules must be adopted. For example banks should be forbidden from issuing banknotes of small denomination.[23]

> To restrain private people, it may be said, from receiving in payment the promissory notes of a banker, for any sum whether great or small, when they themselves are willing to receive them, or to restrain a banker from issuing such notes, when all his neighbours are willing to accept of them, is a manifest violation of that natural liberty which it is the proper business

[22] We are thus quite far from the asymmetry between lenders and borrowers which is studied by contemporary economists, based on the fact that the latter know their projects better than the former.

[23] See Sylvie Diatkine (2002).

> of law not to infringe, but to support. Such regulations may, no doubt, be considered as in some respects a violation of natural liberty. But those exertions of the natural liberty of a few individuals, which might endanger the security of the whole society, are, and ought to be, restrained by the laws of all governments, of the most free as well as of the most despotical. The obligation of building party walls, in order to prevent the communication of fire, is a violation of natural liberty exactly of the same kind with the regulations of the banking trade which are here proposed. (WON, 324)

The Confusion Between Money and Capital: Relations Between Lenders and Borrowers

However, it must be asked whether prudential banking regulations are sufficient to ensure the stability of the financial system. Indeed, the remarkable mistrust shown in the *Wealth of Nations* is not limited only to the relationship between banks and projectors. It extends to financial markets, for the same reasons. For Smith joint-stock companies should only be created for very specific and limited objectives.

Once again we find the projectors operating in financial markets. Smith knew that a prudent projector might need to borrow capital. But in this case, prudence requires a significant degree of intimacy between the lender and the borrower of a loan (therefore a private relationship) which is nearly the same as in association. The creditor needs to be perfectly informed of the guarantees provided by the borrower, so that the default risk is practically zero:

> Traders and other undertakers may, no doubt, with great propriety, carry on a very considerable part of their projects with borrowed money. In justice to their creditors, however, their own capital ought, in this case, to be sufficient to ensure, if I may say so, the capital of those creditors; or to render it extremely improbable that those creditors should incur any loss, even though the success of the project should fall very much short of the expectation of the projectors. Even with this precaution too, the money which is borrowed, and which it is meant should not be repaid till after a period of several years, ought not to be borrowed of a bank, but ought to be borrowed upon bond or mortgage of such private people as propose to live upon the interest of their money without taking the trouble themselves to employ the capital, and who are upon that account willing to lend that capital to such people of good credit as are likely to keep it for several years. A bank, indeed, which lends its money without the expense of stamped paper, or of attorneys' fees for drawing bonds and mortgages, and which accepts of repayment upon the easy terms of the

> banking companies of Scotland, would, no doubt, be a very convenient creditor to such traders and undertakers. But such traders and undertakers would, surely, be most inconvenient debtors to such a bank. (WON, 307)

Thus:

1. Only private relationships which are therefore direct between lenders and borrowers are prudent. I will return to this first point below.
2. Loans must of course be backed by solid collateral, and this solidity needs to be *well known* by the lender. This condition challenges the anonymity of the market relationship as the endowments of the borrower (which may make up the collateral in question) need to be *known* by the lender. The lender of capital therefore needs to be in a quasi-*private* relationship with the borrower.

Imprudence in economic affairs consists simply of going to the market to finance investment. The financial market is an oxymoron, because it assumes, as a market, anonymity which borrowing relationships necessarily destroy.

Smith's hostility to financial markets is un-alloyed. He considers joint-stock companies, and in particular companies benefiting from situations of privilege (monopolies) such as the East India Company, to be dangerous. Their scope of intervention should be narrow and supervised with strong rules. Having recalled at length the history of the East India Company and shown how this joint-stock company, despite its hold on public revenues in Bengal, quite quickly found itself in financial difficulty leading it to "beg" for financial assistance from the British government. Smith concluded his analysis as follows: "The only trades which it seems possible for a joint stock company to carry on successfully without an exclusive privilege are those of which all the operations are capable of being reduced to what is called a Routine, or to such a uniformity of method as admits of little or no variation. Of this kind is, first, the banking trade; secondly, the trade of insurance from fire, and from sea risk and capture in time of war; thirdly, the trade of making and maintaining a navigable cut or canal; and, fourthly, the similar trade of bringing water for the supply of a great city" (WON, 437–438).

Moreover, for Smith, the separation between ownership and management could only be safe in the case of routine companies, since the managers were not encouraged to risk "immoderate" investments. By contrast, joint-stock companies—often colonial companies—were only able to succeed (which according to Smith was actually quite seldom) due to their exclusive privileges. And we could add that their managers, such as Clive or Dupleix, were able to free themselves from the control of their company's shareholders to become nabobs and conquer India.

So for Smith, joint-stock companies could only survive (with some exceptions) thanks to privileges granted by the government. They were therefore similar in all respects to institutions inherited from mediaeval times, namely guilds, which allowed apprentices to be exploited by masters. Joint-stock companies deserved no more consideration and were not only inefficient but also dangerous.

That is why in Chapter iv of Book II dedicated to interest-bearing loans, Smith shows that the interest rate is independent of the quantity of money, drawing on Hume and arguing against "mercantilist" authors. Smith then goes on to defend the necessity of a legal level of interest, as was then fixed in Great Britain, at 5%: i.e. a little bit more than the 3% rate at which the best borrower (the British government) could borrow at the time. Smith thought that if the legal rate of interest was fixed higher, then only imprudent projectors, who naturally expected higher rates of profit than the ordinary rate, would accept to borrow capital at such a high rate. And he believed that banks would be strongly encouraged to lend such funds. Prudent borrowers—sober men—looking for money would then be crowded out of the loan market.

Holding the legal rate low should create a natural selection whereby sober men (borrowing money) would crowd out borrowers of capital, i.e. imprudent projectors.[24] If this were not the case, overtrading would once again take place:

> No complaint, however, is more common than that of a scarcity of money. Money, like wine, must always be scarce with those who have neither wherewithal to buy it nor credit to borrow it. Those who have either will seldom be in want either of the money or of the wine which they have occasion for. This complaint, however, of the scarcity of money is not always confined to improvident spendthrifts. It is sometimes general through a whole mercantile town and the country in its neighbourhood. Overtrading is the common cause of it. Sober men, whose projects have

[24] This is what J. E. Stiglitz (1981) noted when quoting the *Wealth of Nations*.

> been disproportioned to their capitals, are as likely to have neither wherewithal to buy money nor credit to borrow it, as prodigals whose expense has been disproportioned to their revenue. Before their projects can be brought to bear, their stock is gone, and their credit with it. They run about everywhere to borrow money, and everybody tells them that they have none to lend. Even such general complaints of the scarcity of money do not always prove that the usual number of gold and silver pieces are not circulating in the country, but that many people want those pieces who have nothing to give for them. When the profits of trade happen to be greater than ordinary, overtrading becomes a general error both among great and small dealers. They do not always send more money abroad than usual, but they buy upon credit, both at home and abroad, an unusual quantity of goods, which they send to some distant market in hopes that the returns will come in before the demand for payment. The demand comes before the returns, and they have nothing at hand with which they can either purchase money, or give solid security for borrowing. It is not any scarcity of gold and silver, but the difficulty which such people find in borrowing, and which their creditors find in getting payment, that occasions the general complaint of the scarcity of money. (WON, IV, 437)

Smith's tone is always the same, but another story is unfolding. In Chapter ii of Book II, banks issued too much money by discounting a circulating bill of exchange. In this case, money was scarce because savers had placed their funds into "immoderate" companies.

As can be seen, we do not find exactly the same protagonists as in the description of the over-emission of money. Here, savers are lending funds.

This description of financial panics preceded the Wicksellian analysis of the business cycle, as Morris Perlman (1989) has already noted.[25] In this case, the prudential rules which had to be imposed on banks were no longer sufficient, because all financial relationships are involved. This is why Smith favoured a legal rate of interest which was as low as possible. It is interesting here to observe the proximity of the approaches by Steuart and Smith, and at the same time their major differences.[26] Like Steuart, Smith defended the idea of a legal rate of interest. But in contrast to Steuart, he did not support the idea of a minimum threshold. For both authors, the maximum rate aimed at excluding prodigals from the loan market. Yet Smith also and above all wanted to exclude projectors, as we

[25] See Perlman (1989).

[26] See Sylvie Diatkine and Michel Rosier (1999, pp. 226 and sqq).

have seen. Steuart on the other hand feared that an excessively low rate of interest would only lead to a ruinous rise in land prices. So far as I know, there is no mention of this concern in the *Wealth of Nations*.

The *Wealth of Nations* is thus an important step in the construction of an analysis in real terms, and hence in economic orthodoxy. Paradoxically, this construction seems strangely unfinished and remains largely open to the examination of macroeconomic policy. This paradox can be explained by the double theory of money which I have tried to highlight here. On the one hand, a modern conception of money sees it as the result of banking activity, with gold being limited to the (illusionary) role of guaranteeing bank money. On the other hand, the conception of gold as a global currency is archaic, because at the time some currencies (the Amsterdam florin and the pound sterling) were already means of international payment, relegating gold once again to its ever-illusionary function as a guarantee. But then again, this illusion still had a lot of life left in it.

References

Benetti C. (1991). Le problème de la valeur de la monnaie: F. Galiani et Adam Smith. *Cahiers d'économie politique, 19.*

Diatkine, S. (2002). *Les fondements de la théorie bancaire – des textes classiques aux débats contemporains*. Dunod.

Diatkine, S., & Rosier, M. (1999). Steuart and Smith on banking systems and growth. In R. Tortajada (Ed.), *The economics of James Steuart*. Routledge.

Fogel, & Engerman. (1974). *Time on the cross: The economics of American negro slavery*. New York: W.W. Norton and Company.

Hicks, J. R. (1990, June). The unification of macroeconomics. *The Economic Journal, 100*(401), 528–538.

Hirschmann, A. O. (1977). *The passions and the interests: Political arguments for capitalism before its triumph*. Princeton, Princeton University Press.

Humphrey, T. M. (1981), "Adam Smith and the monetary approach to the Balance of Payments", *Federal Reserve Bank of Richmond Economic Review, 67*(6), 3–10.

Laidler, D. (1981, May). Adam Smith as a monetary economist. *Canadian Journal of Economics, 14*(2), 185–200.

Lapidus, A. (2002). Le profit ou la domination: la figure de l'esclave dans l'économie d'Adam Smith. In F. Célimène & A. Legris (Eds.), *L'Économie de l'esclavage colonial*. Éditions du CNRS.

Marx, K. (1863). *Theories of surplus value*. https://www.marxists.org/archive/marx/works/1863/theories-surplus-value/ch03.htm#s1

Perlman, M. (1989). Adam Smith and the paternity of the real bills doctrine. *History of Political Economy, 21*(1), 77–90.
Stiglitz, J. E. (1981). Credit rationing in markets with imperfect information. *American Economic Review, 71*(3), 393–410.
Viner, J. (1928). Adam Smith and laissez faire. In J. M. Clark et al., *Adam Smith 1776–1926*. Chicago, University of Chicago Press.
Zinn, H. (1980). *A people's history of the United States*. Harper & Row.

Conclusion

I hope to have shown in this book that the questions of economic theory raised by the *Wealth of Nations* are rooted in Smith's political opposition to the mercantile system. This is hardly unusual: major theoretical innovations are often born out of deep political controversies. But it is important to be careful. Showing that economic issues are rooted in political debate does not mean that they are to be confused with it. Theoretical discussion needs to be unscathed and conducted independently of such roots. In the case of the *Wealth of Nations*, I have tried to show that its approach to capitalism is based on three perspectives. The first, which is found in Smith's early writings, is historical, because it sees capitalism as a particular stage in history, namely that of the commercial society. This approach contains elements of a theory of history, which Hegel and Marx extended, each in their own way. Smith's second perspective of capitalism is economic. First and foremost, he sought to understand the dynamics of the capitalist economy characterised by the existence of a rate of profit which is a parameter of natural prices. Smith's third view of capitalism is political. It was the mercantile system which designated capitalism as being governed and thus justified by the principle that the interests of the British Empire were the same as those of its merchants.

To update this discovery required cleaning up, so to speak, Smith's text of the successive readings that have been imposed on it, and by so doing, trying to reconstruct both the political and theoretical questions

D. Diatkine, *Adam Smith and the Wealth of Nations*, Palgrave Studies in the History of Economic Thought, https://doi.org/10.1007/978-3-030-81600-1

the *Wealth of Nations* sought to answer. Hopefully therefore, Smith's text has been lightened of some of its ambiguities here.

These may be the source of Schumpeter's own ambiguous judgement on the *Wealth of Nations*, for example. Schumpeter (1954) has been one of the few major economists who was highly critical of the *Wealth of Nations*. Seeking to define its difficult distinction between the history of economic analysis (which is indeed the title of Schumpeter's book) and the history of economic systems, Schumpeter thus noted: "For instance, A. Smith's *Wealth of Nations* was, in fact as in intention, a system of political economy in the sense just defined and as such it does not interest us". Schumpeter was surely embarrassed by the provocative nature of this proposal for setting aside Smith, and he immediately added: "...it [does] interest us by virtue of the fact that A. Smith's political principles and recipes [...] are but the cloak of a great analytic achievement" (1954, p.38). But what then, is this "great analytic achievement" whose "political recipes" are a "cloak"? When Schumpeter studied the latter (ibid., p. 263), he asserts that he did not find any "really new" ideas there. There can be no better way of saying that the *Wealth of Nations* contains little to satisfy an amateur of economic analysis, and it can only interest superficial dilettantes. In other words, there is nothing under the "cloak"! But I hope to have shown here that the criticism of the systems of political economy which Smith studied, fought against or wished to see emerge are not mere "veils", but rather the soil from which his theoretical questions developed. Paradoxically, these questions were not far from those Schumpeter himself asked: how should capitalism be characterised? And what are the stages of its development? Perhaps this book will make it possible to understand (but not share) Schumpeter's Sibylline judgement.

But this is not the only result of the present research, which includes the following.

1. This book aims to show that the *Wealth of Nations* is the product of Smith's critique of the mercantile system, a system judged as partial, because it confused the general interest (i.e. for recall, the enrichment not only of everyone but also that of the community, and so the British Empire) with the interests of the *class* of merchants and manufacturers (or "capitalists" as Turgot called them). The claim that society is divided into classes, and that these classes are necessarily in conflict with each other is in no way special to the *Wealth of Nations*. This idea is old, and the whole of the English eighteenth century was filled by the conflict (and

by the consciousness of this conflict) between the *landed interest* and the *moneyed interest* as Marx noted.[1] Smith turned the *moneyed interest* into a merchant and manufacturing class, but this did not alter the notion of class relations that Ricardo later emphasised when he tried to demonstrate (in contrast to the *Wealth of Nations*) that the profit rate could fall only as a result of a rise in the real rate of wages. The English classical school thus found its unity in the assertion that class conflicts structured society and thus politics. This highly distinctive claim was probably the source of the attack on "English" political economy from all sides, such as by the German historic school, or, in France, by Auguste Comte.

2. Liberal economists also participated in the rejection of this class-based approach. That is why, while they vociferously denounced the demands for protection that certain interests put to the State, they always did so in the name of the "loyalty" of competition, which the State had to preserve. We owe to these early liberal economists, such as Jean-Baptiste Say (1767–1832), the fact that they emphasised the role of entrepreneurs, who combined "producer services", with the help of their collaborators—the workers. These entrepreneurs substituted the class-based approach for an opposition between "workers" and rentiers. Entrepreneurs (as project managers) could thus replace the capitalist (at best transformed into the capital owner) as employers. Entrepreneurs became the "cornerstones" (metaphors abound) of the economy, while capitalists were relegated to the status of being quasi-rentiers. But, as we have seen, Smith recommended legislators exercise "the greatest distrust, the most suspicious attention" to any proposed law by the merchant and manufacturer class.

3. Smith's attack on the mercantile system is also remarkable because it did not make the latter the simple result of prejudices, which science alone could dispel. Instead, Smith saw this class as the product of European history, as was the commercial society—i.e. capitalism—which had not always existed. At the same time, the mercantile system was an expression of an impressive phenomenon, namely the conquest of the world by European capitalism. This phenomenon was indeed clearly spotted by Smith as he began to write the *Wealth of Nations* during the evident build-up of the American War of Independence. As we have seen, Smith's opus states that "The discovery of America, and that of a passage to the East Indies by the Cape of Good Hope, are the two greatest and most

[1] "With few exceptions it is the struggle between moneyed interest and landed interest which fills the century from 1650 to 1750", Marx K. (1863, book 1).

important events recorded in the history of mankind. Their consequences have already been very great" (WON, II, 240). He added, a few lines further, "In the meantime one of the principal effects of those discoveries has been to raise the mercantile system to a degree of splendour and glory which it could never otherwise have attained to". The expansive nature of capital accumulation, which is the "trademark" of capitalism, could not be better expressed. There is no reason to discuss here the many proposed explanations of this important historical phenomenon. But it is worth emphasising that it marks the awareness of the birth of capitalism, because discovering capitalism involves drawing up its birth certificate in the first instance. Yet this is not the least paradox that we have encountered, namely the identification by the ruling classes of the interests of merchants and manufacturers with the public interest (i.e. the seizure of power by the merchants), an identification which Smith denounced vehemently, was perhaps one of the factors that enabled the unprecedented rise of capitalism.

Capitalism thus appears in the *Wealth of Nations* as a historical phenomenon, and presenting it as such was and is exceptional. Marx was Smith's heir from this point of view, at a time when contemporary economic theories generally found this approach to be incongruous.

4. To understand the accumulation of capital—the heart of capitalism—it is necessary to explain why workers are not impoverished when capitalists get rich. Smith explains enrichment in two ways: first, through the progress of the division of labour, which is conceivable in a non-capitalist society (the "primitive and rude" state), and second, by the accumulation of capital in the commercial society that accelerates enrichment and breeds inequality. These two explanations of enrichment (growth in returns of scale and competition) must be made compatible. Yet this does not follow easily.

Moreover, Book I of the *Wealth of Nations* seeks to show that the interests of the classes of workers and landowners are identical to the general interest, as wage and rent rates tend to rise with the economic growth rate. In contrast, the interests of capitalists are different, because the profit rate of capitalists tends to fall as enrichment continues. This leads merchants and manufacturers to demand protective measures that restrict the scope of the market.

Finally, understanding the accumulation of capital led Smith to build a model of capital accumulation consistent with the "natural progress of opulence", which Smith thought he could detect in nascent form in the

English colonies of North America, and which he saw as being the *inverse* of the historical path he believed can be identified in Europe.

5. This book has aimed to show how the principle of interdependence expressed both by the division of labour and by the accumulation of capital is oriented *over time*, with an upstream and a downstream. It is therefore very different from the synchronic interdependence expressed by both Quesnay's *Economic Table*, and Marx's patterns of reproduction set out in Book II of *Capital*, or indeed Walras's general equilibrium model. In the *Wealth of Nations*, goods that are initially non-traded, joint products of corn given the lack of effective demand, become goods brought to the market by specialised agents when such demand exists.

Of course, most of Smith's answers are rarely acceptable today. But some of them have not really been superseded, such as the importance of the extent of the market in explaining growth and technical progress. Moreover, Smith pointed to the central problem of understanding how the list (not just the quantities) of goods brought to the market grows longer *over time* as capital accumulates. This question is basically about how products (things) are transformed into commodities (marketable goods). It is difficult to answer because a price theory seeking to take into account general interdependence usually assumes that the *list of goods and services* brought to the market is *given*, so that only the market equilibrium quantities and prices of these goods and services remain to be determined. Here I suggest that the lack of price-determination theory in the *Wealth of Nations* was not due to Smith's clumsiness, but the price he paid for his diachronic approach to economic interdependence, compared to a synchronic approach, as already set out by Quesnay.

6. Smith wrote that Quesnay, in his critique of Colbert, had to necessarily "bend the stick too much" to straighten it. The same seems true in the *Wealth of Nations*. Smith sought to show the senselessness of the main purpose of the mercantile system's advocates to ensure the value of money, which in the final analysis was set in the foreign-exchange markets. To do so, he was led to the major assertion that all components of wealth (i.e. goods) have purchasing power, which until Smith was considered to be the specificity of money. Smith thus claimed that what is purchased with money is actually purchased with the products of labour, and thus through labour. This equivalence is the basis of the notion of *real*

wealth, which is one of the most important and, indeed, the most mysterious, components of the Smith's legacy.[2] It is here, perhaps, that this book helps to understand Schumpeter's judgement. Due to his critique of the mercantile system, Smith was forced to assert not that money was neutral (Hume had done so before him), but to attribute all the properties of money to *real* wealth. Smith thus takes to its logical conclusion the approach that Schumpeter later attacked with all the energy that was his. Schumpeter did this in the name of "real-world analysis" (Schumpeter *op. cit*., t. I, p. 389), and which remains dominant today to the point of preventing (in Schumpeter's view) a clear analysis of monetary phenomena.

7. Yet Smith, like Hume, was not far from making another important proposition: aside metallic currency, whose value is identified (probably wrongly) in the *Wealth of Nations* with that of the metal which is its standard, there also exists bank money. This is built, as Smith described very well, around the concept of credit. This may be the problem that stopped Smith. As we saw in Chapter 1 here, Hume broached the idea that goods trade should be based not only on particular credit (the *promises* of private individuals), but also on "general credit" (the *promises* of the entire commercial society): i.e. precisely what bank money may be, under *certain conditions*. Smith took this up, but he identified these conditions strictly: bank credit can only be a substitute for gold, and it must not be a substitute for real savings. The *Wealth of Nations* thus marginalises the place of debt relations to the point of denying any relevance of the money markets, whose main purpose is to manage these relations. But Smith knew relations between banks and their customers could not be left to themselves. This was because banks did not know whether their clients borrowed money that would circulate as capital or as an intermediary in trade, and so there was a requirement for legal intervention to avoid the banking system from collapse, which was always possible. Smith thus argued in favour of banking regulation; therefore, Smith was not far from updating the dependency relationship between borrowers and lenders; a dependency that he in fact identifies with acuity in the wage

[2] The notion of a general price level, which is now used to build real quantities, is a construction of the monetary authorities and is not therefore information transmitted by the decentralised market. Moreover, it would take Robert W. Clower (1967) and its famous proposition that "Money buys goods and goods buy money; but goods do not buy goods", to challenge Smith's attribution of purchasing power to all goods.

relationship. Indeed, Smith's classical culture was strong enough to make it clear that getting into "dependency" on one's master *cannot* be the result of a *free* choice between working for oneself or working for some else. It is precisely because workers generally do not have the means to work on their own account, that is, because their labour has no utility for themselves that they are *obliged* to enter the service of another. The supply of such labour is therefore not the result of a choice and so is not really a real form of supply, economically speaking.

8. Finally, it is important to emphasise how the *Wealth of Nations* was extended in two key ways. The first involves reading Smith's work in the light of new questions raised by economists like Ricardo. I have shown here how Smith opposed Quesnay about the possibility of a plurality of accumulation regimes, and hence of price systems that ensure the reproduction of the body politic. In my view, Ricardo raised a *new* question about the theoretical conditions of *measuring* the value of capital, which requires a unique system of natural (or equilibrium) prices that such measurement cannot do without. Ricardo could therefore not be satisfied with plurality opposing Smith and Quesnay. It was this new requirement that likely led political economy (or economic analysis for that matter) to finding a theory of price determination, which had probably never been a question asked by Smith. This is borne out by the fact the latter had no difficulty in assuming the natural rates of profit and salary as being given simultaneously. By contrast, it is well known that determining the laws governing these rates (the theory of distribution) was the main problem of political economy.

The second extension of Smith's work is quite different, and resulted from an unsuccessful but clearly formulated project. In Smith's *Advertisement* to the last edition of the TSM, he argues that the *Wealth of Nations* is only an important part of a much larger project, which was his "endeavour to give an account of the general principles of law and government, and of the different revolutions they have undergone in the different ages and periods of society" (TSM, pp. 19–20; Smith had already shared this project with the Duke of La Rochefoucauld in 1785).[3] I have

[3] "I have [...] two other great works upon the anvil; the one is a sort of Philosophical History of all different branches of Literature, of Philosophy, Poetry and Eloquence; the other is a sort of Theory and History of Law and Government", Smith (*Correspondence...op. cit*, 1977, p. 287). See Lieberman (2006, pp. 214–245).

shown here how much Smith shared Hume's thesis that law and government are artefacts. More specifically, however, Smith distinguished himself from Hume by arguing that they are the products of history. This raises the question of how we establish such general principles of politics. How can we understand this historical construction?

Of course, today it is impossible to imagine how Smith would have answered this question, had he had the time. But this book suggests a path through Smith's outline of reforming the British Empire, which the *Wealth of Nations* offers as a "utopia": adjust the size of the ruled Empire so that its States General (to be created) could bring together legislators/spectators whose impartiality would be ensured by the optimal distance between them and the Empire's classes/actors. This optimal (and unknown) distance would allow them (perhaps) to *adjust* laws to the common good.

Such thinking was not new. Determining the constitution of a polis that would allow citizens to act in accordance with the common good was, as we know, a question already raised by classical political philosophy. Translated into Smith's words, the theory of law and government needed to determine which political organisation (which constitution) would be able to master capitalism.

This approach, which is naturally less-known to economists,[4] thus led on from Smith's work to Hegel, towards a rational-state theory as the ultimate product of History and its relationship to Civil Society.

Two paths of further inquiry thus emerged from the *Wealth of Nations*. One that should have led to a science of history, and which remains largely to be discovered. The other led to the theory of price determination. This was the path economists would take. Yet both routes remain to be explored.

References

Clower R. W. (1967). A reconsideration of the microfundations of monetary theory. *Economic Inquiry, 6*(11), 1–8.

Lieberman, D. (2006). Adam Smith on justice, rights, and law. In K. Haakonssen (Ed.), *The Cambridge companion to Adam Smith*

[4] Although the question was explored by philosophers such as N. Waszeck (1988).

(Cambridge Companions to Philosophy). Cambridge University Press.

Marx, K. (1863). *Theories of surplus value*. https://www.marxists.org/archive/marx/works/1863/theories-surplus-value/ch03.htm#s1 (Book 1).

Schumpeter, J. A. S. (1954). *History of economic analysis*. George Allen and Unwin.

Bibliographical References

A. Works by Adam Smith

The Glasgow edition of the works and correspondence of Adam Smith, Oxford University Press (Clarendon Press), 1976–1983.
I: *The theory of moral sentiments*, ed. by D. D. Raphael and A. L. Macfie, 1976.
II: *An inquiry into the nature and causes of the wealth of nation*, ed. by R. H. Campbell and A. S. Skinner, 1976.
III: *Essays on philosophical subjects, with Dugald Stewart's 'Account of Adam Smith'*, ed. by W. P. D. Wightman, J. C. Bryce and I. S. Ross, 1980.
IV: *Lectures on Rhetoric and Belles Lettres*, ed. by J. C. Bryce, R. H. Campbell, D. D. Raphael and A. S. Skinner, 1983.
V: *Lectures on jurisprudence*, ed. by R. L. Meek, D. D. Raphael and Peter Stein, 1978.
VI: *Correspondence* ed. by E. C. Mossner, I. S. Ross, 1977.
Two additional volumes are associated with this edition:
1. *Essays on Adam Smith*, éd. par A.S. Skinner et T. Wilson, 1975.
2. *Life of Adam Smith*, par I. S. Ross, 1995.

B. Other Sources

Albon, Comte d'. (1775). *Eloge historique de François Quesnay*. de Knapen.
Aristotle. (1948). *Politics* (C. D. C. Reeves, Trans.). Heckett Publishing Company.
Bentham, J. (1787–1952). *Jeremy Bentham's economic writings*. Allen & Unwin.

D. Diatkine, *Adam Smith and the Wealth of Nations*,
Palgrave Studies in the History of Economic Thought,
https://doi.org/10.1007/978-3-030-81600-1

Hume, D. (1739–1740, 1983). *A treatise of human nature*. (L. A. Selby-Bigge, Ed., 2nd éd., with text revised and notes by P. H. Nidditch). Clarendon Press.

Hume, D. (1777–1994). *Political essays* (K. Haakonssen, Ed.). CUP.

Locke J. (1632–1704). *Some considerations of the consequences of the lowering of interest*.... https://la.utexas.edu/users/hcleaver/368/368LockeSomeConsiderationsAlltable.pdf

Mirabeau, V. R. (1763). *Philosophie rurale ou Economie générale et politique de l'agriculture*. Libraires associés.

Mun, T. (1664–1895). *England's treasure by forraign trade* or *the Balance of forraign trade is the rule of our treasure*. https://en.wikisource.org

Quesnay, F. (2005). *Œuvres économiques complètes et autres textes* (C. Théré, L. Charles, & J.C. Perrot, Eds.). INED.

Stewart, D. (1793). Account of the life and writings of Adam Smith. In *Essays on philosophical subjects*.

Turgot, A. R. J. (1970). *Ecrits Economiques*. Calmann-Lévy.

C. Other References

Arrow, K., & Hahn, F. (1971). *General competitive analysis*. North Holland.

Aspromourgos, T. (2009). *The science of wealth: Adam Smith and the framing of political economy*. Routledge.

Audard, C. (2009). *Qu'est-ce que le libéralisme?* Gallimard.

Benetti C. (1991). Le problème de la valeur de la monnaie: F. Galiani et Adam Smith. *Cahiers d'économie politique, 19*.

Benetti, C., & Cartelier, J. (1980). *Marchands, salariat et capitalistes*. PUG Maspero.

Berlin, I. (1958). *Two concepts of liberty*. Clarendon Press.

Berry, C. J., Paganelli, M. P., & Smith, C. (Eds.). (2013). *The Oxford handbook of Adam Smith*. Oxford University Press.

Berthoud, A. (1981). *Aristote et l'argent*. PUG Maspero.

Biziou M. (2003). *Adam Smith et l'origine du libéralisme*. P.U.F.

Blaug, M. (1968). *Economic theory in retrospect*. Cambridge University Press.

Bowen, H. V. (1998). British India 1765–1813: The metropolitan context. In P. J. Marshall (Ed.), *Oxford history of the British Empire, the eighteenth century*. Oxford University Press.

Braudel, F. (1979). *Civilisation matérielle, Economie et Capitalisme, XV–XVIII siècle, t. III*. Armand Colin.

Brewer, A. (1995). The concept of growth on eighteenth century economics. *History of Political Economy, 27*(4), 609–638.

Brewer, J. (1989). *The sinews of power: War, money and the English state, 1688–1783*. Unwin Hyman.

Brown, V. (1994). *Adam Smith's discourse*. Routledge.

Caillois, R. (1958). *Les jeux et les hommes*. Gallimard.
Cain, P. J., & Hopkins, A. G. (2016). *British imperialism, 1688–2015*. Rouotledge.
Campbell Mossner, C. (1960). Of the principle of moral estimation: A discourse between David Hume, Robert Clerk, and Adam Smith, an unpublished MS by Adam Ferguson. *Journal of the History of Ideas, 21*(2), 222–232.
Chamley, P. (1963). *Économie politique et philosophie chez Steuart et Hegel*. Dalloz.
Clark, J. M., et al. (1928). *Adam Smith 1776–1926*. University of Chicago Press.
Clower, R. W. (1967). A reconsideration of the microfundations of monetary theory. *Economic Inquiry, 6*(11), 1–8.
Coats A. W. (1975). Adam Smith and the mercantile system. In A. Skinner & T. Wilson, *Essays on Adam Smith*. Clarendon Press.
Cropsey, J. (1957). *Polity and economy: An interpretation of the principles of Adam Smith*. Martinus Nijhoff.
Deleule, D. (1979). *Hume et la naissance du libéralisme économique*. Aubier.
Deleuze, G. (1953). *Empirisme et subjectivité*. Presses Universitaires de France.
Démier, F., & Diatkine, D. (Ed.). (1996). *Le libéralisme à l'épreuve: de l'empire aux nations (Adam Smith et l'économie coloniale)*. Cahiers d'Economie Politique, n° 27–28.
Diatkine, D. (1989). Hume et le libéralisme économique. *Cahiers d'Economie Politique*, n° 17.
Diatkine, D. (1991). *«Présentation» of La richesse des nations*. Flammarion.
Diatkine, D. (1996). Smith et le projet colonial ou l'avenir d'une illusion. *Cahiers d'Economie Politique*, n° 27–28.
Diatkine, D. (2007). Le suffrage et le marché: la critique par Smith du système mercantile est-elle libérale ? *Cahiers d'Economie Politique*, n° 52.
Diatkine, D. (2010, September). Vanity and the love of system in theory of moral sentiments. *The European Journal of the History of Economic Thought, 17*(3), 383–404.
Diatkine, D. (2014). Les capitalistes et les législateurs: à propos du système de la liberté naturelle selon Adam Smith. *Revue Economique, 65*.
Diatkine, D. (2016). David Hume (1711–1776). In G. Faccarello & H. Kurz (Eds.), *Handbook on the history of economic analysis*. Edward Elgar.
Diatkine, S., & Diatkine, D. (1991). Division du travail et marché du travail chez Adam Smith. *Cahiers d'Economie Politique, 19*, 69–84.
Diatkine, S. (2002). *Les fondements de la théorie bancaire – des textes classiques aux débats contemporains*. Dunod.
Diatkine, S., & Rosier, M. (1999). Steuart and Smith on banking systems and growth. In R. Tortajada (Ed.), *The economics of James Steuart*. Routledge.
Ditchfield, G. (2002). *George III, an essay in Monarchy*. Palgrave.

Duboeuf, F. (2004). Prix réels, prix naturels dans la Richesse des Nations: de la réflexion éthique à l'analyse économique. *Oeconomia, Economie et Sociétés, 38*(8–9).
Dumont, L. (1977). *Homo aequalis*. Gallimard.
Dupuy, J. P. (1992). *Libéralisme et justice sociale -le sacrifice et l'envie*. Hachette.
Ege, R., & Iggersheim, H. (Eds.). (2011). *Freedom and happiness in economic thought and philosophy*. Routledge.
Evensky, J. (2015). *Adam Smith's wealth of nations*. Cambridge University Press.
Fleischaker, S. (2004). *On Adam Smith's wealth of nations*. Princeton.
Forbes D. (1976). Sceptical whiggism, commerce and liberty. In A. Skinner & T. Wilson (Eds.), *Essays on Adam Smith*. Oxford University Press.
Friedman, M. (1976). *Adam Smith's relevance for 1976* (Selected Papers Series, n°50b). University of Chicago.
Gauthier, D. (1992). Artificial virtues and the sensible knave. *Hume Studies, 18*(2), 401–427.
Gide, C., & Rist, C. (1944). *Histoire des doctrines économiques, depuis les Physiocrates jusqu'à nos jours*. Larose et Tenin.
Graeber, D. (2011). *Debts: The first 5000 years*. Melville House.
Grampp W. (2000). What Did Smith Mean by the Invisible Hand?. *Journal of Political Economy, 108*(3).
Griswold, C. L. (1999). *Adam Smith and the virtues of enlightenment*. Cambridge University Press.
Groenewegen, P. D. (1968). Turgot and Adam Smith. *Scottish Journal of Political Economy, 15*(3), 271–287.
Groenewegen, P. D. (2009). Adam Smith, the Physiocrats and Turgot. In J. T. Young T. (Ed.), *Elgar companion to Adam Smith*. Edward Elgar.
Haakonssen, K. (1981). *The science of a lagislator*. Cambridge University Press.
Halévy, E. (1926). *The growth of philosophic radicalism*. The Macmillan Company.
Hamilton, H. (1956, April). The failure of the Ayr Bank, 1772. *The Economic History Review, 8*(3), 405–417.
Harrison, J. (1981). *Hume's theory of justice*. Oxford University Press.
Hayek, F. (1946). *Individualism: True and false*. Blackwell.
Hicks, J. R. (1990, June). The unification of macroeconomics. *The Economic Journal, 100*(401), 528–538.
Hill, L. (2009). Adam Smith on war (and peace). In I. Hall & L. Hill (Eds.), *British international thinkers from Hobbes to Namier*. Palgrave Macmillan.
Hirschmann, A. O. (1977). *The passions and the interests: Political arguments for capitalism before its Triumph*. Princeton, Princeton University Press.
Hollander, S. (1973). *The economics of Adam Smith*. The University of Toronto Press.
Hont, I. (2005). *Jealousy of trade*. Harvard University Press.

Hont, I., & Ignatieff, M. (Eds.). (1981). *Wealth and virtue. The shaping of political economy in the Scottish enlightenment*. Cambridge University Press.

Hoppit, J. (1986). Financial crises in eighteenth-century England. *The Economic History Review, New Series, 39*(1), 39–58.

Humphrey, T. M. (1981), "Adam Smith and the monetary approach to the Balance of Payments", *Federal Reserve Bank of Richmond Economic Review, 67*(6), 3–10.

Jacquet, J. (2007). *L'Économie politique smithienne et l'histoire: les rapports entre la Richesse des nations et l'école historique écossaise* (PhD). Université d'Évry-Val d'Essonne.

Jeck, A. (1974). The macrostructure of Adam Smith's theoretical system: A reconstruction. *The European Journal of the History of Economic Thought, 1*(3), 551–576.

Keynes, J. M. (1926). *The end of Laissez-Faire*. Hogarth Press.

Kindelberger, C. P. (1976). The historical background. Adam Smith and the industrial revolution. In T. Wilson & A. S. Skinner (Eds.), *The Market and the State: Essays in Honour of Adam Smith*. Oxford University Press.

Koehn, N. (1994). *The power of the commerce*. Cornell University Press.

Kurz, H. (1992). Adam Smith on foreign trade: A note on the 'vent for surplus' argument. *Economica, 59*(236), 475–481.

Laidler, D. (1981, May). Adam Smith as a monetary economist. *Canadian Journal of Economics, 14*(2), 185–200.

Lapidus, A. (2002). Le profit ou la domination: la figure de l'esclave dans l'économie d'Adam Smith. In F. Célimène & A. Legris (Eds.), *L'Économie de l'esclavage colonial*. Éditions du CNRS.

Lavisse, E. (Ed.). (1921). *Histoire de la France contemporaine*. Hachette.

Lecaldano, E. (2009). Hume's theory of justice, or artificial virtue. In E. S. Radcilffe (Ed.), *A companion to David Hume*. Blackwell.

Littré. (1863–1872). *Dictionnaire de la langue française*. Hachette.

Lieberman, D. (2006). Adam Smith on justice, rights, and law. In K. Haakonssen (Ed.), *The Cambridge companion to Adam Smith* (Cambridge Companions to Philosophy). Cambridge University Press.

Mackie, J. L. (1980). *Hume's moral theory*. Routledge.

Magnusson, L. (1994). *The shaping of an economic language*. Routledge.

Marouby, C. (2004). *l'économie de la nature essai sur Adam Smith et l'anthropologie de la croissance*. Le Seuil.

Marshall, P. J. (1998). The British in Asia: Trade to dominion, 1700–1765. In P. J. Marshall (Ed.), *The Oxford history of British Empire* (Vol. III). Oxford University Press.

Marx, K. (1867). *The capital*. https://www.marxists.org/archive/marx/works/download/pdf/Capital-Volume-I.pdf

Marx, K. (1863). *Theories of surplus value*. https://www.marxists.org/archive/marx/works/1863/theories-surplus-value/ch03.htm#s1
Mathiot, J. (1990). *Adam Smith Philosophie et Economie*. PUF, coll. Philosophie.
Medema, S. G., & Samuels, W. J. (2005). Freeing Smith from the "free market": On the misperception of Adam Smith on the economic role of government. *History of Political Economy, 37*(2), 219–226.
Meek, R. L., Raphael, D.D., & Stein, P. J. (1978). Introduction. In A. Smith, *Early Drafts of the Wealth of Nations*.
Meek, R. (1971). Smith, Turgot and the four stages theory. *History of Political Economy, 3*, 1.
Middlekauff, R. (1982). *The glorious cause: The American revolution, 1763–1789*. Oxford University Press.
Mill, J. S. (1888). *Principles of political economy* (6th ed.). Longmans.
Miller, D. (1981). *Philosophy and ideology in Hume's political thought*. Oxford University Press.
Mizuta, H., & Sugiyama, C. (1993). *Adam Smith, international perspectives*. Macmillan Press.
Mizuta, H. (1996). Kaleidoscope of the colonial discussion. *Cahiers d'Economie Politique*, n° 27–28.
Mizuta, H. (1967). *Adam smith library*. Cambridge University Press.
Montes, L. (2004). *Adam smith in context*. Palgrave Macmillan.
Moreau, P. F. (1992). *Le récit utopique*. Presses Universitaires de France.
Pack, S. (1991). *Adam smith's critique of the free market economy*. Billing & Sons.
Pack, S. (2005). Freeing Smith from the "free market": On the misperception of Adam Smith on the economic role of government. *History of Political Economy, 37*(2), 219–226.
Perlman, M. (1989). Adam Smith and the paternity of the real bills doctrine. *History of Political Economy, 21*(1), 77–90.
Pitson, A. E. (1988). Hume on promises and their obligation. *Hume Studies, XIV*(1), 176–190.
Pockock, J. G. A. (1975). *The Machiavellian moment: Florentine political thought and the Atlantic republican tradition*. Princeton University Press.
Raphael, D. D. (1975). The impartial spectator. In A. S. Skinner & T. Wilson (Eds.), *Essays on Adam Smith*. Oxford University Press.
Ray, R. K. (1998). Indian society and the establishment of British supremacy, 1765–1819. In P. J. Marshall (Ed.), *The Oxford history of the British Empire, the eighteenth century*. Oxford University Press.
Rey, J. M. (2002). *Le temps du crédit*. Desclée De Brouwer.
Ricardo, D. (1817–1951). *On the principles of political economy and taxation*. Cambridge University Press.
Robbins, L. (1935). *An essay on the nature and significance of economic science*. (pp. 68–69). Macmillan. Traduction de l'auteur

Rockoff, H. (2009). Adam Smith on money, banking, and the price. In Berry, Paganelli & Smith, *Oxford handbook of Adam Smith*, op. cit., p. 314.
Ross, I. S. (1995). *The life of Adam Smith*. Oxford University Press.
Rothbard, M. (2006). *An Austrian perspective on the history of economic thought* (Vol. 1). Mises Institute.
Rothschild, E. (2002). *Economic sentiments. Adam Smith, Condorcet and the Enlightment*. Harvard University Press.
Rotwein, E. (1955). *David hume: Writings on economics*. University of Wisconsin Press.
Schumpeter, J. A. S. (1954). *History of economic analysis*. George Allen and Unwin.
Skinner, A. (1996). Adam Smith: The demise of the colonial relationship with America. *Cahiers d'Economie Politique*, n° 27–28.
Skinner, Q. (1998). *Liberty before Liberalism*. Cambridge University Press.
Stiglitz, J. E. (1981). Credit rationing in markets with imperfect information. *American Economic Review, 71*(3), 393–410.
Tilly, C. (1989). Cities and states in Europe 1000–1800. *Theory and Society, 18*(5), 563–584.
Tribe, K. (1999). Adam Smith, critical theorist? *Journal of Economic Literature, 37*(2), 609–632.
Turgot. (1970). *Ecrits Economiques*. Calmann-Lévy.
Vaggi, G. (1987). *The Economics of François Quesnay*. Palgrave Mac Millan.
Viner, J. (1928). Adam Smith and laissez faire. In John Maurice Clark et al., *Adam Smith 1776–1926*. Chicago, University of Chicago Press.
Waszeck, N. (1988). *The Scottish enlightenment and Hegel's account of 'civil society.'* Dordrecht.
Wennerlind, C. (2001). The link between David Hume's a treatise of human nature and his fiduciary theory of money. *History of Political Economy, 33*(1), 139–160.
Wennerlind, C., & Schabas, M. (2008). *David's Hume political economy*. Routledge.
West, E. (1990). *Adam Smith and modern economics*. Edward Elgar.
Winch, D. (1978). *Adam Smith's politics*. Cambridge University Press.
Winch, D. (1996). *Adam Smith's Politique Coloniale*. Cahiers d'Economie Politique, n° 27–28.
Witztum, A. (2010). Interdependence, the invisible hand, and equilibrium in Adam Smith. *History of Political Economy, 42*(1), 155–192.
Young, J. T. (1997). *Economics as a moral science*. Edward Elgar.
Young J. T. (Ed.). (2009) *Elgar companion to Adam Smith*. E. Elgar.
Zinn, H. (1980). *A people's history of the United States*. Harper & Row.

Index

D. Diatkine, *Adam Smith and the Wealth of Nations*, Palgrave Studies in the History of Economic Thought, https://doi.org/10.1007/978-3-030-81600-1

GPSR Compliance
The European Union's (EU) General Product Safety Regulation (GPSR) is a set of rules that requires consumer products to be safe and our obligations to ensure this.

If you have any concerns about our products, you can contact us on

ProductSafety@springernature.com

In case Publisher is established outside the EU, the EU authorized representative is:

Springer Nature Customer Service Center GmbH
Europaplatz 3
69115 Heidelberg, Germany

www.ingramcontent.com/pod-product-compliance
Ingram Content Group UK Ltd.
Pitfield, Milton Keynes, MK11 3LW, UK
UKHW020835290926
15470UKWH00004B/1356
* 9 7 8 3 0 3 0 8 1 5 9 9 8 *